IRVING BURSTINER, Ph.D., is an associate professor of Marketing at Baruch College, City University of New York. In addition to his 35 years of business experience before becoming a professor, Dr. Burstiner has operated his own mail order business, conducted intensive seminars in creative management and leadership, and owns a consulting firm. He is the author of numerous articles and books, including *Run Your Own Store, The Small Business Handbook, Management,* and *An Essential Guide to Management,* all published by Prentice-Hall, Inc.

Irving Burstiner, Ph.D.

# Mail Order Selling

## How to Market Almost Anything by Mail

A SPECTRUM BOOK

PRENTICE-HALL, INC.
Englewood Cliffs, N.J. 07632

*Library of Congress Cataloging in Publication Data*

Burstiner, Irving.
  Mail order selling.

  "A Spectrum Book."
  Includes bibliographies and index.
  1. Mail-order business.  I. Title.
HF5466.B88      658.8'72      82-3733
                              AACR2

*Dedicated to my wife Razel for her patience and encouragement.*

A SPECTRUM BOOK

0-13-545855-2

0-13-545848-X {PBK.}

10  9  8  7  6  5  4  3  2  1

Printed in the United States of America

Editorial/production supervision by Cyndy Lyle Rymer
Manufacturing buyer: Barbara Frick
Cover design by Jeannette Jacobs
Cover illustration by Jim Kinstrey

Prentice-Hall International, Inc., *London*
Prentice-Hall of Australia Pty. Limited, *Sydney*
Prentice-Hall of Canada, Inc., *Toronto*
Prentice-Hall of India Private Limited, *New Delhi*
Prentice-Hall of Japan, Inc., *Tokyo*
Prentice-Hall of Southeast Asia Pte. Ltd., *Singapore*
Whitehall Books Limited, *Wellington, New Zealand*

# CONTENTS

# PREFACE

I designed *Mail Order Selling* to help those among you who fit any of the following descriptions:

- You are struggling to keep abreast of inflation, live with high tax rates, and cope with a sluggish economy.
- You prefer to keep your present job for the time being, so you can continue to buy food and clothing, pay the rent, and take care of other necessities. But you need to earn more.
- You have been looking for ways to convert your idle time into extra dollars.
- You find you must stay at home, yet you would like to bring additional income into your household.
- Although retired, you know you must earn more money so that you can pay for an occasional vacation, a new car, or some other luxury.
- You have the courage and initiative to dream about owning a business of your own, even though you are not sure of the type of business to go into.
- You haven't enough capital to warrant investing in machinery and a plant, or a new store.
- You want to know more about the potential of a mail order enterprise.

From the outset, my intent was to write a complete, practical, and easy-to-follow guidebook for starting and running a successful mail order operation. I planned to remove much of the mystery that seems to surround this field and to expose those "secrets of the trade" that are presumed to be known to only a few. At the same time, I studiously sought to tone down those exaggerated visions of potential wealth that reputedly hypnotize the aspiring mail order entrepreneur.

I will not promise to set you squarely on a fast, sure track to riches. The truth of the matter is that mail order selling is not a quick, certain, no-sweat path to wealth. To succeed in this field, just as in any other kind of business, you need courage, know-how, innovativeness, and dogged perseverance. You must also have some money to invest. Even with these requirements, you still face a great deal of hard work—and uncertainty.

Yet, mail order does have its attractive features. Some of them are unique. For example, there is no need to commit yourself to renting business premises. Nor do you have to shelve your present job. Moreover, you can launch your own business with a much smaller investment than is typically required for other types of enterprise.

You can earn an excellent, full-time livelihood selling by mail. You may even succeed in making a lot of money; many people do. But perhaps the most rewarding payoff in this business is the fun and excitement you will enjoy all along the way.

*Mail Order Selling* covers a wide spectrum of valuable topics: those preliminary steps you will need to take before launching your new business, the proper management of your firm's finances, how to write copy and create advertisements that pull, the basics of print production, the care and treatment of mailing lists, direct mail possibilities, information on both print and broadcast media, and much more.

Many of the books and manuals on the market are quite weak in specifics, or bog down in trivial details, or are unrealistic in their appraisal of eventual rewards. Few show more than a cursory treatment of "prestart" activities, so important to securing a foothold in the field. One or two are much too technical, too advanced—and designed to serve mostly as texts for advanced courses in advertising. They are not for the beginner, but rather for the larger, well-established operation.

There are some unusual features to this book: an entire chapter devoted to showing you how to prepare a comprehensive business plan, another that furnishes insights into the selling process itself, and two final chapters on growth, expansion, and possible evolution of your successful mail order business.

The book also contains comparative information on magazine rates for both display and classified mail order advertising. It lists the names, addresses, and telephone numbers of mailing list houses. It provides up-to-date facts about postage meters, imprints, mail classes, postage rates, and services offered by the U.S. Postal Service—as well as recommended mail room practices that will hold down your expenses and produce greater efficiency in your mailing activities. You will learn the details of money management, how to keep accurate records, what insurance coverages to seek, the taxes you will be responsible for, and more.

I'll be looking for your mail order ads. Good luck; and I hope you make a mint of money!

IRV BURSTINER

**1**

# THE WONDERFUL WORLD OF MAIL ORDER SELLING

How many times have you thought about starting a business of your own? Of the opportunity to be your own boss, answering to no one but your own conscience? Of escaping from the tedium of your job? Of pursuing the vision of an eventual fortune, long before the end of the road?

You are not alone. Each year, millions of people have the same thoughts and desires—and hundreds of thousands do try their hand at launching a small enterprise. Some succeed, others fail. Each new business represents a considerable gamble.

What holds most people back? Perhaps the realization that most types of business require a sizable investment. Perhaps not knowing how to go about opening a business. Or being too comfortable and not open to change. Or the fear of failure. Or too little self-confidence.

**MAIL ORDER: MYTH AND REALITY**

To many of us, there is an enchantment that surrounds those two words: *mail order*. We are fascinated with the dream of making a big score, of being inundated by sacks of mail bulging with checks and money orders, of firmly stepping out on the road to riches, of independence and self-sufficiency. It all seems so easy, too: find a unique product, write and place an advertisement, and the orders soon begin to arrive. All you then need do is address labels and cart off packages each day to the post office; and, of course, make your daily deposits at the local bank.

We believe we can do all this on little more than a shoestring. We can do it in our spare time. We need no office, no place of business; a table in the basement or the kitchen should suffice.

**1**

This widespread, positive attitude is encouraged by the many books, pamphlets, and manuals on the market. All of them preach how easy it is for you to make a fortune, to be financially independent in next to no time at all.

Yes, people can and do strike it rich in the mail order business. But overnight successes are well nigh impossible. Despite what you may have been led to believe, you probably will not get rich by the end of the first six months of operation. Nor in a year. It may take you 5 or 10 years—or you may never become rich at all. What you most likely can do is earn a living, a *good* living. Eventually, too, you will get to be most comfortable.

The purpose of this book is to help show you how to attain that objective.

## The Mail Order Dilettante

Probably, many of you have already experimented once or twice with marketing merchandise by mail. A typical scenario runs something like this:

You come across an interesting product. You believe it can sell for at least two or three times its cost, which gives you the kind of markup that makes the item "workable" for selling by mail. From the manufacturer or other source, you obtain a glossy 8 x 10 photograph of the product. You prepare copy and suggested layout for a small advertisement, then schedule space in a forthcoming issue of a magazine. The advertisement comes out—and you await the results.

Then you discover that the orders you have received do not even cover your advertising cost. Chastened, you pull back, considering yourself lucky to have gotten out of the "mail order business" with such a small loss.

Or, you may have tried to play it smart. Instead of springing for the cost of a magazine display advertisement, you composed a small classified one. You ran it for three days, or for a full week, or in the Sunday edition of a large metropolitan newspaper. This way, you almost recouped your advertising expense. You may have even earned a bit of profit. But then you decided it wasn't worth all the effort, and you gave up on mail order.

Some among you may have succumbed to the attractions of those frequently seen advertisements that offer ready-made catalogs for sale. The companies that distribute these "beautiful, four-color, professionally prepared, order-pulling catalogs" promise all sorts of glowing rewards. They remind you that you could never hope to duplicate such catalogs for even twice their cost, or more. You can buy them by the thousand, and have your firm's name and address imprinted on the covers. You then address them to your list of names, affix postage, and mail them. The catalog companies will handle all your orders, on a "drop-ship" basis.

Even as you and I and many others have discovered, you then found out the profit on the merchandise you sold was insufficient to cover even your postage costs. By way of consolation, however, you should understand that you were not in the mail order marketing business at all. You simply dabbled your toes in the stream, gambling and losing. You had done no serious planning. Few first advertisements or direct mail efforts turn a profit. You have to place many advertisements, realizing that some may produce losses, several may break even, and an occasional one will prove profitable. All along, you need to keep careful records so that you can determine your "cost per order" or "cost per inquiry." You need to build, however slowly, a mailing list of customers who buy from you. The mail order business is built on *repeat sales*. Above all, you need to study, learn how to write copy that "pulls," do your homework, prepare a comprehensive business plan, and so on—long before you start up your operation.

There are opportunities galore in this business. And many success stories can be told. Although the facts are necessarily scanty, look for some common denominators in the reports that follow:

**OPPORTUNITIES IN MAIL ORDER SELLING**

---

**FIGURE 1-1. The mail order business.**

MAIL ORDER—two words that both inspire and excite the mind of the business entrepreneur. More so, perhaps than any other business, mail order conjures up visions of enormous wealth, easy living, and the proverbial "pot of gold" at the end of the rainbow.

There is a magic—a mystic—a magnetic attraction that draws people to mail order. Like other types of businesses, mail order has its advantages and disadvantages—its share of successes and failures. It is not a quick, easy, effortless road to riches.

Yet it is also true that mail order, as a way of doing business, has been good to many people. The success stories are countless of people who have not only made a good living selling products and services by mail, but have amassed fortunes—starting on a kitchen table, garage or spare room. It is likewise the fact that many people attempt, flounder about, and lose money in the effort to establish a successful mail order enterprise.

Despite the greater mobility of people throughout the nation, abundance of shopping centers, convenience of telephone shopping, boom and recession economies, mail order continues to grow. Mail order sales to date totals approximately $60 billion and represents about 12 percent of all consumer purchases. That's over a billion dollars a week of products and services purchased by mail.

---

**Source:** Paul Muchnick, "Selling by Mail Order," *Small Business Bibliography No. 3* (Washington, D.C.: Small Business Administration, revised September 1977), p. 2.

In the early 1970s, a young schoolteacher/retailer experimented with selling patterns for wooden toys by mail, as a part-time venture. Dale Prohaska placed a classified advertisement in *Workbench* at a cost of $16. Pleased with the results, he followed with display advertising and later on sent out catalogs to his customer list. By

1980, sales at Love-Built Toys and Crafts, Inc., of Tahoe City, California, were at the quarter-million-dollar mark. Dale Prohaska still believes in testing new product ideas in the classified sections before investing in space advertising.[1]

Jerry and Anita Gentry launched the mail order company called Annie's Attic in 1975, from a small town in Texas. They chose to specialize in craft items; patterns and kits. Their first effort was a modest test mailing to 1,000 names. Today, their pillow dolls (especially Sunbonnet Sue and Overall Sam) are big sellers. And their mailings are instantly recognized by recipients; they are packaged in brown paper bags instead of envelopes.[2]

Lawrence Selman, a former professor of organic chemistry, built a sound specialty business, selling (and buying) paperweights through the mails. Working through classified advertisements in hobby magazines, he tries to reach people who buy expensive collectibles and who are interested in antiques.[3]

Until December 1975, Burton Bank was president of a firm that manufactured pants and jeans. Intrigued by the potential he saw in mail order marketing, he reviewed the literature in the field, read books, and took evening courses in advertising. In January 1976, he launched the Chesapeake Bay Trading Company (Pikesville, Maryland), planning to sell denim clothing and related merchandise by mail. His first advertisement appeared in the *National Observer*. It was successful, bringing in between $3,000 and $4,000 in orders. Through subsequent space advertising and catalog business, he managed to reach a half million dollars in sales his first year.[4]

Retailer Jerry Gunderson, president of American Golf of Florida, Inc. (Deerfield Beach, Florida), owns a mail order subsidiary. When he began his mail order operation in 1975, he owned three retail stores. Now he has seven. He runs advertisements in such publications as *Golf Magazine* and *Golf Digest,* and finds that the average mail order sale runs about $50.[5]

Ed Stern, a vice president at the publishing house of Grosset & Dunlap, authored a book called *Prescription Drugs and Their Side Effects*. He decided to promote it himself, running test advertisements in regional editions of *TV Guide*. He followed up with full-page advertisements nationally in that same publication, and others in regional editions of both *Parade* and *Redbook*. This mail order effort was successful. The approach he used can be a "model" of sorts for persons who are able to create or invent a product that can be sold through the mails.[6]

[1]Mary Kentra Ericsson, "Selling via a Mail Order Catalog," *In Business* (February 1981), pp. 52–53.

[2] "Homey Touch of Annie's Attic Uses Brown Paper Bag as Mailer," *Direct Marketing* (May 1976), pp. 22–23ff.

[3] "Selling Paperweights by Mail Shows Promise to Ex-Professor," *Direct Marketing* (December 1975), pp. 29–33ff.

[4] "Manufacturer Sells Business to Go into Mail Order Sales," *Direct Marketing,* (May 1977), pp. 32ff.

[5] "Florida Firm Finds Success Selling Golf Clubs by Mail," *Direct Marketing,* (August 1977), pp. 28–32.

[6] "How to Create a Product for Mail Order Success," *Direct Marketing* (June 1977), pp. 24–26.

All these stories reflect the following characteristics:

- Carefully selected target groups of prospects to approach
- Offers of specialized merchandise
- Some investment in inventory and in advertising
- A knowledge of advertising media
- Seizing opportunities that were not perceived by competitors
- Courageous persons who were not afraid of taking chances
- People with tenacity—the determination to see things through

Just about anything that can be sold at all can be sold by mail: products, services, even knowledge.

**What Should You Sell?**

Chapter 3 is devoted to the subject of locating suitable mail order items; consequently, we will touch on that topic only briefly at this point.

You should explore your skills, talents, special knowledge, and hobbies for ideas for your new business. Learn how to put these things to work, earning money for you. As one example, consider the vast field of handicrafts. If you have expertise in any one of the crafts listed below, be assured that there are ways to develop that expertise into a thriving mail order operation (with some creative thinking on your part, of course).

| | |
|---|---|
| basket weaving | macramé |
| ceramics | metal enameling |
| crocheting | metalwork |
| drawing | mosaics |
| flower arranging | needlepoint |
| glassmaking | painting |
| graphic arts | rug making |
| jewelry making | sculpture |
| knitting | sewing |
| lamp making | weaving |
| leatherwork | woodcarving |

Some of you may already be operating a business at home. If so, you will find that you can expand it quite readily by selling your products or services *via* the mails. Here are a few examples of home businesses that can benefit from this avenue of distribution:

| | |
|---|---|
| antiques | jewelry repair |
| art instruction | music instruction |
| bookkeeping service | pet care information |
| clock and watch repair | rubber stamps |
| coins for collectors | shopping service |
| craft instruction | small appliance repair |
| dressmaking | stamps for collectors |
| handbag repair | typing service |

If you discuss your mail order plans with friends, family, or business associates, you can be sure that some of them will try to discourage you. They may suggest that the field is too overcrowded, that it is impossible to make it any longer in mail order, that the heyday of

**Don't Let the Pessimists Get You Down**

such businesses is long past. Postage today is far too costly, they are bound to say. They will remind you of the good old pre-ZIP code days, back when the penny postcard really cost a penny and a two-cent stamp carried your letter cross country and with dispatch. Or, they will try to convince you of the futility of attempting to compete with the big mail order houses, telling you that you could never hope to: (1) buy merchandise as cheaply as they are able to do, or (2) put out the kinds of weighty, four-color catalogs they issue. Others may chatter on about how people love to shop at today's beautiful stores and fine shopping centers, how consumers like to see and touch what they're buying, and why there isn't much interest in buying by mail.

Don't let any of them dampen your enthusiasm. Mail order selling is alive, well, and prospering.

## Why Mail Order Is Growing and Will Continue to Grow

Despite the hue and cry every time the basic postage rates increase, neither the enthusiasm nor the vitality of the mail order merchant has been dampened. Customers enjoy the convenience of shopping by mail, especially from reputable companies that will stand firmly by this motto: "Satisfaction fully guaranteed, or your money will be cheerfully refunded." People also love the fact that they can save on expenses. Nowadays, most of us think twice before hopping into gas guzzlers to go shopping; fuel is just too expensive. Public transportation costs are up, too. Visa, MasterCard, and other credit cards have made it easier to order merchandise by mail. So have the charge accounts maintained by the larger mail order houses, telephone WATS lines, and toll-free 800 numbers.

All of these factors have contributed to the rapid growth of direct marketing activity across the country. In 1977, government statistics showed some 11,000 mail order companies in operation, up about 37.5 percent from 1972. Over the same five-year period, the total annual sales of these firms increased from $4.6 to $7.6 billion, for a growth of 65.2 percent.[7] These figures are quite misleading, however. They do not include the many thousands of part-time mail order operators, or the hundreds of thousands of retail stores that carry on mail order activities. Estimates of the total monies being spent annually by all types of firms in direct marketing exceed $100 billion.

## THE ATTRACTIONS OF MAIL ORDER SELLING

You stand to gain from going into any business of your own. There are, however, a good many additional advantages to starting a mail order enterprise. Here is a list of some of the benefits.

1.  You experience the joy and challenge of running a small business of your own.
2.  You can start in your spare time, without conflicting with your regular job.
3.  You have a chance to supplement your income, to earn those extra dollars to purchase some of the luxuries you cannot now afford.

[7]Bureau of the Census, *Census of Business, 1972; Statistical Abstract of the United States: 1979,* 100th ed. (Washington, D.C., 1979).

4. Age, sex, race, creed, or handicap present no barriers to your eventual success.

5. If you are already retired, this business gives you an opportunity to add to your social security and/or pension.

6. Location is never a problem; you can work from your home in any section of the country.

7. If you operate on a full-time basis, you will save costs of transportation to and from a job, and you will not need to worry about proper office or work clothing.

8. Your overhead expenses will be minimal; additional labor might be supplied by your spouse and children.

9. You can work at your own pace.

10. You have the potential for eventual expansion into store retailing or wholesaling to stores or through agents.

11. If your business meets with success, you will be able to set up your own retirement plan, life and health insurance coverage, and other benefits.

## THE ELEMENTS THAT MAKE FOR SUCCESS

The statistics on new business ventures are always disheartening. Year after year, they show that a high percentage of "new starts" go out of business within the first two or three years of operation. This attrition rate is variously attributed to the owner's lack of know-how or experience, inadequate financing, insufficient sales volume, weak management ability, or—in the case of store retailing—poor location.

Your chances for succeeding in mail order will be affected by these same factors. As would be true in any other type of enterprise, you not only need knowledge, adequate financing, and management talent, but also the courage to take chances and the sense to plan thoroughly. People enthused by the entrepreneurial spirit tend to rush ahead precipitously. Be cautious. Proceed slowly. Learn all you can before giving yourself the "go" signal. Don't become a statistic in the "failure" column.

Here are the elements that make for success, the major topics with which you should become familiar (all are covered in subsequent chapters);

- Money and its management
- Customer knowledge
- Merchandise or services to offer
- Details of starting up and record-keeping
- Your business plan
- Developing and maintaining a mailing list
- How to write copy and create advertisements
- Learning about printing
- Direct mail advertising
- The print media: newspapers and magazines
- The broadcast media: radio and television

Good luck to you—and to your new business!

**FIGURE 1-2. An introduction to mail order.**

The mail-order business is a distinctive type of retailing because it uses the United States Postal Service to carry its advertising message, receive consumer orders, and make delivery of its products. A mail-order business makes its offers through catalogs, flyers, newspapers, magazines, or even a single printed sheet. In addition, some mail-order business is solicited by radio and television advertising.

Launching a successful mail-order business requires an aptitude for merchandise selection, a knowledge of markets, organizational ability, capital investment, and time. If all, or a good part, of these requirements are present, there is no guarantee that the mail-order business is an easy road to riches. But it has been done, as thousands of small, independent, and thriving mail-order businesses in the United States will attest.

Many small mail-order businesses are started with a single item presented on a single page through the mails, or in a small magazine or newspaper coupon advertisement. The item is usually unique, perhaps exclusive, or not widely distributed. If the item is wanted by a substantial number of consumers, and the offer reaches those consumers attractively presented and priced, a successful mail-order business is possible.

Related items also encourage multiple sales and a higher average order. A presentation in a small flyer or booklet might well become the foundation for a catalog mail-order empire.

Proceed cautiously and keep in mind that few miracles occur in any business endeavor. Rule out luck and use ability, perseverance and judgment to utilize all attributes of a successful business person. Keep costs at a minimum, use what's available, start from home, and keep it simple.

**Source:** Richard J. Patton, "Selling by Mail Order," *Small Business Bibliography No. 3* (Washington, D.C.: Small Business Administration, revised August 1974), p. 2.

**FIGURE 1-3. Principles to follow in your mail order business.**

1. Enter the mail-order business on a small scale. Operate from home and use the family car and home address.
2. Choose products that are unique, attractively priced, and not widely distributed.
3. Buy quality products from dependable suppliers and develop loyalties.
4. Build dependable relationships with customers through honest advertising and by shipping what has been promised.
5. Fill all orders promptly or give reason for delay and offer the option of a refund.
6. Offer a money-back guarantee if merchandise is not satisfactory.
7. Select and keep records on all customers.
8. Keep careful financial records.

Entering the mail-order business carries with it a serious responsibility, because it is a business based on trust. It takes only a few fast-buck operators to give the entire business a bad name. Most mail-order businesses are run by the rules, by honest people, who care about their customers.

**Source:** Richard J. Patton, "Selling by Mail Order," *Small Business Bibliography No. 3* (Washington, D.C.: Small Business Administration, revised August 1974), p. 5.

HOGE, CECIL C., SR., *Mail Order Moonlighting*. Berkeley, Calif.: Ten Speed Press, 1976.

JOFFE, GERARDO, *How You Too Can Make at Least $1 Million (But Probably Much More) in the Mail Order Business*. San Francisco: Advance Books, 1978.

MARTYN, SEAN, *How to Start and Run A Successful Mail Order Business*. New York: David McKay, 1971.

METALLO, WILLIAM R., *A Fortune Awaits You in Mail Order*. Orlando, Fla: American Enterprise, 1979.

POWERS, MELVIN, *How to Get Rich in Mail Order*. No. Hollywood, Calif.: Wilshire Book, 1980.

SHINN, BEV, and DUANE SHINN, *Thirty-Three Mail Order Businesses You Can Operate from Your Home*. Central Point, Ore.: Duane Shinn, 1978.

SIMON, JULIAN L. and JULIAN SIMON ASSOCIATES, *How to Start and Operate a Mail Order Business*, 2nd ed. New York: McGraw-Hill, 1976.

STERN, A. L., *How Mail Order Fortunes Are Made*. Belfast, Me.: Porter, Bern, 1977.

STONE, BOB, *Successful Direct Marketing Methods*, 2nd ed. Chicago: Crain Books, 1979.

**Suggested Reading**

**Books**

### Small business bibliographies

#1 GRAY, ROBERT W., "Handicrafts," reprinted December 1973.

#2 WEBER, JUDITH EICHLER, "Home Businesses," revised September 1977.

#3 MUCHNICK, PAUL, "Selling by Mail Order," revised September 1977. From the Superintendent of Documents**

**Free Materials from the Small Business Administration***

### Starting and managing series

#1 METCALF, WENDELL O., "Starting and Managing a Small Business of Your Own," *The Starting and Managing Series, Vol. 1,* 3rd ed. Washington, D.C.: Small Business Administration, 1973. (Stock #045-000-00123-7)

**To Order from the Superintendent of Documents**

*These and many other printed aids are available free from the Small Business Administration, P.O. Box 15434, Fort Worth, Tex. 76119. (Write for your copy of order form 115A.) The toll-free number is 800-433-7212; in Texas, 800-872-8901.

**Write to the Superintendent of Documents, Government Printing Office, Washington, D.C. 20402.

**2**

# KNOWING
# YOUR
# CUSTOMERS

A favorite, centuries-old adage among retailers is "know your customer." This applies just as firmly to selling through the mails. To succeed in this business, you must know exactly *who* is your customer. This means that you first need to target in on selected prospects and then study them in depth. You must learn all you can about them, get to understand them fully, find out their needs and wants. Only after you have done your homework can you set out to prepare the right combinations of merchandise, pricing strategy, offers, advertisements, and the like to sell them with comparative ease.

**CONSUMER BEHAVIOR**

You need to know those to whom you plan to sell in two lights: as individuals and as members of groups. The first approach embraces a thorough grounding in human psychology, the second, a firm grasp of the fundamentals of social psychology; for the way we behave in situations involves many factors. We are affected by both inborn traits and acquired characteristics, by our environment as well as by what we have inherited. Some of our needs and wants are innate; others we acquire as we go through life. We form and maintain attitudes toward both animate and inanimate objects, develop value systems that support us, and personalities we project to others. In many ways, we are much the same, yet we differ markedly from one another because each of us is the individual sum of our particular heredity and background.

To market goods and/or services successfully, you must know why—and how—people come to buy what they buy. You need to become familiar with those factors that influence purchasing behavior. Since about the late 1950s, investigations in this area have led to the accumulation of a sizable body of knowledge known as "consumer behavior." (For more in-depth understanding, read several books on this subject listed at the end of this chapter.)

Today, we know a good deal about why people buy, the motives behind their purchasing. We know what attracts them more readily to certain stores rather than to others, or to specific brands of goods. We know that our buying behavior is affected by a number of outside forces: family influences, the various kinds of groups we belong to, social class, life-style, and so on. Other more personal influences include sex, age, income level, type of occupation, and the like. Then there are still other determinants of behavior, such as our perceptions, beliefs, attitudes, and values.

## Some Common Motives

Here are some of the things people want:

| | |
|---|---|
| affection | love |
| beauty | money |
| comfort | peace of mind |
| companionship | pleasure |
| convenience | praise |
| ego-satisfaction | recognition |
| enjoyment | security |
| entertainment | self-actualization |
| friends | self-confidence |
| good health | self-esteem |
| happiness | self-improvement |
| knowledge | spiritual well-being |

People also want to:

| | |
|---|---|
| accomplish | enjoy a good standard of living |
| achieve | express their creativity |
| acquire possessions | express their individuality |
| be accepted | get ahead |
| be appreciated | have fun |
| be attractive | laugh |
| be fashionable | play |
| be liked | relax |
| be successful | save money |
| belong | save time |

People seek to avoid:

| | |
|---|---|
| confusion | fear |
| danger | grief |
| deprivation | hunger |
| embarassment | hurt |
| failure | illness |

| loss   | tension |
|--------|---------|
| pain   | thirst  |
| sorrow | worry   |

**Culture**

One's culture is a reflection of the society in which one lives. It embraces everything, all that is material, intellectual, artistic. It represents the sum total of that society, its values, attitudes, philosophy, language, ideas, goods, publications, tools, and artifacts. Included, too, are the laws and regulations, the ethics, morals, and scruples, and the ways of living.

Given a fair amount of innate characteristics and traits, we are born into our culture and are then "accultured" or socialized by it throughout our lifetimes. This is so because we are constantly surrounded by all of its trappings, literally immersed in them. And it is perpetuated throughout generations by our schools and our institutions.

It influences the way we think and perceive.

**Social Classes**

As members of the American culture, we tend to hold attitudes toward ourselves and toward others. We are able to discern differences. We stratify our society into different levels. We recognize that some people have higher status than we do. Some we look up to, others we may look down on, still others we feel are right on our level. Differences *do* exist, although many of us would like to ignore this fact of life since we believe in and practice democracy, where everyone is supposed to be equal.

Social scientists identify a person's social class by studying such factors as occupation, type and place of residence, income, educational level, and the like. But most of us have an instinctive capacity for judging another's social class, albeit in a very rough manner. In the way others live, we are able to perceive differences among at least three major classes: upper, middle, and lower. A college course in either social psychology or consumer behavior indicates that each of the three classes can be subdivided into two, resulting in six social classes. The two upper classes, the upper-upper and the lower-upper, together comprise only a small fraction of our total population. Far bigger in size are the two middle and the two lower classes.

The class you belong to affects your buying behavior.

**Subcultures**

Within our larger American culture, substantial numbers of people share traits and attitudes peculiar to those segments and in addition to the characteristics of the greater society. These are called *subcultures,* and they may be segmented along racial, religious, geographic, age, and other lines. According to one textbook, the members of a particular subculture "possess beliefs, values, and customs that set them apart from other members of the same society; at the same time, they hold to the dominant beliefs of the overall society."[1]

For example, blacks account for some 11 or 12 percent of the American population, have a higher birth rate, a younger median age,

[1] Leon G. Schiffman and Leslie Lazar Kanuk, *Consumer Behavior* (Englewood Cliffs, N.J.: Prentice-Hall, Inc., 1978), p. 393.

and a far lower median family income than do whites.[2] Differences exist between black and white shoppers in both product and media usage. Similarly, belonging to the Jewish, Mexican-American, midwestern, youth, or other subcultures will be reflected in purchasing behavior.

## SEGMENTATION

Once you have peeled an orange, you can proceed to separate it into neat slices by pulling it apart along the natural creases in its spherical surface. Each of these orange slices may also be called a segment. Or, you cut your favorite pie into a number of portions: these portions, too, are segments. A *segment* is a slice, portion, part, section, or subdivision of something whole.

*Segmentation* is a popular marketing term. It describes various approaches to the same problem: how to locate and separate sections, called *groups*, from among the total consumer population; or, if your selling efforts are to be directed at business, industry, and other kinds of organizations, from among their entire populations.

Modern marketing theory underscores the futility of trying to sell to every individual or organization, of trying to be all things to all customers. Some will never, never be interested in what you may have to offer. You would have problems attempting to sell room air-conditioners to Eskimos, twin-engined speedboats to people who earn less than $10,000 a year, toupees to healthy young women, or hair dryers to bald septuagenarians.

Instead, you must look for specific groups or types of people or firms toward whom to aim your sales efforts. Because they share one or more characteristics in common, ones that may indicate an interest in or the ability to pay for the kinds of products you will be selling, they may be likely prospects for you. By concentrating on such groups, you will not be scattering your advertising dollars like buckshot to the wind.

### Demographic Segmentation

This is the earliest, and still the most useful, approach to "carving up the consumer pie." Often, it is referred to simply as *demographics*, from the word *demography*—the statistical study of populations with attention to specific characteristics. Marketing professionals look for those aspects that affect people's purchasing behavior, such as sex, age, income, level of education, race, nationality, and so on.

Women, for example, clearly represent the major market for perfumes, cosmetics, and feminine hygiene products. And, obviously, teenagers haven't the slightest interest in some of the products and services that senior citizens use regularly.

As a mail order hopeful, you will need to bone up on what we consumers really are like. Reading a book or two on "consumer behavior," such as those listed at the end of this chapter, will provide many insights into the psychological and sociological foundations. An hour or two in consultation with the latest copy of the *Statistical*

[2]Del I. Hawkins, Kenneth A. Coney, and Roger J. Best, *Consumer Behavior: Implications for Marketing Strategy* (Dallas, Tex.: Business Publications, Inc., 1980), pp. 127–43.

*Abstract,* in the quietude of the reference section at your local library, will yield lots of worthwhile data.

In the meanwhile, here are some broad generalities to mull over. They may help in your thinking about the market segments you may choose to go after in your new business.

1.   *We are faced with a declining birth rate.* This means fewer babies being born each year per 1,000 population, lessening demand for infant wear and baby medicines and foods, proportionately fewer young children to feed, clothe, and otherwise maintain over the next decade. On the other hand, zero population growth still eludes us. The total continues to increase, and we will most likely reach the 250 million mark well before the century's end. Naturally, more goods and services will be needed than we now use—and more manufacturers and distributors to provide them. Ample room exists for thousands of new firms and for expansion on the part of established businesses.

2.   *Our population is growing older.* Our median age is inching up, year by year. The age bracket between 35 and 55 appears to be increasing far more rapidly than other age groups, making it a most desirable target at which to aim selling efforts. The numbers of senior citizens are also increasing.

3.   *Family incomes continue to rise.* Fewer than one-third of all households had annual incomes of over $15,000 in 1970. Ten years before that, only one person in 10 earned over $25,000 a year. With the passage of time, inflation, and the growth of two- and three-income families, that $25,000 figure may well represent the median family income before 1990.

4.   *People are more educated.* With more education, consumers can be more knowledgeable and more efficient buyers. Some two-thirds of all adults over the age of 25 are high school graduates; of these, many have had some college as well.

5.   *More and more women are entering the work force.* The percentage of married women now working approaches 45 percent. This indicates a need for the time- and energy-saving products and services, for quicker shopping.

**Other Ways to Segment the Consumer Market**

Since about 1960, other approaches to market segmentation have been explored and found to be of merit. These include psychographic, life-style, and usage segmentation. In psychographic segmentation, consumer groups are segregated according to personality, value systems, attitudes, interests, and the like. Life-style segmentation calls for pinpointing people segments whose ways of living are quite similar, or homogeneous. Both these methods have, in the main, been used by the larger corporations. They require more intricate study and analysis, including the use of psychological instruments. They are usually well outside the grasp of the smaller firm.

Usage segmentation is simpler to employ. People are first dichotomized into two groups: *users* and *nonusers* of a particular product or brand. Nonusers are thereafter ignored; the only consumers of interest to the company are the users, who are then separated into three subgroups: *heavy, moderate,* and *light* users. Heavy users of a product—for example, beer—may purchase over a year up to 10 times (or more) the amount that the light user will buy.

Another useful illustration is bingo, a common American diversion. Some people never play; they detest the game, think it's utterly devoid of challenge, and so on. These are the nonusers. Others play occasionally; still others play as often as three to five times or more each and every week of the year (barring holidays, of course!). These latter are the heavy users—and of far more importance to the bingo hall than all the rest.

Often, a simple questionnaire is enough to categorize people according to their usage of the product or service.

## SELLING THE "NON-CONSUMER"

You may, of course, elect not to sell to the final consumer, and aim instead at selling to organizations. You can count these in the millions, rather than in the hundreds of millions that comprise the consumer market. This makes it far easier for you to target in on specific types and groups. Moreover, individual orders stemming from such organizational customers are generally much larger than those that emanate from the consumer sector.

These may be industrial or business organizations such as manufacturers, wholesalers, retailers, and service enterprises. Or, they may be government organizations at all levels: federal, state, county, and local. Indeed, government is the biggest buyer of them all, Massive purchasing of goods and services goes on continuously, to support military forces, schools and hospitals, public works, police and fire departments, and so on. There is also a huge agricultural market that needs to be maintained.

These markets require raw and semiprocessed materials, components, equipment, machinery, and supplies of every conceivable kind. You can reach them through placing advertisements in trade publications and by direct mail. In fact, thousands of different mailing lists are readily available; they are organized not only by SIC (Standard Industrial Classification) number, but also by organizational size, annual sales volume, number of employees, and the like. Directories of industrial and commercial firms, of government agencies and offices, and other types of organizations are also available.

If you plan to sell to organizations, you will need to learn a great deal about them beforehand—about their ways, their needs, and their preferences. You will discover that their purchasing agents are far more qualified and knowledgeable than is the typical consumer buyer. They are skilled in the intricacies of negotiating prices and terms, in contract dealings, and in their awareness of the quality and prices of competitive products.

The rewards, however, may well make it worth your while to investigate this area.

## Suggested Reading

### Books

ENGEL, JAMES F., ROGER D. BLACKWELL, and DAVID T. KOLLAT, *Consumer Behavior,* 3rd ed. Hinsdale, Ill.: Dryden Press, 1978.

HAWKINS, DEL I., KENNETH A. CONEY, and ROGER J. BEST, *Consumer Behavior: Implications for Marketing Strategy.* Dallas, Tex.: Business Publications, 1980.

Reynolds, Fred D., and William D. Wells, *Consumer Behavior*. New York: McGraw-Hill, 1977.

Schiffman, Leon G., and Leslie Lazar Kanuk, *Consumer Behavior*. Englewood Cliffs, N.J.: Prentice-Hall, Inc., 1978.

Walters, C. Glenn, *Consumer Behavior: Theory and Practice,* 3rd ed. Homewood, Ill.: Irwin, 1978.

### Management aids

#236 Smith, Ivan C., "Tips on Getting More for Your Marketing Dollar," December 1978.

### Small marketers aids

#114 Laws, Dwayne, "Pleasing Your Boss, the Customer," June 1965.

#167 Laumer, J. Ford, Jr., James R. Harris, and Hugh J. Guffey, Jr., "Learning About Your Market," April 1979.

### Small business management series

#22 Semon, Thomas T., "Practical Business Use of Government Statistics," *Small Business Management Series No. 22.* Washington, D.C.: Small Business Administration, 1975. (Stock #045-000-00131-8.)

**Free Materials from the Small Business Administration**

**To Order from the Superintendent of Documents**

**3**

# DECIDING
# WHAT
# TO SELL

In Chapter 1, you were introduced to the exciting potential of mail order selling, a business you could start at home in your spare time. In Chapter 2, you learned about people and about organizations. Now, you need to know about the merchandise or services you may wish to sell in this new enterprise. Decisions must be made. Many people in mail order maintain that the single most important ingredient contributing to success is *what you sell*. It is thought of as the one vital component of your "mail order marketing mix." Indeed, you cannot hope to start the business without one or two products in which you have confidence.

So, you now have a problem: what shall I choose to sell—at least at the start?

To get on the right track, use this excellent point of departure. Ask yourself: "What would my customers be interested in?"

If you are targeting your efforts at consumers, as do the majority of direct marketers, you might begin by exploring *your own* attitudes, interests, needs, and wants. After all, you are a consumer yourself—and aren't you somewhat (at least) representative of the rest of us?

Try to come up with a short list of the things you hold most dear. Chances are that, with a bit of soul-searching, you will devise one that is similar to the following:

- Health (physical, mental, emotional)
- Personal appearance
- Family
- Friends

- Home
- Work
- Play
- Saving money

Granted, these areas of concern might paint you as somewhat self-centered. But, really, aren't we all?

Now tackle each area in turn, devoting time and thought to spark literally dozens of product ideas for your mail order business. Consider, for example, the first item on the list: health. This has to be a prime area for possibilities, for good health is something all of us earnestly desire. With several minutes of thinking, you might come up with such ideas as: health foods, jogging shoes, vitamins, gym equipment, diets of all kinds, skin care products, books on psychology or on self-control, and the like. An hour spent on this task might yield another one or two dozen thoughts. Moreover, each idea can in turn be broken down into more dozens of specific items, so that you will never lack for product possibilities.

Then you can progress down the list to the next item, personal appearance, and repeat the process once more.

Later on, you will find suggestions as to the kinds of products, knowledge, or services you may be able to sell by mail.

Whatever product or product lines you finally decide to sell, try to match them against this idealized picture of the "good" mail order item.

- It should satisfy a real customer need.
- It should be novel, unusual, interesting.
- It must not be readily available in stores.
- It must offer good value for the price.
- It should provide a gross margin percentage of between 60 and 75 percent of the selling price.
- It should be easy to mail or ship.
- The mailing cost should be modest.
- A potential for repeat orders should exist.

---

**FIGURE 3-1.   What sells by mail?**

There is, of course, no single or simple answer to this basic question. The stories are common of the unusual sales of items such as the ant farm, pet rock, and others. These are exceptions! Like lightning, they do not strike too often. Generally speaking, products that sell well by mail are usually those not readily available in stores or other sources.

To discover such items requires studying many trade publications, attending product shows, such as giftwares, housewares, stationery, jewelry, boutique, and other consumer merchandise, contacting manufacturers, and answering ads. Talk to friends, relatives and business associates and use any other means to find the elusive small order money-maker.

Make a thorough study of magazines and newspapers and review the ads appearing there over a period of time. Note ads that run consistently, month after month or several times a year. Answer ads that are particularly interesting. Carefully study the catalogs, sales letters, brochures and sales literature received. Study particularly all follow-up mailings received. Learn from the promotion of the successful mail order firms that this will be a competitive market and know well what the competition is doing.

Ideally, the most profitable mail order product is one which customers will buy repeatedly, or a variety of products from which customers may make repeated purchases. Rarely is a profitable mail order business established through the sale of a single product or any kind of one-shot offer.

**Source:** Paul Muchnick, "Selling by Mail Order," *Small Business Bibliography No. 3*, (Washington, D.C.: Small Business Administration, revised September 1977), p. 3.

## WHERE TO GO FOR INFORMATION

Where do you begin? What sources can you turn to in your hunt for products with sales potential for your new mail order enterprise?

The buying committees at the central headquarters of large supermarket chains have a continuous problem; they must screen several thousands of new products every year for their shelves. The manufacturers and wholesalers who present this merchandise to them are anxious to benefit from the tremendous purchasing power behind these retailers. They will not be visiting your premises, of course, but you can read about these and other new items in the various trade publications. Nearly every product field is represented by some trade journal.

Perhaps your most fertile field for gathering merchandise ideas is the advertising of other mail order companies. These are to be found in both men's and women's magazines, in the shelter publications, in the large numbers of special interest magazines, and in many newspapers. (See Chapters 12 and 13 for details on the print media.)

You will see new products promoted on television, too, and hear about them over radio. Other sources include trade shows, trade directories, and directories of importers. New items offered by manufacturers are reviewed (and often advertised) in just about every issue of *Direct Marketing*. This publication should be required reading for every mail order distributor.

Last but certainly not least, there is the National Mail Order Association, with offices at 5818 Venice Boulevard, Los Angeles, Calif. 99919 (213-934-7986). Join the association; it is a valuable source of information for the mail order dealer. Its newsletter, the *Mail Order Digest,* is full of new product mentions, helpful merchandising methods, developments in the mail order field, list sources, and the like. If you are interested, for example, in learning of new items of merchandise and where to get them, the association can send you, at nominal cost, lists such as "50 U.S. Drop Shipment Firms," "30 Hong Kong Suppliers," "30 European Suppliers," and so on. You can receive information about list brokers and compilers, envelope manufacturers, printers, mailing services, stock photos, clip art, and so on.

## THOUGHTS AND SUGGESTIONS ABOUT MERCHANDISE

Some mail order companies are general merchandisers, much like our traditional department stores. They offer an extensive assortment of merchandise lines; from furniture, curtains and draperies, lamps, and other home furnishings through both large and small appliances and sporting goods to clothing for the entire family. The giants among them, like Sears, Roebuck and Montgomery Ward, stock thousands of different products. Their big catalogs, running hundreds of pages, contain some items of interest to just about everyone.

Other mail order firms are content to specialize in one or a few major merchandise lines. It may be that they realize full well their inability to compete on equal terms with the larger distributors, and so prefer to carve out niches for themselves among particular consumer segments. Within each product line, they carry a broader variety of merchandise than the general house finds it profitable to do, and they maintain more depth as well. Some specialize in scientific instruments or musical instruments; others in sporting goods, giftwares and novelties, educational games and toys, kitchen utensils, country music (on tapes or cassettes), ladies' sportswear, ceramic ware, or hundreds of other lines.

What ought you to carry? First, you must realize that rarely can a direct marketing firm succeed over the long term with a lone product, no matter how popular the item may prove to be. You need to think in terms of a number of products in the mail order game. Pause and reflect for a moment. Most likely, you will spend scads of money advertising your first product or two in the print media, or perhaps through direct mail efforts, to add a goodly number of names to your customer list. Wouldn't it seem a terrible waste of your investment if you failed to follow up by seeking additional sales from those buyers, either through circulars or folders ("bouncebacks") that you enclose with every package you send out or through your own catalog? Think ahead to that point when you will have accumulated an extensive list of people who have bought from you, and to the line of products with which you intend to keep selling to them.

There are always new products to be found or to be developed. For years, the simple hand magnifying glass has been sold by mail without much difficulty, because it fills a strong need in those people who have trouble reading the fine print in a book. And this is true despite the availability of the hand magnifying glass in many variety stores. Yet, not long ago there was an advertisement that featured a new variation on an old theme: a plastic product that magnifies an entire page at one time, yet is so thin that you can use it as a bookmark to hold your place when you put the book down.

So, when you scan the following list of just a few of the merchandise possibilities, keep your imagination flowing freely. With a little twist or adjustment, an old-line, longtime seller may become an exciting novelty with excellent sales potential. Remember, too, that each listing represents an entire category within which you may be able to find 10 or as many as 50 distinct product possibilities.

apparel
aquarium supplies
arts and crafts supplies

astrological charts and
   medallions
beaded novelties

beauty supplies
billfolds
binoculars
books
brassware
bridal items
build-it-yourself kits
burglar alarms
business opportunities
calculators
cameras
car care products
ceramic items
chairs
cheeses
chemicals
chinaware
cleaning compounds and
    supplies
clocks
coins
computers
confectionery
construction sets
cookies
cooking
cookware
correspondence courses
cosmetics
cutlery
decorative accessories
diet aids
diet foods
do-it-yourself manuals
doll houses
dolls
educational toys
electrical appliances
electronic games
employment information
fabrics
farm supplies
fashion hints
figurines
films
fire alarms
fire extinguishers
fireplace accessories
fishing equipment and supplies
flashlights
flower arrangements
foods
footwear
formulas
furniture
garden items

giftwares
glassware
gloves
gourmet foods
gymnastic equipment
handbags
handicrafts
health foods
health-related products
hearing aids
heaters and heating
    equipment
hobby supplies
home furnishings
home gardening supplies
home study courses
hunting equipment and
    supplies
jewelry
keychains
knitting supplies
knives
lawn care items
loans
luggage
magazines
magic tricks
magnifying glasses
medallions
medical appliances
medical supplies
medicines
metalwork
microscopes
mirrors
models and kits
newsletters
nursery stock
office supplies
paintings
paperweights
perfumes
photographic equipment and
    supplies
piece goods
porcelain items
postage stamps (for collectors)
power tools
rainwear
recipes
records, cassettes, and tapes
reducing aids
religious items
scientific equipment
scissors
sculptures

| | |
|---|---|
| seafood | stationery |
| searchlights | telescopes |
| seeds | toiletries |
| sewing supplies | tools and utensils |
| shoes | towels |
| skates | toys |
| skin care items | vitamins |
| souvenirs | wagons |
| spice racks | watches |
| sporting goods and equipment | woodenware |
| | work clothing |

## KNOWLEDGE FOR SALE

Opportunities abound in the knowledge area for the mail order marketer, for buyers must surely exist somewhere for every conceivable kind and type of information. We all thirst for knowledge often during our lifetimes, all 230 million of us. So do some 12 or 13 million business firms and countless other organizations of all descriptions.

Obviously, you cannot hope to reach every customer or every organization. Nor should you think about trying to do so. You will accomplish far more by searching out specific segments of the population, groups of people who share common ideas, interests, aspirations, attitudes, and life-styles. Your challenge is to locate those types—of individuals or organizations—whose "profile" indicates that they would be prime prospects for the knowledge you intend to sell. You then study these selected targets to find out more about their needs and wants, and then prepare the material that would satisfy them.

If you have had worthwhile and broad experience in a particular trade or occupation, or you can claim expertise in any subject area, you should be able to find interested parties who will pay for your knowledge—provided, of course, that you "package" it in a leaflet, booklet, pamphlet, or other type of printed work. If you are not well versed by virtue of your own "hands-on" experience, you can still tackle whatever subjects attract you by doing some heavy research. You can even seek to purchase information from others, then write it up yourself, or have someone who is a more accomplished writer prepare it for you. And make sure you hold the copyright!

Such "products" reflect many of the characteristics of the successful mail order item. They cannot be obtained in stores or from other mail order dealers (unless you sell them to these retailers); you can set the kind of selling price that will provide the big markup you need; there are no problems with breakage or perishability in mailing the item; handling is extremely easy; and the postage cost is minimal.

To whet your appetite, here is just a sprinkling of possibilities for consumer group targets. (In a similar fashion, firms and organizations may be broken down into innumerable classifications.)

| | |
|---|---|
| arthritis sufferers | card players |
| bicyclists | college students |
| car owners | dieters |

executives
hobbyists
home gardeners
housewives
investors
jobseekers
joggers

mechanics
parents
pet owners
seafood lovers
sports fans
teenagers
veterans

Here is an abbreviated list of topic areas to really spark your thinking:

appliance repair
arts and crafts (how to draw,
    paint, sculpt, etc.)
attracting opposite sex
beauty suggestions
blueprints
boating
build-it-yourself plans
business opportunities
car care
collecting (stamps, gemstones,
    many other collectibles)
cooking
correspondence courses
dancing
decorating (home, office)
designing clothes
diets
doll making
employment
entertaining
entrepreneurship
exploring
fashions
finances
flower arranging
formulas
glassmaking
health improvement
history
hobbies
home gardening
home protection
homeowners' hints
horoscopes
hunting
inventing
investments
jewelry making
jewelry repair

joke telling
knitting
leisure activities
making clothes
making money
medical facts
metalwork
needlepoint
party suggestions
patternmaking
personal care
photography
physical development
playing instruments
pottery
raising animals, fish, pets
real estate
résumé preparation
sailing
self-defense
self-improvement
self-protection
self-publishing
seminars and workshops
sewing
skiing
solving puzzles
sports
stock market
toymaking
travel
treasure hunting
vacationing
weaving
weight reduction
winning (at bingo, cards,
    dice, horse racing, etc.)
winning contests
woodworking
writing

The most interesting aspect of selling a service by mail is the **SERVICES** assurance of repeat sales. A satisfied customer will continue to use your service and may be induced to recommend other prospective clients to you. With this kind of "product," total sales income will continue to increase along with the passage of time—just so long as you deliver what you promise and people continue to have confidence in your service.

If you have had considerable experience in a particular line of trade, or if you have published articles or books in some field and thereby built a reputation, you may be able to transfer your background and expertise to a useful service business.

Here are some of the many services being sold successfully by mail:

advertising agency
advisory service
appliance repair
clipping bureau
commercial art supplier
consulting service
correspondence club
equipment leasing
jewelry repair
letter remailing
machinery repair
musical instrument repair
newsletter
personalizing products

photography (prints, enlargements, miniatures, photo stamps, etc.)
printing
public relations agency
publicity firm
reminder service
research bureau
résumé preparation
shopping service
stationery
tax form preparation
toy repair
translation bureau

## PATENTING OR COPYWRITING YOUR CREATIONS

One way to assure a steady supply of unique products to sell by mail is to create your own. In that way, you need not fear competition. If you have an active imagination and a creative bent, you may be able to invent useful gadgets, tools, toys, and thingamajigs that people will want to buy. Or, you may write up information that will answer needs not now being met by anyone else.

When you patent your inventions, you can exclude others from making or selling them for a period of 17 years, long enough to make yourself a small fortune if the item (or items) proves popular. You should seek professional assistance since a patent search is usually needed. File your application with the Commissioner of Patents and Trademarks, Washington, D.C. 20231. There is a filing fee, some printing charges, and a final fee to be paid. Contact the SBA's Texas headquarters for two helpful *Management Aids*—No. 240, "Introduction to Patents" and No. 248, "Can You Make Money with Your Idea or Invention?" (Write to: U.S. Small Business Administration, P.O. Box 15434, Fort Worth, Tex. 76119.)

Most of us are not inventors, but many of us can write or put together a printed piece. Under the old Copyright Act of 1909, publication and registration were the keys to obtaining statutory copyright. No longer is this true. Unpublished as well as published works are automatically protected by copyright. So long as the work has been fixed in a tangible form of expression—written, typed, recorded on tape or phonograph record, and so on—the copyright becomes the property of the author. Publication, however, has its advantages; the main benefit is that it establishes a public record of the copyright claim—which can be useful in infringement suits.

Under the Copyright Act of 1976, your protection begins at the time the piece is created, and extends for your lifetime plus 50 years thereafter. For complete information, write to the Register of Copyrights, Library of Congress, Washington, D.C. 20559. Ask also for Form TX, the application form for published and unpublished nondramatic literary works. To register a work, you must send them a completed application form, a check for $10 (the fee), and two complete copies of the published work.

**4**

# PRACTICAL MONEY MANAGEMENT

You've heard it before: to make money, you need money. Sure, it's an old axiom. But it's so true! Enthusiasm, hard work, and perseverance won't do the job! If you have no money of your own that you can afford to gamble with, it would be prudent to remain at your present job until you have saved up a hefty sum of, say, several thousand dollars. Or, find yourself a better job and postpone your dream of owning your own business for another year or two.

Any business must run on money. Even to launch a modest, part-time, run-from-your-home venture requires financial support. This is just as true of a new mail order business as it is of any other type of enterprise. Luckily, the mail order game often does not call for as heavy an initial outlay of funds as do most other business types.

You will need some funds to register your business name, pay for a partnership agreement, or file for a corporate form. You will need much more money to purchase stock and equipment, pay for media advertising and for stationery, buy postage stamps to affix to your letters and parcels, and so on. If you start on a full-time basis, you will need back-up funds to live on until your business begins to generate profit.

**MONEY SOURCES**

Essentially, there are only three ways to go when it comes to getting the capital you need. You can provide your own money. You can borrow funds. You can sell part of your business to others, thus trading equity for ready funds.

**29**

**Your Own Money**

Using your own funds is usually best. Certainly, it is the one approach most recommended by bankers and other financial advisors—and by other business executives. If you have your own money to use, you won't have to worry about paying back loans directly or even by installments. Nor about struggling to pay those high interest rates. Neither will you have to give away any piece, large or small, of your business.

Bear in mind, too, that most businesses cannot afford to pay their owners even a minimum salary for the first six or eight months after starting up.

**Borrowing Funds**

You might consider borrowing *some* money, to add to your own nest egg, from a close relative or two, or from one or two good friends. If you do, make sure you do it in a businesslike manner. Give them promissory notes to make things official. And be sure you pay those notes when they come due. You might also pay them interest on what they have loaned to you at a fair rate. After all, they will be losing potential bank interest all along.

### Passbook loans

This is a relatively inexpensive way of borrowing. If you have some money in a savings account, you might consider taking out a passbook loan. Your account continues to earn interest at the regular rate while you pay the bank back, usually in regular monthly payments. Of course, this does tie up the money you have in your account, at least to the extent of the current balance owed.

### Other bank loans

If you have been steadily employed all along, earn a fair income, and have little outstanding debt, chances are that many banks will be willing to extend a personal loan on your signed application. Depending on your earnings and credit evaluation, you may be able to borrow anywhere from a few hundred to several thousands of dollars without having to put up collateral. It helps, too, if you own an automobile, boat, home, or other property such as stocks or bonds. If you do have worthwhile assets, you can put some of these up as collateral for larger loans.

### Borrowing against life insurance

If you carry life insurance policies on which you have been paying premiums for years (except, of course, for term insurance), you may have accumulated substantial cash equity in those policies. Although you probably do not wish to cash them in by surrendering them, you can borrow against the cash accumulation, generally at a very low rate, often five percent per year, which is a fantastic bargain nowadays. Whether you eventually pay back the loan is your decision. If you should die before repaying the loan, the outstanding indebtedness will be deducted from the face value of the policy when payment is made to your beneficiary.

### Mortgages and other loans on property

If you own your own home or apartment, or, perhaps, a summer cabin or bungalow, look into the possibilities of getting a mortgage on your property. This applies, too, to any business property you may own. If you already have a mortgage, you may be able to refinance it, or obtain a second mortgage. (In these days of excessively high interest rates, you might be inclined to forego this approach, unless, of course, there is just no other way to raise money.) The same thinking can apply to other items of value, such as a car, truck, or boat.

### Small Business Administration loans

This federal agency may be a valuable source of additional funds, especially if you have already approached several banks and have been turned down for a large loan. The SBA offers a variety of arrangements to help small companies with capital for construction, expansion, purchase of equipment and supplies, working capital, and so on. Also available are economic opportunity loans (designed for minority group members and the disadvantaged) and loans to small firms run by handicapped individuals. Visit your nearest SBA office to discuss the various programs and secure an application form.

### Small business investment corporations

Some companies are licensed and regulated by the Small Business Administration. They can provide the smaller company with either equity capital or long-term loan financing; often, management assistance is offered as well. There are also MESBICs, similar institutions devoted to helping small firms that are run by members of minority groups. (The prefix ME stands for "Minority Enterprise.")

### Venture capital companies

Some institutions, corporations, and small groups of private investors conduct business by financing the expansion and growth of other companies. They may invest substantial sums in firms that show promise and otherwise meet their criteria; in return, they become part owners. Yet, their major interest is in making capital gains. They usually prefer to recoup their investment, plus perhaps some 300 or 400 percent profit on that investment, within a few years.
Venture capitalists are generally not interested in furnishing initial capital to a company that is just starting up; they prefer to come in after the firm is well established, shows a good financial picture, and is ready to move ahead at a more rapid pace.

### Trade credit

If your credit has been good, many of your suppliers will extend credit on the merchandise or supplies you buy. Usual trade terms are one or two percent, 10 days, net 30 days. This means that you will have up to 30 days to pay your invoices for the merchandise you buy. Or, should you pay your bills early (within 10 days of the invoice date), you can deduct one or two percent from the amount indicated on the bill when you send out your check. Effectively, then, you will have the loan of your vendors' money for anywhere from a few days up to an entire month.

Along somewhat similar lines, an occasional vendor may let you buy merchandise on consignment. This means that you need not pay for the goods until you have sold them. Usually, return privileges go along with sales on consignment. If you have not succeeded in disposing of all the merchandise within a certain period of time, you can return the balance to your supplier.

### Leasing

A somewhat indirect way of "financing" your operation, leasing can free money that ordinarily would have to be allocated to equipment, fixtures, or machinery. (Of course, this aspect would be much more important if you have a manufacturing, wholesale, or retail business along with your mail order operation.) Instead of purchasing such goods outright, you rent them from willing suppliers.

## Selling Part of the Company

If you have incorporated your new business, there is the possibility of selling shares of stock in it to friends, relatives, acquaintances, and even employees. (This does not refer to a public offering, of course. It would be in your best interest to consult both your lawyer and your accountant about this approach.)

## BASIC ACCOUNTING STATEMENTS

The operator of any type of business must become thoroughly familiar with all the details of the two major accounting statements: the *balance sheet* and the *income statement*. A working knowledge of both forms is essential to executive decision-making and to the success of the business itself. It is needed, too, before you think about launching your new business, so that you can work out just how much capital you will need to begin your operation.

Chapter 6 will provide ample opportunity to work up these two reports for your first year of operation, well in advance of starting up. From the two proforma statements you will create, you will be able to compute not only your expected sales, expenses, and profits, but also the amount of money needed to get started and to ensure the building of a successful enterprise.

## The Balance Sheet

Like other business owners, you need to prepare (or have your accountant prepare) a balance sheet at least once each year. This is done after the close of business on December 31 if you operate on a calendar year basis, or perhaps after June 30, if yours is a fiscal year operation. In accounting terms, you will be "closing the books."

The balance sheet is a summary of the assets, liabilities, and net worth of your business at a point in time. It is called a balance sheet because of its format; typically, it is a single sheet of paper divided down the middle so that the two halves are shown side by side. In the left-hand section are the firm's assets; in the right-hand section, the firm's liabilities and net worth. Bottom-line figures in both halves are identical, or "in balance."

Figure 4-1 shows a rather simplified balance sheet. (Note, however, that the two parts are not displayed side by side, as is usually the case.) You will see that the last entry in the first section shows a figure for "total assets" of $25,970, and that this sum is the same as the total "liabilities and net worth" shown in the second section.

Following the figure, all terms that appear in it are explained.

---

**FIGURE 4-1.   A simple balance sheet.**

### DINKY'S TOYS & GADGETS

*Balance Sheet*
*For: Year Ended December 31, 19XX*

#### ASSETS

Current Assets:
  Cash on hand and in bank . . . . . . . . . . . . . . . . . . . . . . $8,450
  Marketable Securities . . . . . . . . . . . . . . . . . . . . . . . . . .  780
  Accounts receivable (less allowance for bad debts)  570
  Merchandise inventory . . . . . . . . . . . . . . . . . . . . . . . .  7,120
  Inventory supplies . . . . . . . . . . . . . . . . . . . . . . . . . . . .  1,140
    Total current assets . . . . . . . . . . . . . . . . . . . . . . . . . . . . $18,060

Fixed Assets:
Office machinery and equipment (less depreciation) . . . . .  3,630
Furniture (less depreciation) . . . . . . . . . . . . . . . . . . . . . . . .  2,380
Leasehold improvements . . . . . . . . . . . . . . . . . . . . . . . . . . .  1,900
  Total fixed assets . . . . . . . . . . . . . . . . . . . . . . . . . . . . . . .   7,910
  TOTAL ASSETS . . . . . . . . . . . . . . . . . . . . . . . . . . . . . . . .  25,970

#### LIABILITIES AND NET WORTH

Current Liabilities:
  Accounts payable . . . . . . . . . . . . . . . . . . . . . . . . . . . . . . $4,150
  Notes payable within year . . . . . . . . . . . . . . . . . . . . . . .  1,100
  Accrued taxes . . . . . . . . . . . . . . . . . . . . . . . . . . . . . . . . .  740
    Total current liabilities . . . . . . . . . . . . . . . . . . . . . . . . . . . $5,990

Long-term Liabilities:
  Note payable, 1987 . . . . . . . . . . . . . . . . . . . . . . . . . . . .  1,000
  Note payable, 1988 . . . . . . . . . . . . . . . . . . . . . . . . . . . .  1,000
    Total long-term liabilities . . . . . . . . . . . . . . . . . . . . . . . .   2,000
    TOTAL LIABILITIES . . . . . . . . . . . . . . . . . . . . . . . . . . . . $ 7,990
Net Worth (Owner's Equity) . . . . . . . . . . . . . . . . . . . . . . . . . .  17,980
    TOTAL LIABILITIES AND NET WORTH . . . . . . . . . . . . . . $25,970

---

### Assets

On the first half of your balance sheet, indicate the value of all assets, or resources, owned by your company: money, merchandise, machinery, equipment, and other items of capital. These resources are grouped into "current" and "fixed" assets.

### Current assets

These are the resources of the firm that are actively employed in conducting business operations over the year. Cash, merchandise, and supplies, such as stationery and packaging materials, are examples.

### Cash on hand and in bank

Actually, this label is somewhat of a misnomer, for you will also include in this category all checks and money orders not yet deposited in the bank; so, too, with any sum in your petty cash fund. Moreover, if you run a retail store operation in conjunction with your mail order business, you must add the total amount in your "store bank"; that is the coins (loose and in rolls) and small bills you keep on the premises so that you can make change for customers each day.

### Marketable securities

Enter in this category the current market value of all business-owned stocks, debentures, and other securities that can be readily converted into cash if necessary.

### Accounts receivable

If you encourage purchases on credit, you must set up an individual record, called an "account," for each customer. In these accounts, you carefully record all such sales and all payments subsequently made. The balance sheet entry indicates the sum total of all outstanding balances owed. (This term is often shortened to "receivables.")

### Allowance for bad debts

You will find that some of your accounts receivable may never be fully paid up. Not every person is ethical or trustworthy. In recognition of this sorry fact, you should deduct a small percentage of the outstanding balance (say, one percent) from the total receivables figure and enter only the net result on your balance sheet. In this way, the accounting statement reflects a more accurate appraisal of your financial status.

### Inventories

Like most types of stores, the mail order firm typically maintains a merchandise inventory. It stocks articles of merchandise so that incoming orders may be filled without delay. The overall figure that appears here is calculated at your cost or at the current market value of the goods, whichever is lower. Indeed, some mail order companies may resemble the manufacturer even more than the retailer. Such firms may manufacture the products they sell; others assemble or package merchandise on their premises. Consequently, they may maintain several different types of inventories: (1) raw materials, (2) semiprocessed goods ("work-in-progress"), and (3) finished, or "ready," merchandise. The balance sheet will, of course, show these inventories separately.

Finally, all enterprises maintain supplies necessary to operations. Examples of such material in a mail order business include packing materials of all sorts—cartons, shipping tubes, wrapping paper and the like, envelopes and letterheads, typewriter ribbons, paper clips, and index cards. The total value of your supplies is also entered on the balance sheet.

### Fixed assets

Among those assets of a more permanent (or fixed) nature owned by the company are office equipment, machinery, perhaps a delivery truck, furniture, and so on. If the firm owns the building in which it is located, or the land on which the building has been erected, these are also fixed assets.

### Depreciation

With the exception of land, the value of a firm's fixed assets declines with the passage of time. This is readily grasped by visualizing the effects of normal wear and tear alone, over the years, with an office mimeograph or a small panel truck. Generally, you will need to set up a depreciation schedule for each group of your fixed assets according to Internal Revenue Service regulations. (Request a copy of their Publication 534, "Depreciation.")

### Leasehold improvements

This term applies to the cost of any and all improvements made by a lessee on property leased for use in the business.

### Liabilities

This is a collective term for all your outstanding business debts: what you owe your suppliers, your employees, the advertising media (or agency), the banks from whom you borrowed, various levels of government (for taxes due), and the like.

### Net worth

Subtract the sum total of your liabilities from that of your assets; what is left is the "net worth" of your business. For the owners of sole proprietorships and partnerships, this is also known as "Owner's, or Owners', Equity." If you run your business as a corporation, this section of the balance sheet will show the amount of common stock held by your stockholders, plus any "retained" (not distributed) earnings.

### Current liabilities

Under this classification, list all obligations you will need to pay back within the next 12 months.

### Accounts payable

As with all of your accounts receivable, you need to keep records of all firms and individuals from which you buy on credit. Enter here the total amount owed to these suppliers.

### Notes payable

A note is simply a written acknowledgement of a debt, and a promise to repay that debt. These are obligations you have contracted with banks and other lenders to pay back during the next 12 months (as against notes/loans shown under "long-term liabilities").

### Accrued taxes

The verb *to accrue* means to collect, gather, or add to in an orderly fashion. Here you need to indicate the sum you have set aside to pay upcoming tax obligations.

### Long-term liabilities

These are debts your business is obligated to repay in the future, beyond the next 12 months.

## The Income Statement

This is also commonly referred to as the operating statement, the profit and loss statement, or simply the P and L. It summarizes the outcome or results of operating the business for a period of time. Like the balance sheet, it is typically prepared once each year. However, many firms will make up an income statement quarterly, even monthly, so that management can keep on top of just what is happening in the business and so that decisions may be made promptly and with full knowledge of results along the way. Frequently, it is far too late to do much about a business operation after an entire year has gone by.

The major "parts" of an income statement are:

- Net sales for the period
- Cost of goods sold
- Gross margin
- Operating expenses
- Operating profit
- Total income before income taxes
- Net income (or net profit) after taxes

More details are shown in the sample P and L, Figure 4-2.

---

**FIGURE 4-2.   A profit and loss statement.**

### HANDICRAFTS BY ROSLYN

*Profit and Loss Statement*
*For: Year Ended December 31, 19XX*

Net Sales. . . . . . . . . . . . . . . . . . . . . . . . . . . . . . . . . . . . . . . . . . . . . . $73,750

Less cost of goods sold:

| | | |
|---|---|---|
| Opening inventory, January 1 | $1,740 | |
| Purchases during year | 30,230 | |
| Freight charges | 320 | |
| Total goods handled | $32,290 | |
| Less ending inventory, December 31 | 2,120 | |
| Total cost of goods sold | | 30,170 |

Gross Margin .................................................. $43,580

Less operating expenses:

| | | |
|---|---|---|
| Salaries and wages | $12,270 | |
| Payroll taxes | 1,750 | |
| Utilities | 1,610 | |
| Telephone | 1,020 | |
| Rent | 4,250 | |
| Office supplies | 660 | |
| Postage | 4,730 | |
| Maintenance expenses | 550 | |
| Insurance | 1,280 | |
| Interest expense | 340 | |
| Depreciation | 1,160 | |
| Advertising | 8,670 | |
| Dues and contributions | 160 | |
| Miscellaneous expenses | 110 | |
| Total operating expenses | | 38,560 |

Operating Profit ................................................ 5,020

Other income:

| | | |
|---|---|---|
| Dividends on stock | 150 | |
| Interest on bank account | 270 | |
| Rental of mailing list | 500 | |
| Total other income | | 920 |
| Total income before income tax | | $ 5,940 |
| Less provision for income tax | | 1,700 |
| Net profit | | $4,240 |

## Net sales

The word *net* in this category should alert you to the fact that the term *gross sales* also exists. Your gross sales are the total amount of dollars taken in by selling merchandise during the period covered by the operating statement. From this amount, you must subtract debits, such as returns from customers, employee and customer discounts, and other allowances, to derive your net sales.

## Cost of goods sold

In this section, you enter those computations that enable you to arrive at your total cost of the merchandise sold during the period. To clarify the procedure, let us go through the steps for a single month, instead of trying to take the entire year into account.

1. Compute the total cost of all merchandise you have in stock at the beginning of the month.

2. Tally the costs of all stock you purchased during the month. (Generally, you ascertain the amounts from the invoices for the goods, less any returns you may have made to vendors. You also deduct any cash discounts earned.)

3. If you had to pay freight charges on any of the shipments, these must also be counted.

4. Add the amounts in 1 to 3 above. This gives you the complete cost of all merchandise handled.

5. From 4 above, subtract end-of-the-month inventory value, at cost, of course. The resulting sum represents your cost of what you have actually "moved."

### Gross margin

Some people refer to this as "gross profit." Either way, it represents the difference between net sales and cost of goods. For you to operate successfully, whether in the mail order field or in any other type of business, your gross margin must be large enough to pay all of your business expenses and still yield some net profit.

### Operating expenses

These are the costs you need to cover while operating your business during the time period covered by the statement. (See Figure 4-3 for a listing of the more common classifications of expenses.)

### Operating profit

Subtract your operating expenses total from the gross margin figure. The resulting amount is the profit earned from the actual running of the business.

### Other income

You may find that extra dollars come into your business from sources other than your usual operation, for example, interest earned on your business savings account. (Naturally, excess cash should be put to work!) Other income would include dividends from stocks or bonds, money collected by selling an old piece of equipment, and so on.

### Total income before income tax

Both your operating profit and the other income entry are combined to form this category. It represents the business earnings before income taxes are deducted.

### Net profit

This last figure is an exacting measurement of the performance of your business. It tells you how much profit your firm has earned after taxes. Its position on the operating statement indicates why it is commonly referred to as the "bottom line."

**FINANCIAL RECORD-KEEPING**

Few owners of small-scale enterprises enjoy doing the tedious paperwork necessary to maintain the firm's records for supporting tax claims. Such people are generally much more attuned to action than to desk work. Yet, the proper handling of the financial aspects of your business is essential to its successful operation. By setting up your records properly at the outset, you will be able to spot trends, pinpoint problem situations, and arrive at decisions more easily.

For purposes of taxation, you may be surprised to learn that the federal government mandates no specific bookkeeping approach. If your mail order business will be run as a sole proprietorship, record-keeping can be quite simple. Your basic needs will include a checkbook, records of cash receipts and of cash disbursements (payouts), and a petty cash record.[1] All sales must be recorded, as does everything that you pay out. If possible, all cash disbursements should be made by check so that your checkbook can become your record of disbursements, especially if each check stub carries all the details: the firm to which it has been issued, the kind of expense (for merchandise, stationery, and so on), the number of the invoice paid, and the like.

Some items do not warrant making out a check. An example might be when you pick up a roll of parcel post tape or a couple of typewriter ribbons at a local stationer's. These and other little items might be paid out of your petty cash fund. Of course, each time you tap the petty cash, be sure to fill out a petty cash slip on which you note the reason for the purchase.

You should find a competent accountant at the outset, preferably one who has had some experience with mail order companies. He or she can advise you on how the books should be set up, not only for tax reasons, but also to help you keep on top of what is going on in your business. The accountant will teach you how to make all entries on a daily basis and handle things yourself until your operation has grown in size to the point where you may want to consider hiring a part-time bookkeeper.

According to one SBA pamphlet, the requirements of a good record-keeping system include:

Simple to use
Easy to understand
Reliable
Accurate
Consistent
Designed to provide information on a timely basis[2]

A discussion of the principles of bookkeeping is beyond the scope of this book. However, simplified one-book systems are available for use, as are other double-entry systems.[3]

Even under the simple bookkeeping approach mentioned earlier, there are additional records you may need to maintain. These

[1]William C. Greene, "Getting the Facts for Income Tax Reporting," *Small Marketers Aids No. 144* (Washington, D.C.: Small Business Administration, 1970), p. 3.

[2]John Cotton, "Keeping Records in Small Business," *Small Marketers Aids No. 155* (Washington, D.C.: Small Business Administration, 1974), p. 2.

[3]See Nathan H. Olshan, "Recordkeeping Systems—Small Store and Service Trade," *Small Business Bibliography No. 15* (Washington, D.C.: Small Business Administration, 1977 revision).

depend on the size and type of business you operate. Among these other records can be:

- Payroll records—if you have employees
- Accounts receivable records, generally kept together in one ledger—if you sell goods or services on credit
- Records of the assets of the firm, depreciation schedules, and insurance coverages
- Copies of previous years' tax returns
- Legal documents

Corporations, of course, are a special case. For example, you will need to keep records of the minutes of stockholders' meetings, among other things.

For further details on record-keeping, refer to Figures 4-4 and 4-5. (The latter deals with the important subject of records retention, or how long records of different types should be kept on file.)

---

**FIGURE 4-3. Sample classification of accounts.**

*Assets (Debit)*

100—Cash in Banks
101—Petty Cash Fund
102—Accounts Receivable
105—Materials and Supplies
107—Prepaid Expenses
108—Deposits
120—Land
121—Buildings
122—Reserve for Depreciation—Buildings (Credit)
123—Tools and Equipment
124—Reserve for Depreciation—Tools and Equipment (Credit)
125—Automotive Equipment
126—Reserve for Depreciation—Automotive Equipment (Credit)
127—Furniture and Fixtures
128—Reserve for Depreciation—Furniture and Fixtures (Credit)
130—Organization Expenses (to be amortized)

*Liabilities (Credit)*

200—Accounts Payable
201—Notes Payable
205—Sales Taxes—Payable
206—FICA Taxes—Payable
207—Federal Withholding Taxes
208—State Withholding Taxes
209—Unemployment Taxes
220—Long-Term Debt—Mortgages Payable
221—Long-term Debt—SBA Loan
225—Miscellaneous Accruals

*Capital Accounts (Credit)*

300—Common Capital Stock
301—Preferred Capital Stock } for Corporations

or

300—Proprietorship Account
301—Proprietor's Withdrawals } for Proprietorship
305—Retained Earnings

*Sales Accounts (Credit)*

400—Retail Sales
401—Wholesale Sales
402—Sales—Services
405—Miscellaneous Income

*Expenses (Debit)*

500—Salaries and Wages
501—Contract Labor
502—Payroll Taxes
503—Utilities
504—Telephone
505—Rent
506—Office Supplies
507—Postage
508—Maintenance Expense
509—Insurance
510—Interest
511—Depreciation
512—Travel Expense
513—Entertainment
514—Advertising
515—Dues and Contributions
520—Miscellaneous Expenses

The use of too many accounts should be avoided. Break down sales into enough categories to show a clear picture of the business. Use different expense accounts covering frequent or substantial expenditures, but avoid minute distinctions which will tend to confuse rather than clarify. Use Miscellaneous Expense for small unrelated expense items.

**Source:** John Cotton, "Keeping Records in Small Business," *Small Marketers Aids No. 155* (Washington, D.C.: Small Business Administration, May 1974), pp. 5–6.

**FIGURE 4-4.  Your business checkbook.**

All major payments should be made by checks drawn on a bank account used only for business transactions. If your business is typical, you will have to write checks for merchandise purchases, employees' salaries, rent, utilities, petty cash, payroll taxes, and various other expenses.

### Your Checkbook

Your business checkbook should be the large desk-type checkbook. Such a checkbook usually has three checks to a page and large stubs on which to write a full description of each expenditure. It may have the name and address of your business printed on each check, and the checks should be prenumbered.

As each check is written, enter on the stub the date, payee, amount, and purpose of the payment. A running balance of the amount you have in the bank is maintained by subtracting the amount of each check from the existing balance shown on the check stub.

When a check is spoiled, tear off the signature part of the check to prevent any possibility of the check's being used, write "VOID" prominently on the check and on the stub, and staple the torn check to the back of its stub. This assures you that the check has not been used in an unauthorized way.


### Supporting Documents

Every check should have some sort of written document to support it—an invoice, petty-cash voucher, payroll summary, and so on. If such support is not available for some good reason, a memo should be written stating what the check is for.

Each of these supporting documents should be approved, by signature or initials, by you or someone you have authorized to do so. The signature should indicate that the goods or services have been received, that the terms and price are correct, and that no error has been made in computing the amount to be paid. It is especially important to see that cash discounts, when offered, are correctly computed and deducted.

When each check is written, the supporting document should be marked "Paid" and the date and check number shown. If the checks are prepared for your signature by an employee, you should see the supporting document before you sign the check. Make certain that it is marked in a way to prevent its being paid a second time. After payment has been made, this supporting material should be filed in a paid-bills file in alphabetical order by payee.


### Paying the Bills

Bills are usually paid once a month unless there are special discount terms or special arrangements with suppliers for daily or weekly settlement. Most vendors send monthly statements, often in addition to delivery tickets and/or invoices for each individual purchase. Before the monthly statement is paid, the items on it should be checked against the individual invoices for correctness and to make sure that no item on the statement has already been paid on the basis of its invoice. Any balance brought forward from an earlier month should also be carefully checked to make sure that it is correct and has not already been paid.


### Reconciling Your Bank Statement

The bank will periodically send you your canceled checks and a statement of your bank account. Some banks send out statements once a month, on various days of the month. Others, particularly in the case of accounts without much activity, send out statements less often. However, you can arrange with your bank to have your statement sent each month as of the last business day of the month. This will make it easier for you to *reconcile* your records with the bank statement—that is, to compare the two records and account for any differences.

Reconciling your bank statement every month without fail is an important step in keeping accurate records. Even if someone else does the rest of your recordkeeping, you should do the bank reconciliation yourself.

**Source:** Robert C. Ragan, "Financial Recordkeeping for Small Stores," *Small Business Management Series No. 32,* revised printing. (Washington, D.C., Small Business Administration, 1976), pp. 19–21.

## FIGURE 4-5.   Records retention.

Accounting Records

*Journals, Ledgers, Registers:* As the basic accounting summary, the general ledger should be retained indefinitely. Books of original entry, such as the cash receipts book and the cash disbursements book, should be retained for at least six years. They would be essential, for example, to support challenged items on income tax returns.

*Accounts Payable (cancelled checks, vouchers):* Cancelled general checks should be kept for the number of years required by your state's Statute of Limitations. Such laws range from three to twenty years and average 6 years. Many companies keep payroll checks for only three years. Vouchers may be divided into plant vouchers (retain indefinitely) and petty cash vouchers (retain for one to two years).

*Accounts Receivable (billing copies of invoices, credit-memo invoices, accounts receivable ledger):* Your chief concern is in the unpaid invoices. Paid invoices often may be disposed of within three to four years because few complaints are received after that time. Your accounts receivable ledger—as a basic summary of credit sales—need be kept only so long as it is a ready index to invoices or total daily sales.

*Tax Records:* These are important, since they may be audited by local, state, and federal taxing authorities. For sales and use taxes most states and local jurisdictions require that the tax return forms be retained three years. After that, these jurisdictions would ordinarily not conduct an audit of the return. State and Federal income tax returns and the records which back up the figures on the tax returns should be kept at least six years. The Statute of Limitations which applies to normal tax returns may be extended if the taxing authorities can prove the tax returns to have been fraudulently prepared.

Legal Papers

A small business may have many other types of records which should be kept for legal reasons. Some of them are evidences of ownership and, for that reason, are assets that should be guarded zealously while they have value. Typically, a copyright, a letter of patent, and a trademark registration should be kept indefinitely even though they have a definite expiration date. The possibility of having to prove ownership of such assets in law suits may arise even after the ownership has expired. Similarly, deeds and right-of-way and easement records should be kept indefinitely. Contracts and leases, on the other hand, can be destroyed 6 years after they expire (unless renewed annually). Records on law suits should be retained from six to ten years after they are settled.

When a business is a corporation, its by-laws, minutes of stockholders' meetings, and annual reports are usually retained indefinitely. Cancelled stock certificates, except for those corporations regulated by the Securities and Exchange Commission, may be destroyed at the discretion of the company as long as a record of such destruction is kept (10 years as a general rule). Since corporations are governed by some State agency, it is a good idea to check with the appropriate agency to see that the records being kept are the proper ones.

Payroll and Personnel Records

Information on employee wages and hours must be retained for three years to comply with the Fair Labor Standards Act. The records do not have to be kept on any particular form. Supporting data, such as timecards and piecework tickets, need to be kept only two years. Microfilm copies of such documents are generally acceptable.

*Payroll records* which include wage payments and deductions for Federal income taxes and Social Security must be retained for at least 4 years after the tax becomes due or is paid, whichever is later. You should check your State and local authorities because some of these jurisdictions require that payroll records be kept longer than four years.

*Pension records* should be retained at least a year after the death of the pensioner. *Personnel records,* such as employee applications, however, can be retained according to your needs.

Production Records

*Production records,* such as job tickets, production orders, maintenance records, and operating reports, have a short life as far as retention is concerned. Job tickets can be discarded after a job is completed; the production order may be retained one year or longer. If a company is audited, all production records should be kept until the audit is completed. *Maintenance records* are kept usually for the life of the equipment on which the data are compiled.

*Purchasing (purchase orders, requisitions, and receiving reports):* Major purchase records, particularly where specifications are included, should be kept for six years. Routine items may be cut to three years and still be within legal requirements for tax purposes on proof of cash and charge purchases of supplies and other items used in the business. Purchase requisitions need be retained only until the items are received. Receiving reports are usually supporting documents for the accounts payable vouchers and are retained accordingly.

*Traffic (bills of lading, freight bills, packing lists):* The only legal requirement on these items is by the Department of Labor, Wage and Hour and Public

Contracts Divisions, on "order, shipping and billing records" and calls for retention for two years.

**Source:** Robert A. Shiff, "Records Retention: Normal and Disaster," *Management Aids No. 210.* (Washington, D.C.: Small Business Administration, September 1973 reprint).

As we all know only too well, the federal government insists on collecting its just share of our earned income. This is the case no matter what form that income takes: salaries, commissions, stock dividends, capital gains on the sale of property, gambling winnings, interest on bank accounts, and profits from operating a business.

**COMMENTS ABOUT TAXES**

Most states also have the same attitude. To further compound the problem, some of our country's larger cities also impose an income tax.

As the owner of a new mail order company, you will face the same situation. You will be liable for income tax on the profits it generates and for various other taxes. It would be wise, then, to find out as much as you can about tax liabilities—and responsibilities—as a business owner, even before you start your business. You need to know what to expect. Remember, the lack of knowledge is no defense (to the Internal Revenue Service, that is).

There is little room here for more than a cursory treatment of the subject of taxation. For a more detailed understanding, a helpful book can be obtained from your local office of the Internal Revenue Service. It is called Publication 334, "Tax Guide for Small Business." (You can have it mailed to you.) It carries detailed instructions regarding accounting methods, how to determine your gross profit and net income or loss, information on the acquisition and disposal of business assets, sample filled-in tax forms (for sole proprietorships, partnerships, and corporations), information regarding tax credits, and so on.

If you have one or more employees working for you, ask also for the "Employer's Tax Guide, Circular E." And request a copy of Publication 534, "Tax Information on Depreciation." This booklet will help in working out depreciation schedules for your business assets.

Different legal forms of business call for different approaches to the federal tax on income. If you are the owner of a small business, have no partners, and did not select the corporate form, you are a sole proprietor. Tax laws require you to file annually the same Form 1040 you used while you were working at your job. This is the case whether you use your own name for the business or have assumed a trade name (which, of course, you registered). You will show your company's name on the proper line on Schedule C, where you must report your business results for the year. Schedule C is titled "Profit or Loss From Business or Profession—Sole Proprietorship" (see Figure 4-6).

**Federal Income Tax**

If you are one of the partners (a principal) in a partnership, you still file Form 1040 at income tax time. On it, you will report your

**SCHEDULE C**
(Form 1040)

Department of the Treasury
Internal Revenue Service

# Profit or (Loss) From Business or Profession
(Sole Proprietorship)

Partnerships, Joint Ventures, etc., Must File Form 1065.

▶ Attach to Form 1040 or Form 1041.  ▶ See Instructions for Schedule C (Form 1040).

**1980**

09

Name of proprietor

Social security number of proprietor

**A** Main business activity (see Instructions) ▶ _____ ; product ▶ _____

**B** Business name ▶

**C** Employer identification number

**D** Business address (number and street) ▶ _____
City, State and ZIP Code ▶ _____

**C**

**E** Accounting method: **(1)** ☐ Cash  **(2)** ☐ Accrual  **(3)** ☐ Other (specify) ▶ _____

**F** Method(s) used to value closing inventory:
**(1)** ☐ Cost  **(2)** ☐ Lower of cost or market  **(3)** ☐ Other (if other, attach explanation)

| | Yes | No |
|---|---|---|

**G** Was there any major change in determining quantities, costs, or valuations between opening and closing inventory? . . If "Yes," attach explanation.

**H** Did you deduct expenses for an office in your home? . . . . . . . . . . . . . . . . . . . .

**I** Did you elect to claim amortization (under section 191) or depreciation (under section 167(o)) for a rehabilitated certified historic structure (see Instructions)? . . . . . . . . . . . . . . . . . .
(Amortizable basis (see Instructions) ▶ _____ )

## Part I  Income

| | | | | |
|---|---|---|---|---|
| **1 a** Gross receipts or sales . . . . . . . . . . | **1a** | | | |
| **b** Returns and allowances . . . . . . . . | **1b** | | | |
| **c** Balance (subtract line 1b from line 1a) . . . . . . . . . . . | | **1c** | | |
| **2** Cost of goods sold and/or operations (Schedule C–1, line 8) . . . . . . . . . . | | **2** | | |
| **3** Gross profit (subtract line 2 from line 1c) . . . . . . . . . . . . | | **3** | | |
| **4** Other income (attach schedule) . . . . . . . . . . . . . . . | | **4** | | |
| **5** Total income (add lines 3 and 4) . . . . . . . . . . . . . . ▶ | | **5** | | |

## Part II  Deductions

| | | | | | | |
|---|---|---|---|---|---|---|
| **6** Advertising . . . . . . . | | | **31 a** Wages . . | | | |
| **7** Amortization . . . . . . | | | **b** Jobs credit | | | |
| **8** Bad debts from sales or services . | | | **c** WIN credit | | | |
| **9** Bank charges . . . . . . . | | | **d** Total credits | | | |
| **10** Car and truck expenses . . . . | | | **e** Subtract line 31d from 31a . | | | |
| **11** Commissions . . . . . . . | | | **32** Other expenses (specify): | | | |
| **12** Depletion . . . . . . . . | | | **a** | | | |
| **13** Depreciation (explain in Schedule C–2) . | | | **b** | | | |
| **14** Dues and publications . . . . | | | **c** | | | |
| **15** Employee benefit programs . . | | | **d** | | | |
| **16** Freight (not included on Schedule C–1) . | | | **e** | | | |
| **17** Insurance . . . . . . . . | | | **f** | | | |
| **18** Interest on business indebtedness . | | | **g** | | | |
| **19** Laundry and cleaning . . . . | | | **h** | | | |
| **20** Legal and professional services . | | | **i** | | | |
| **21** Office supplies . . . . . . | | | **j** | | | |
| **22** Pension and profit-sharing plans . | | | **k** | | | |
| **23** Postage . . . . . . . . . | | | **l** | | | |
| **24** Rent on business property . . . | | | **m** | | | |
| **25** Repairs . . . . . . . . . | | | **n** | | | |
| **26** Supplies (not included on Schedule C–1) . | | | **o** | | | |
| **27** Taxes . . . . . . . . . . | | | **p** | | | |
| **28** Telephone . . . . . . . . | | | **q** | | | |
| **29** Travel and entertainment . . . | | | **r** | | | |
| **30** Utilities . . . . . . . . . | | | **s** | | | |

| | | |
|---|---|---|
| **33** Total deductions (add amounts in columns for lines 6 through 32s) . . . . . . . . . . ▶ | **33** | |
| **34** Net profit or (loss) (subtract line 33 from line 5). If a profit, enter on Form 1040, line 13, and on Schedule SE, Part II, line 5a (or Form 1041, line 6). If a loss, go on to line 35 . . . . . | **34** | |

**35** If you have a loss, do you have amounts for which you are **not** "at risk" in this business (see Instructions)? . . ☐ Yes ☐ No

**FIGURE 4-6**

share of the partnership's income. However, another form for information purposes only must be sent to the Internal Revenue Service, Form 1065, "U.S. Partnership Return of Income." The

## SCHEDULE C–1.—Cost of Goods Sold and/or Operations (See Schedule C Instructions for Part I, line 2)

| | | |
|---|---|---|
| 1 Inventory at beginning of year (if different from last year's closing inventory, attach explanation) . | 1 | |
| 2 a Purchases . . . . . . . . . . . . . . . . . .   2a | | |
|    b Cost of items withdrawn for personal use . . . . . .   2b | | |
|    c Balance (subtract line 2b from line 2a) . . . . . . . . . . . . . . | 2c | |
| 3 Cost of labor (do not include salary paid to yourself) . . . . . . . . . . . . . | 3 | |
| 4 Materials and supplies . . . . . . . . . . . . . . . . . . . . | 4 | |
| 5 Other costs (attach schedule) . . . . . . . . . . . . . . . . . | 5 | |
| 6 Add lines 1, 2c, and 3 through 5 . . . . . . . . . . . . . . . . . | 6 | |
| 7 Inventory at end of year . . . . . . . . . . . . . . . . . . . ▶ | 7 | |
| 8 Cost of goods sold and/or operations (subtract line 7 from line 6). Enter here and on Part I, line 2 . ▶ | 8 | |

## SCHEDULE C–2.—Depreciation (See Schedule C Instructions for line 13)
### If you need more space, please use Form 4562.

| Description of property (a) | Date acquired (b) | Cost or other basis (c) | Depreciation allowed or allowable in prior years (d) | Method of computing depreciation (e) | Life or rate (f) | Depreciation for this year (g) |
|---|---|---|---|---|---|---|
| 1 Total additional first-year depreciation (do not include in items below) (see instructions for limitation) ➞ | | | | | | |
| 2 Other depreciation: | | | | | | |
| | | | | | | |
| | | | | | | |
| | | | | | | |
| | | | | | | |
| | | | | | | |
| | | | | | | |
| | | | | | | |
| | | | | | | |
| | | | | | | |
| | | | | | | |
| 3 Totals . . . . . . . . . . . . . . . . . . . . | | | | | 3 | |
| 4 Depreciation claimed in Schedule C–1 . . . . . . . . . . . . | | | | | 4 | |
| 5 Balance (subtract line 4 from line 3). Enter here and on Part II, line 13 . . . . . . . . ▶ | | | | | 5 | |

## SCHEDULE C–3.—Expense Account Information (See Schedule C Instructions for Schedule C–3)

Enter information for yourself and your five highest paid employees. In determining the five highest paid employees, add expense account allowances to the salaries and wages. However, you don't have to provide the information for any employee for whom the combined amount is less than $25,000, or for yourself if your expense account allowance plus line 34, page 1, is less than $25,000.

| Name (a) | Expense account (b) | Salaries and wages (c) |
|---|---|---|
| Owner . . . . . . . . . . . . . . | | |
| 1 | | |
| 2 | | |
| 3 | | |
| 4 | | |
| 5 | | |

| | Yes | No |
|---|---|---|
| Did you claim a deduction for expenses connected with: | | |
| A Entertainment facility (boat, resort, ranch, etc.)? . . . . . . . . . . . . . . . | | |
| B Living accommodations (except employees on business)? . . . . . . . . . . . . | | |
| C Conventions or meetings you or your employees attended outside the U.S. or its possessions? (see Instructions) . . | | |
| D Employees' families at conventions or meetings? . . . . . . . . . . . . . . | | |
|    If "Yes," were any of these conventions or meetings outside the U.S. or its possessions? . . . . . . | | |
| E Vacations for employees or their families not reported on Form W–2? . . . . . . . . . . . | | |

☆ U S GOVERNMENT PRINTING OFFICE: 1980 –313-259   31-0598032

income tax is levied against you as an individual, not against the partnership (and, of course, against your other partners).

    Corporations are treated differently. Since they have an existence of their own, they are required to pay taxes on profits directly.

Form 1120, "U.S. Corporation Income Tax Return" is used for filing the return, unless you have elected the small business corporation (S-type) form. In that case, you report on Form 1120S, "U.S. Small Business Corporation Income Tax Return."

Although the corporation itself will have to pay income tax, you—as an employee of the corporation—still must complete Form 1040 when you file.

It should also be pointed out that a sole proprietor or a partner generally needs to file a declaration of estimated tax (Form 1040ES) along with the Form 1040, and pay any tax due in four installments throughout the year. (The entire amount may be paid in full, if this is desired.) Corporations also need to pay estimated tax and deposit payments at regular intervals.

## Other Kinds of Taxes

At the federal level, you must be concerned with your employees' income taxes (and withholding rules), FICA taxes, and FUTA taxes. State taxes will differ—in regulations, dates of payment, and amounts—from one state to the next. There are unemployment taxes, sales taxes, and income taxes. And, locally, you need to think about real estate taxes and, possibly, sales and/or personal property taxes, too.

Contact all taxing authorities in your area for information. Your accountant can help you tremendously. So can your state department of labor, if you employ help.

You also should know that if you operate your mail order company as either a sole proprietorship or a partnership, you must pay a self-employment tax. This is in lieu of the social security tax you paid in the past as an employee (unless you are still working at a job and are conducting business as a sideline). This tax is computed on Schedule SE and submitted along with your Form 1040 (see Figure 4-7). In this connection, obtain a copy of IRS Publication 533, "Information on Self-Employment Tax."

## SUGGESTED READING

### Books

BARNES, JOHN, *How to Cut Your Taxes.* West Caldwell, N.J.: William Morrow, 1976.

BOWER, JAMES B., and HAROLD Q. LANGENDERFER, *Income Tax Procedure.* Cincinnati: South-Western, 1979.

HARTLEY, W. C. F., and YALE L. MELTZER, *Cash Management: Planning, Forecasting and Control.* Englewood Cliffs, N.J.: Prentice-Hall, Inc., 1979.

Internal Revenue Service, "Tax Guide for Small Business, 1980," Publication 334. Washington, D.C.: Internal Revenue Service, 1980.

LANE, MARC J. *Legal Handbook for Small Business.* New York: American Management Associations, 1978.

Prentice-Hall Editorial Staff. *Federal Tax Handbook, 1980 Edition.* Englewood Cliffs, N.J.: Prentice-Hall, Inc., 1979.

WALKER, ERNEST W., and J. WILLIAM PETTY II, *Financial Management of the Small Firm.* Englewood Cliffs, N.J.: Prentice-Hall, Inc., 1978.

**SCHEDULE SE (Form 1040)**
Department of the Treasury
Internal Revenue Service

## Computation of Social Security Self-Employment Tax

▶ See Instructions for Schedule SE (Form 1040).
▶ Attach to Form 1040.

**1980**
23

Name of self-employed person (as shown on social security card) | Social security number of self-employed person ▶

**Part I** Computation of Net Earnings from FARM Self-Employment

| | | | |
|---|---|---|---|
| **Regular Method** | | | |
| 1 Net profit or (loss) from: | | | |
| a Schedule F (Form 1040) | 1a | | |
| b Farm partnerships | 1b | | |
| 2 Net earnings from farm self-employment (add lines 1a and 1b) | 2 | | |
| **Farm Optional Method** | | | |
| 3 If gross profits from farming are: a Not more than $2,400, enter two-thirds of the gross profits; b More than $2,400 and the net farm profit is less than $1,600, enter $1,600 | 3 | | |
| 4 Enter here and on line 12a, the amount on line 2, or line 3 if you elect the farm optional method | 4 | | |

**SE**

**Part II** Computation of Net Earnings from NONFARM Self-Employment

| | | | |
|---|---|---|---|
| **Regular Method** | | | |
| 5 Net profit or (loss) from: | | | |
| a Schedule C (Form 1040) | 5a | | |
| b Partnerships, joint ventures, etc. (other than farming) | 5b | | |
| c Service as a minister, member of a religious order, or a Christian Science practitioner. (Include rental value of parsonage or rental allowance furnished.) If you filed Form 4361 and have not revoked that exemption, check here ▶ ☐ and enter zero on this line | 5c | | |
| d Service with a foreign government or international organization | 5d | | |
| e Other (specify) ▶ | 5e | | |
| 6 Total (add lines 5a through 5e) | 6 | | |
| 7 Enter adjustments if any (attach statement, see page 29 of Instructions) | 7 | | |
| 8 Adjusted net earnings or (loss) from nonfarm self-employment (line 6, as adjusted by line 7) | 8 | | |
| Note: *If line 8 is $1,600 or more* **or** *if you do not elect to use the Nonfarm Optional Method, skip lines 9 through 11 and enter amount from line 8 on line 12b.* | | | |
| **Nonfarm Optional Method** | | | |
| 9 a Maximum amount reportable under both optional methods combined (farm and nonfarm) | 9a | $1,600 | 00 |
| b Enter amount from line 3. (If you did not elect to use the farm optional method, enter zero.) | 9b | | |
| c Balance (subtract line 9b from line 9a) | 9c | | |
| 10 Enter two-thirds of gross nonfarm profits or $1,600, whichever is smaller | 10 | | |
| 11 Enter here and on line 12b, the amount on line 9c or line 10, whichever is smaller | 11 | | |

**Part III** Computation of Social Security Self-Employment Tax

| | | | |
|---|---|---|---|
| 12 Net earnings or (loss): | | | |
| a From farming (from line 4) | 12a | | |
| b From nonfarm (from line 8, or line 11 if you elect to use the Nonfarm Optional Method) | 12b | | |
| 13 Total net earnings or (loss) from self-employment reported on lines 12a and 12b. **(If line 13 is less than $400, you are not subject to self-employment tax. Do not fill in rest of schedule)** | 13 | | |
| 14 The largest amount of combined wages and self-employment earnings subject to social security or railroad retirement taxes for 1980 is | 14 | $25,900 | 00 |
| 15 a Total "FICA" wages (from Forms W-2) and "RRTA" compensation — 15a | | | |
| b Unreported tips subject to FICA tax from Form 4137, line 9 or to RRTA — 15b | | | |
| c Add lines 15a and 15b | 15c | | |
| 16 Balance (subtract line 15c from line 14) | 16 | | |
| 17 Self-employment income—line 13 or 16, whichever is smaller | 17 | | |
| 18 Self-employment tax. (If line 17 is $25,900, enter $2,097.90; if less, multiply the amount on line 17 by .081.) Enter here and on Form 1040, line 48 | 18 | | |

U.S. GOVERNMENT PRINTING OFFICE: 1980— 313-265 23-188-5979

**FIGURE 4-7**

### Free Materials from the Small Business Administration

*Management aids*

#170 Staff Members, Financial Assistance, Small Business Administration, "The ABC's of Borrowing," revised April 1977.

#210 SHIFF, ROBERT A., "Records Retention: Normal and Disaster," September 1973.

#234 GOULET, PETER G.,"Attacking Business Decision Problems with Break-even Analysis," March 1978.

#235 Hosmer, LaRue Tone, "A Venture Capital Primer for Small Business," August 1978.

*Small business bibliographies*

#15 "Recordkeeping Systems—Small Store and Service Trade," revised May 1977.

*Small marketers aids*

# 71 "Checklist for Going into Business," revised September 1977.

#130 ABRAHAM, ALFRED B., "Analyze Your Records to Reduce Costs," reprinted July 1977.

#142 RADICS, STEPHEN P., JR., "Steps in Meeting Your Tax Obligations," revised January 1975.

#144 GREENE, WILLIAM C., "Getting the Facts for Income Tax Reporting," June 1970.

#147 MURPHY, JOHN F., "Sound Cash Management and Borrowing," reprinted July 1977.

#149 CALEY, JOHN D., "Computers for Small Business: Service Bureaus or Time-Sharing," reprinted August 1973.

#155 COTTON, JOHN, "Keeping Records in Small Business," May 1974.

#165 BHANDARI, NARENDRA C., "Checklist for Profit Watching," May 1978.

**To Order from the Superintendent of Documents**

*Small business management series*

#15 ZWICK, JACK, "A Handbook of Small Business Finance," *Small Business Management Series No. 15,* 8th ed. Washington, D.C.: Small Business Administration, 1975. (Stock #045-000-00139-3.)

#32 RAGAN, ROBERT C., "Financial Recordkeeping for Small Stores," *Small Business Management Series No. 32.* Revised printing. Washington, D.C.: Small Business Administration, 1976. (Stock #045-000-00142-3.)

**5**

# MORE PRELIMINARIES TO SETTING UP YOUR OPERATION

Now that you have some knowledge of the financial end of running a business, you must begin thinking about its administrative management. This chapter will help you to understand and clarify several important problem areas, such as:

- Where to go for counsel and assistance
- Which legal form of business to choose
- How to protect your business (and yourself) against serious losses
- How to set up and run your "operations center"

In the Appendix is a valuable Checklist for Going into Business, available free from the Small Business Administration. Spend a lot of time working through this guide; it is an excellent preparation for Chapter 6, which covers setting up your own business plan.

**SOURCES OF ASSISTANCE**

If you are like the majority of people who go into business for the first time, you have had little or no prior management training. Or management experience. Or knowledge of where to go for advice or to ferret out information you may need. Several of these resources are discussed in this section.

**The Small Business Administration**

In your new role as mail order entrepreneur, you will find the Small Business Administration to be a valuable source of information and help. Created by congressional action in the 1950s, this federal agency exists to serve the needs of—and encourage the growth of—small enterprises in America.

If you were a manufacturer, or in a wholesale business, the agency could help you with government procurement assistance and in subcontracting. Since you are in mail order, however, their most important contributions will be in the areas of providing management help and advice and financial assistance. Field offices of this organization are spotted throughout the country in more than 90 locations. (See Figure 5-1 for a complete listing of addresses.) You can make an appointment by telephone to see one of their SCORE or ACE counselors. (SCORE stands for Service Corps of Retired Executives; ACE, for the Active Corps of Executives.) You will get worthwhile advice from former business owners.

At these offices are management assistance officers who set up business management courses, workshops, conferences, and business clinics in their areas. They also work with small business institutes at colleges and universities.

Scores of booklets and pamphlets are also available free of charge. In fact, many of them are noted at the ends of chapters in this book. For an order form and copies of these publications, call toll-free 800-433-7212. (If you live in Texas, call 800-792-8901.) If you prefer to write, address your letter to the Small Business Administration, P. O. Box 15434, Fort Worth, Tex. 76119.

Most people in small business think of the SBA in terms of the financial assistance it can render. The agency can provide loans for a variety of purposes: construction, expansion, the purchase of machinery, even working capital. They may loan money to a business directly or, more commonly, enter into a participation agreement with a bank. There are also special SBA programs for disaster, physical damage, and economic injury loans, as well as loans for the handicapped and the economically disadvantaged. Other programs include lease guarantee, surety bond, and minority enterprises. The agency also licenses small business investment companies (SBICs) to work with small firms and makes loans to state and local development companies. Visit your local office for full details.

---

**FIGURE 5-1.  Offices of the Small Business Administration.**

| | |
|---|---|
| Boston | Massachusetts 02114, 150 Causeway Street |
| Holyoke | Massachusetts 01050, 302 High Street |
| Augusta | Maine 04330, 40 Western Avenue, Room 512 |
| Concord | New Hampshire 03301, 55 Pleasant Street |
| Hartford | Connecticut 06103, One Financial Plaza |
| Montpelier | Vermont 05602, 87 State Street, P.O. Box 605 |
| Providence | Rhode Island 02903, 57 Eddy Street |
| | |
| New York | New York 10007, 26 Federal Plaza, Room 3100 |
| Albany | New York 12210, 3100 Twin Towers Building |

| | |
|---|---|
| Elmira | New York 14901, 180 State Street, Room 412 |
| Hato Rey | Puerto Rico 00919, Chardon and Bolivia Streets |
| Melville | New York 11746, 425 Broad Hollow Road |
| Newark | New Jersey 07102, 970 Broad Street, Room 1635 |
| Camden | New Jersey 08104, 1800 East Davis Street |
| Rochester | New York 14014, 100 State Street |
| Syracuse | New York 13260, 100 South Clinton Street, Room 1071 |
| Buffalo | New York 14202, 111 West Huron Street |
| St. Thomas | Virgin Islands 00801, Federal Office Building, Veterans' Drive |
| Philadelphia | Bala Cynwyd, Pennsylvania 19004, One Bala Cynwyd Plaza |
| Harrisburg | Pennsylvania 17101, 100 Chestnut Street |
| Wilkes-Barre | Pennsylvania 18702, 20 North Pennsylvania Avenue |
| Baltimore | Towson, Maryland 21204, 8600 La Salle Road |
| Wilmington | Delaware 19801, 844 King Street |
| Clarksburg | West Virginia 26301, 109 N. 3rd Street |
| Charleston | West Virginia 25301, Charleston National Plaza, Suite 628 |
| Pittsburgh | Pennsylvania 15222, 1000 Liberty Avenue |
| Richmond | Virginia 23240, 400 N. 8th Street, Room 3015 |
| Washington | D.C. 20417, 1030 15th Street, NW., Suite 250 |
| Atlanta | Georgia 30309, 1720 Peachtree Road, NW |
| Biloxi | Mississippi 39530, 111 Fred Haise Boulevard |
| Birmingham | Alabama 35205, 908 South 20th Street |
| Charlotte | North Carolina 28202, 230 South Tryon Street, Suite 700 |
| Greenville | North Carolina 27834, 215 South Evans Street |
| Columbia | South Carolina 29201, 1801 Assembly Street |
| Coral Gables | Florida 33134, 2222 Ponce de Leon Boulevard |
| Jackson | Mississippi 39201, 200 East Pascagoula Street |
| Jacksonville | Florida 32202, 400 W. Bay Street |
| West Palm Beach | Florida 33402, 701 Clematis Street |
| Tampa | Florida 33602, 700 Twiggs Street |
| Lousiville | Kentucky 40202, 600 Federal Place, Room 188 |
| Nashville | Tennessee 37219, 404 James Robertson Parkway, Suite 1012 |
| Knoxville | Tennessee 37902, 502 South Gay Street, Room 307 |
| Memphis | Tennessee 38103, 167 North Main Street |
| Chicago | Illinois 60604, 219 South Dearborn Street |
| Springfield | Illinois 62701, 1 North Old State Capitol Plaza |
| Cleveland | Ohio 44199, 1240 East 9th Street, Room 317 |
| Columbus | Ohio 43215, 85 Marconi Boulevard |
| Cincinnati | Ohio 45202, 550 Main Street, Room 5028 |
| Detroit | Michigan 48226, 477 Michigan Avenue |
| Marquette | Michigan 49885, 540 West Kaye Avenue |
| Indianapolis | Indiana 46204, 575 North Pennsylvania Street |
| Madison | Wisconsin 53703, 122 West Washington Avenue |
| Milwaukee | Wisconsin 53202, 517 East Wisconsin Avenue |
| Eau Claire | Wisconsin 54701, 500 South Barstow Street, Room B9AA |
| Minneapolis | Minnesota 55402, 12 South Sixth Street |

| | |
|---|---|
| Dallas | Texas 75242, 1100 Commerce Street |
| Albuquerque | New Mexico 87110, 5000 Marble Avenue, NE |
| Houston | Texas 77002, 1 Allen Center, 500 Dallas Street |
| Little Rock | Arkansas 72201, 611 Gaines Street |
| Lubbock | Texas 79401, 1205 Texas Avenue |
| El Paso | Texas 79902, 4100 Rio Bravo, Suite 300 |
| Lower Rio Grande Valley | Harlington, Texas 78550, 222 East Van Buren |
| Corpus Christi | Texas 78408, 3105 Leopard Street |
| Marshall | Texas 75670, 100 South Washington Street, Room G12 |
| New Orleans | Louisiana 70113, 1001 Howard Avenue |
| Shreveport | Louisiana 71101, 500 Fannin Street |
| Oklahoma City | Oklahoma 73102, 200 N.W. 5th Street |
| San Antonio | Texas 78206, 727 East Durango, Room A-513 |
| | |
| Kansas City | Missouri 64016, 1150 Grand Avenue |
| Des Moines | Iowa 50309, 210 Walnut Street |
| Omaha | Nebraska 68102, Nineteenth and Farnam Streets |
| St. Louis | Missouri 63101, Mercantile Tower, Suite 2500 |
| Wichita | Kansas 67202, 110 East Waterman Street |
| | |
| Denver | Colorado 80202, 721 19th Street |
| Casper | Wyoming 82601, 100 East B Street, Room 4001 |
| Fargo | North Dakota 58102, 657 2d Avenue, North, Room 218 |
| Helena | Montana 59601, 301 South Park |
| Salt Lake City | Utah 84138, 125 South State Street, Room 2237 |
| Rapid City | South Dakota 57701, 515 9th Street |
| Sioux Falls | South Dakota 57102, 8th and Main Avenue |
| San Francisco | California 94105, 211 Main Street |
| Fresno | California 93712, 1229 N Street |
| Sacramento | California 95825, 2800 Cottage Way |
| Honolulu | Hawaii 96850, 300 Ala Moana |
| Agana | Guam 96910, Pacific Daily News Building |
| Los Angeles | California 90071, 350 South Figueroa Street |
| Las Vegas | Nevada 89101, 301 East Stewart |
| Reno | Nevada 89505, 50 South Virginia Street |
| Phoenix | Arizona 85012, 3030 North Central Avenue |
| San Diego | California 92188, 880 Front Street |
| | |
| Seattle | Washington 98174, 915 Second Avenue |
| Anchorage | Alaska 99501, 1016 West Sixth Avenue, Suite 200 |
| Fairbanks | Alaska 99701, 101 12th Avenue |
| Boise | Idaho 83701, 1005 Main Street |
| Portland | Oregon 97204, 1220 South West Third Avenue |
| Spokane | Washington 99120, Courthouse Bldg., Room 651 |

**Other Government Agencies**

Help is available from other government agencies besides the SBA, not only at the federal, but also often at state and local levels. Among the federal agencies, the Bureau of Census of the Department of Commerce is probably the biggest supplier of information (see Figure 5-2). The Department of Labor puts out the *Survey of Consumer Expenditures;* the Federal Reserve System issues, on a monthly basis, the *Federal Reserve Bulletin;* and so on. New York State, for example, issues a guide for small business.

A number of organizations can be useful in managing your new enterprise. There are also several publications oriented toward small business in particular; these seem to contain valuable information in most issues.

In addition to those organizations of interest to business in general, such as the American Management Associations (135 West 50th Street, New York, N.Y. 10020) and the American Marketing Association (222 Riverside Plaza, Chicago, Ill. 60606), you might contact these organizations for advice and assistance: the International Entrepreneurs Association and the National Mail Order Association.

---

**FIGURE 5-2.   Some useful sources of government statistics.\***

Publications of the Bureau of the Census, Suitland, Md. 20233

*Census of Business for 1977. Retail—Area Statistics—U.S. Summary.* Final figures from the 1977 Census of Retail Trade. Includes statistical totals for each region, state, city, and standard metropolitan statistical area—tabulated by type of establishment.

*Census of Manufacturers for 1977.* Five-volume report about manufacturing industries. Location of manufacturing plants tabulated by state and counties.

*Census of Wholesale Trade for 1977.* Two-volume report of wholesalers, including geographical breakdowns by states, cities over 5,000 population, and standard metropolitan statistical areas.

*Census of Selected Service Industries for 1977.* Two-volume report of more than 150 kinds of service industries.

*Census of Population for 1970.* Most complete source of population data in the United States. (Census is taken every 10 years; results of the 1980 census will not be published for some time.)

*County Business Patterns.* Published annually. Shows employment, payrolls, and number of "reporting units" in detail for all kinds of business, for the United States and for states, counties, and SMSA's. (Individual state books can be purchased separately.)

*County and City Data Book.* Provides a wide variety of statistical information—population, agriculture, finance, trade, manufacturing, local government finances, climate, home equipment, etc. for counties, for cities of 25,000 population or more, for SMSA's, and for urbanized areas.

*Statistical Abstract of the United States.* Published annually. A general review of statistical data collected by the U. S. government and other public and private organizations. A good source of secondary data. (Available in most public libraries.)

Publications of the Department of Commerce, Washington, D. C. 20230

*Survey of Current Business.* Contains a wide variety of statistics and economic indicators dealing with all aspects of business—trade, finance, manufacturing, imports/exports, labor, construction, etc.—on a monthly basis.

*Business Statistics*. Biennial. A historical record of the statistics presented monthly in the *Survey of Current Business*.

---

*All publications may be ordered from the Superintendent of Documents, U.S. Government Printing Office, Washington, D.C. 20402.

**Source:** Keith K. Cox, James E. Stafford, and Art Palmer, "Marketing for Small Business," *Small Business Bibliography #89* (Washington, D.C.: Small Business Administration, revised November 1978), p. 5; and Thomas T. Semon, "Practical Business Use of Government Statistics," *Small Business Management Series No. 22* (Washington, D.C.: Small Business Administration, 1975), pp. 26–27.

### International Entrepreneurs Association (IEA)

This nonprofit organization, with well over 50,000 members, is located at 631 Wilshire Boulevard, Santa Monica, Calif. 90401 (213-394-3787). It was launched in 1973, via a one-inch advertisement in the *Wall Street Journal,* by Chase Revel, a successful multibusiness entrepreneur. The IEA provides in-depth research information on new business and offers manuals and plans for all kinds of enterprises, as well as management advice. It sponsors small business seminars and expositions around the country. The IEA also publishes the attractive and informative *Entrepreneur Magazine.*

### National Mail Order Association

This association, at 5818 Venice Boulevard, Los Angeles, Calif. 90019 (213-934-7986), provides a variety of worthwhile services for persons involved in mail order and direct marketing. A tremendous help is the monthly newsletter, *Mail Order Digest*. In addition to news from Washington and abroad, each issue contains valuable suggestions, new product listings, and other information for members.

### Other publications

*In Business,* a bi-monthly magazine published by The JG Press, Inc., Box 323, Emmaus, Pa. 18049 (215-967-4135), has a circulation of some 15,000. Readers are mostly owners of small businesses and entrepreneurs. Its own advertising material labels it "The Survival Guide for Human-Sized Enterprises," and it tries to live up to that label.

The *Journal of Small Business Management* is a more academic periodical, published on a quarterly basis by the International Council for Small Business. Each issue contains a number of highly informative articles about small business and its environment. It also lists resources and reports on new books in the field. For information, write to ICSB Executive Office, 929 North Sixth Street, Milwaukee, Wis. 53203.

*Inc.,* established in 1978, is a national business magazine "edited specifically for the owners and managers of smaller, growing companies whose annual sales are typically in the $1–30 million range." The typical month's issue contains how-to articles, summaries of experiences that confront its readers, profiles of entrepreneurs, provocative "think pieces," special reports, and so on. Its circulation has exceeded 400,000. The address: 38 Commercial Wharf, Boston, Mass. 02110 (617-227-4700).

There is also the all-important *Direct Marketing*—at least for everyone involved in selling products or services via the mails or through the mass media. Reading a number of issues is a must, just as an introduction to the field of mail order selling. And it is even more vital for you to know this publication if you are intent on succeding in this business. Every issue yields valuable insights into direct marketing. List compilers, brokers, and managers advertise in the book; so do manufacturers of items suitable for mail order—and manufacturers of all kinds of supplies you will need in your operation. This is the Bible for the field. The address is 224 Seventh Street, Garden City, N.Y. 11530 (516-746-6700).

## FORM OF OWNERSHIP

There are three common legal forms of ownership through which you can launch your new mail order business: sole proprietorship, partnership, and corporation. Each of these forms has its attractions and its drawbacks. Consider the following details with care; they can help to shape your decision.

### Sole Proprietorship

This is the most popular form of ownership. Sole proprietorships by far outnumber both corporations and partnerships combined in our economy. That is because the sole proprietorship is the easiest way to initiate a business enterprise, and it costs you practically nothing.

If you plan to do business under your own name, all you need to do in most locales is start your operation. In some places, you may have to place an announcement of intent to carry on business in the local newspaper, or, perhaps, register that intent with the local or county authorities. Most new business owners, however, tend to operate under a company or trade name. If you do, you will have to file a certificate of conducting business under an assumed name, often referred to as a D/B/A form ("doing business as"). See Figure 5-3 for a sample of the type of form you must file, usually with the county or city clerk.

The sole proprietorship gives you the widest possible latitude for making decisions (and mistakes), and the owner gets to keep all the profit (less taxes, of course).

But a major disadvantage is that you can be held personally liable for business debts, should your firm not be able to pay off its liabilities, or for judgments against the business awarded to people who sue you. There is no distinction at all made between you as an individual and you as the owner of a business. (The same is true of the partnership form.)

Sole proprietorship will also affect your income tax responsibilities. For example, any money you earn at a job while operating a part-time enterprise will be added to your firm's profits to ascertain your total taxable income. This puts you into a higher tax bracket.

There are some other disadvantages to the sole proprietorship. Since you are in business by yourself, you will not have the benefit of partners to supplement your talents or help you do some of the work.

**FIGURE 5-3. Certificate of conducting business under an assumed name.**

X 201—Certificate of Conducting Business under an Assumed Name
For Individual

JULIUS BLUMBERG, INC., LAW BLANK PUBLISHERS

# Business Certificate

I HEREBY CERTIFY *that I am conducting or transacting business under the name or designation*

*of*

*at*

*City or Town of*      *County of*      *State of New York.*

*My full name is\**

*and I reside at*

I FURTHER CERTIFY *that I am the successor in interest to*

*the person or persons heretofore using such name or names to carry on or conduct or transact business.*

IN WITNESS WHEREOF, *I have this*     *day of*     *19*   *, made and signed this certificate.*

.......................................................................................................

\* Print or type name.
\* If under 18 years of age, state "I am...............years of age".

*STATE OF NEW YORK*
*COUNTY OF*    } *ss.:*

*On this*    *day of*     *19*   *, before me personally appeared*

*to me known and known to me to be the individual described in and who executed the foregoing certificate, and he thereupon duly acknowledged to me that he executed the same.*

**Source:** Legal forms reprinted with the permission of and available from Julius Blumberg, Inc., New York, New York 10013.

Investors generally shy away from contributing equity capital to a one-person business since it is somewhat dangerous to do. After all, should you get sick or die, the business is defunct, and their investment goes down the drain.

Partnership

If at all possible, try to avoid taking on a partner. Although this form of ownership does have attractive qualities, too many such businesses end up in disagreement, at times quite violent. In a partnership, you split not only the profits and losses, but the work and all the decisions as well. This means you are not entirely your own boss, and that, at times, your partner may make decisions you don't like. Yet, you have to live by them, legally!

Why, then, you may ask, are there partnerships at all? Most often, they exist because more capital is needed initially to get the new business off the ground, and the would-be entrepreneur does not have enough of it. Other reasons for taking on one or more partners include: (1) getting someone in with skills you don't have, but need, (2) because the work load is expected to be too heavy for one person, and (3) because the new business owner does not have the courage to go it alone.

When you start up a partnership, you will most likely want to use a company name. So, you will file a Certificate of Partners planning to conduct business under an assumed name (see Figure 5-4).

You should also find a good attorney and have him or her prepare a formal partnership agreement before you go any further.

## Corporation

Most small businesspersons would do best to form a corporation at the outset, for three good reasons:

1. Barring any fraudulent acts on your part, your personal holdings are not placed in jeopardy. You cannot be held personally liable for the corporation's debts.
2. This is the only permanent legal form of business. A corporation exists independently of its owners (the stockholders). Business continues, even though the stockholders come and go. Moreover, stock ownership itself is readily transferred.
3. The corporation enjoys a more favorable income tax rate than the individual or partner, when your new company really starts to earn money.

Other features of the corporate form of ownership include the fact that banks and other lenders—as well as investors—are far more attracted to the corporation than to sole proprietorships or partnerships. This attitude stems from a mix of reasons: the corporation has its own "life," more owners are involved than in the other two forms of ownership, more capital is usually invested in the business, and so on. Another feature is that the corporation can raise capital by selling shares of stock from its treasury.

What about the disadvantages? The biggest single disadvantage is what is known as "double taxation." In addition to you paying income tax on your own earnings from working in the business (salary, bonuses, and the like), the corporation must pay a corporation income tax on profits earned. If you are the major stockholder in the company and you have set it up in the first place, you may feel especially put out because of being hit twice in the wallet. And in many states, you have to pay a state income tax from both directions, too!

Of the three forms of business ownership, the corporation is the most closely scrutinized and highly regulated by the government. And record-keeping is quite complex.

To open a corporation, you must file a certificate of incorporation in the state in which you plan to do business (with the Secretary of

**FIGURE 5-4.   Certificate for partners conducting business.**

State). You also must pay a fee to the state for incorporating and, annually, another fee for conducting business in this form. Do not try to start a corporation yourself, despite the books and manuals you may see advertised as "doing it yourself." Have an attorney set this up for you (See Figure 5-5 for a sample certificate of incorporation.)

**YOUR INSURANCE PROGRAM**

Like politics, the topic of insurance sparks both favorable and unfavorable comments, especially life or fire insurance. Some people make such statements as "I don't believe in it," "it's a big ripoff," or "the insurance companies get richer and richer." They will gladly tell you how they hate to pay premiums, year after year, on their automobile or fire insurance policies, and never collect a dime. Of course, the premiums are always far too high.

Other people are "insurance happy"; they try to take out

**FIGURE 5-4. (continued)**

State of New York, County of                                    ss.:                    CORPORATE ACKNOWLEDGMENT

   On this                day of                                        19        , before me personally appeared

to me known, who being by me duly sworn, did depose and say, that        he resides in

that    he is the                                        of

the corporation described in and which executed the foregoing certificate; that    he knows the seal of said
corporation; that the seal affixed to said certificate is such corporate seal; that it was so affixed by order
of the Board of                                    of said corporation, and that    he signed h        name thereto
by like order.

INDEX No.

**Certificate of Partners**

CONDUCTING BUSINESS UNDER
THE NAME OF

State of New York, County of                                    ss.:                    INDIVIDUAL ACKNOWLEDGMENT

   On this                day of                                        19        , before me personally appeared

to me known and known to me to be the individual    described in, and who executed the foregoing
certificate, and    he    thereupon                    duly acknowledged to me that    he    executed the same.

**Source:** Legal forms reprinted with the permission of and available from Julius Blumberg, Inc., New York, New York 10013.

insurance against almost any eventuality, perhaps because they fear all sorts of dire consequences if they are not protected. Or perhaps because they are gamblers who like to "play the odds."

There is one redeeming feature here, however; the corporate tax rates are lower than individual rates. The rates for 1980 were:

| Taxable Income | Corporation Tax (federal) |
|---|---|
| $0. to $25,000 | 17% |
| $25,000 to $50,000 | $ 4,250 + 20% of amount over $ 25,000 |
| $50,000 to $75,000 | $ 9,250 + 30% of amount over   50,000 |
| $75,000 to $100,000 | $16,750 + 40% of amount over   75,000 |
| $100,000 and over | $26,750 + 46% of amount over  100,000 |

**FIGURE 5-5. Certificate of incorporation.**

Still others are somewhere in between these two extremes. They carry insurance that is within their means; they protect themselves against the kinds of perils that can seriously affect their finances; and they shy away from covering unimportant or insignificant aspects.

How do *you* feel about insurance for your mail order business? Before you make up your mind, consider the following explanation from an S.B.A. booklet. It may help you to develop a more precise understanding of—and a healthy attitude toward—the business of insurance:

Insurance has been defined as a system in which "winners pay losers." Those who are lucky enough to avoid loss contribute through premium payments to the unlucky ones who do suffer loss. If you never collect from your insurance, consider yourself ahead, because you are one of the

**FIGURE 5-5.   (continued)**

A 234—Certificate of Incorporation
Business Corporation Law §402 : 9-75

COPYRIGHT 1975 BY JULIUS BLUMBERG. INC., LAW BLANK PUBLISHERS
80 EXCHANGE PL AT BROADWAY. N. Y. C. 10004

### Certificate of Incorporation of

*under Section 402 of the Business Corporation Law*

IT IS HEREBY CERTIFIED THAT:

*(1) The name of the proposed corporation is*

*(2) The purpose or purposes for which this corporation is formed, are as follows, to wit:*

*The corporation, in furtherance of its corporate purposes above set forth, shall have all of the powers enumerated in Section 202 of the Business Corporation Law, subject to any limitations provided in the Business Corporation Law or any other statute of the State of New York.*

winners. If you suffer a loss for which you are insured, you have the security of knowing that the other members of the insurance system will relieve you of most of your burden.

In this sense, you come out ahead either way. Your premiums are the price you pay for freedom from worry about economic loss from conditions outside your control.[1]

By this time, you have invested both money and time in your new business. Shouldn't you want to protect your investment?

Every business needs some types of insurance coverages. Some are truly essential, like fire and liability insurances, because losses in these areas can totally ruin your business. You may want to consider

[1]Mark R. Greene, "Insurance Checklist for Small Business," *Small Marketers Aid No. 148* (Washington, D.C.: Small Business Administration, 1971), pp. 2–3.

FIGURE 5-5.   Certificate of incorporation. (continued)

(3)  *The office of the corporation is to be located in the*

                                (city) (town) (incorporated village)

*of*                                        *County of*                          *State of New York.*

(4)  *The aggregate number of shares which the corporation shall have the authority to issue is*

other types because they have special application to your business, or your personal situation, or because it makes sense for some other reason. These become even more attractive as you begin to make profits from your operation.

For a complete rundown, talk over your insurance needs with a good insurance representative. Select someone locally, so that he or she will be available when you need to ask questions. You need someone who is knowledgeable and who, preferably, has had experience insuring other mail order concerns.

Figure 5-6 gives you an overview of how to go about setting up your business insurance program. Figure 5-7 provides some valuable hints on how to save money with your program.

**Types of Insurance**    A fire insurance policy protects you against loss due to fire and lightning. This is the basic coverage, but you can get extended

## FIGURE 5-5. (continued)

(5) The Secretary of State is designated as agent of the corporation upon whom process against it may be served. The post office address to which the Secretary of State shall mail a copy of any process against the corporation served upon him is

(6) The accounting period which the corporation intends to establish as its calendar or fiscal year for reporting the franchise tax shall end on                                    19

The undersigned incorporator, or each of them if there are more than one, is of the age of eighteen years or over.
IN WITNESS WHEREOF, this certificate has been subscribed this          day of                    19
by the undersigned who affirm(s) that the statements made herein are true under the penalties of perjury.

| | |
|---|---|
| ........................................................ | ........................................................ |
| Type name of incorporator | Signature |
| ........................................................ | |
| Address | |
| ........................................................ | ........................................................ |
| Type name of incorporator | Signature |
| ........................................................ | |
| Address | |
| ........................................................ | ........................................................ |
| Type name of incorporator | Signature |
| ........................................................ | |
| Address | |

**Source:** Legal forms reprinted with the permission of and available from Julius Blumberg, Inc., New York, New York 10013.

coverage for a small additional premium that will insure you against such dangers as damage from windstorm, smoke, explosion, and other sources. Note that the standard fire insurance policy does not cover the loss of money or securities, or deeds to property and other items. For that protection, you will need additional coverage.

Liability insurance is also a must. For example, should someone be injured on your premises—or off your premises as well—due to negligence on your part, you may be sued. Judgments today can easily run into the hundreds of thousands of dollars (and more). Of course, anyone can sue you, even if that person really does not have a good case against you. Without liability insurance, you will need to pay legal and court costs yourself, even though the case ends up in your favor. This kind of policy will pay any judgments against you, defend you in court, pay medical and surgical expenses for the injured party, and more. The size of your premium will depend on the limit of liability you select, on where you are located, the size of your premises, and other possible bases.

As far as automobile insurance is concerned, chances are that you already carry it. Because you need your car (or a truck) to take your mailings and packages to the post office, you will be using it for business purposes. Consequently, you will need two types of vehicle coverage: (1) physical damage insurance, in the form of a comprehensive automobile policy—to protect your car against the perils of fire or collision, for example, and (2) auto liability insurance—to cover you in the event of damage to other vehicles, property, or persons caused by your car or truck. You should also note that this second type is necessary to cover *any* vehicles used in or for your business, even if they are not owned by you (or by your corporation, if you have incorporated your mail order enterprise). As an example, your employee uses his or her car to go to the bank for you, to transport some packages to the post office, or to pick up some office supplies. On the way, there is an accident; your employee damages someone else's car or, perhaps, injures another person. You can be sued.

If you have one or more employees working in the business, you need to think about workers' compensation insurance. Discuss this area with your insurance agent. You may be able to cut premium costs in using safety and loss prevention methods.

Check into the pros and cons of these other types, too. Your insurance agent can point out their benefits quite readily. He or she may recommend one or more of them.

- Business interruption insurance
- Key man insurance
- Crime insurance
- Health and disability insurances (group)
- Business life insurance

---

**FIGURE 5-6.   Organizing your insurance program.**

A sound insurance protection plan is just as important to the success of your business as good financing, marketing, personnel management, or any other business function. And like the other functions, good risk and insurance management is not achieved by accident, but by organization and planning. A lifetime of work and dreams can be lost in a few minutes if your insurance program does not include certain elements. To make sure that you are covered, you should take action in four distinct ways:

1. Recognize the various ways you can suffer loss.
2. Follow the guides for buying insurance economically.
3. Organize your insurance management program.
4. Get professional advice.

*Recognize the risks.* The first step toward good protection is to recognize the risks you face and make up your mind to do something about them. Wishful thinking or an it-can't-happen-to-me attitude won't lessen or remove the possibility that a ruinous misfortune may strike your business.

Some businesses will need coverages not mentioned in the checklist. For example, if you use costly professional tools or equipment in your business, you may need special insurance covering loss or damage to the equipment and/or business interruption resulting from not being able to use the equipment.

*Study insurance costs.* Before you purchase insurance, investigate the methods by which you can reduce the costs of your coverage. Be sure to cover the following points:

1. Decide what perils to insure against and how much loss you might suffer from each.
2. Cover your largest loss exposure first.
3. Use as high a deductible as you can afford.
4. Avoid duplication in insurance.
5. Buy in as large a unit as possible. Many of the "package policies" are very suitable for the types of small businesses they are designed to serve, and often they are the only way a small business can get really adequate protection.
6. Review your insurance program periodically to make sure that your coverage is adequate and your premiums are as low as possible consistent with sound protection.

*Have a plan.* To manage your insurance program for good coverage at the lowest possible cost, you will need a definite plan that undergirds the objectives of your business. Here are some suggestions for good risk and insurance management:

1. Write down a clear statement of what you expect insurance to do for your firm.
2. Select only one agent to handle your insurance. Having more than one spreads and weakens responsibility.
3. If an employee or partner is going to be responsible for your insurance program, be sure he understands his responsibility.
4. Do everything possible to prevent losses and to keep those that do occur as low as possible.
5. Don't withhold from your insurance agent important information about your business and its exposure to loss. Treat your agent as a professional helper.
6. Don't try to save money by underinsuring or by not covering some perils that could cause loss, even though you think the probability of their occurring is very small. If the probability of loss is really small, the premium will also be small.
7. Keep complete records of your insurance policies, premiums paid, losses, and loss recoveries. This information will help you get better coverage at lower costs in the future.
8. Have your property appraised periodically by independent appraisers. This will keep you informed as to just what your exposures are, and you will be better able to prove what your actual losses are if any occur.

*Get professional advice about your insurance.* Insurance is a complex and detailed subject. A professionally qualified agent, broker, or consultant can earn his fees many times over.

---

**Source:** Mark R. Greene, "Insurance Checklist for Small Business," *Small Marketers Aids No. 148* (Washington, D.C.: Small Business Administration, 1971), pp. 13–15.

**FIGURE 5-7.  Saving on insurance costs.**

Before purchasing insurance, you should investigate various ways by which you can reduce the costs of your coverage. Among these are the following:

1. Decide which of the different kinds of risk protection will work best and most economically for you. Commercial insurance is only one of the means available for handling risk ... Investigate the other methods—such as loss prevention, self-insurance, noninsurance, risk transfer, and so forth—to see if they offer better coverage for your specific needs. Frequently, you will find that various methods working together will serve you best.

2. Cover your largest loss exposure first, the less severe or more frequent as your budget permits. Use your premium dollar where the protection need is greatest. Some firms insure their automobiles against collision loss, but neglect to purchase adequate limits on their liability coverage. Collision losses seldom bankrupt a firm, but liability judgments often have.

3. Make proper use of deductibles. In many lines of insurance, full coverage is uneconomical because of the high cost of covering the "first dollar" of loss. But if you cannot afford a $1,000 loss, do not select a deductible of this amount. Rather, reduce the deductible to the amount you can afford.

In many cases, however, the rate reduction for accepting a larger deductible will be very small. For example, increasing the waiting period from three months to six months for income disability coverage in group health insurance saves very little in premiums.

4. Review your insurance periodically. Renewing your policies automatically greatly increases the likelihood that you will fail to increase limits of liability where indicated, or that you will deprive yourself of a rate reduction possible when you remove some risk factor previously charged for. Periodic review saves you from insuring property you have disposed of or have written off as valueless. And you also avoid overlaps and gaps in coverage.

5. Check the market occasionally to see if you are getting your insurance for a reasonable price. You should not switch insurers each time a lower price is quoted, but you should keep aware of average costs for the amount and types of coverage you require.

6. Analyze insurance terms and provisions. When a firm attempts to save money by purchasing a "cheaper" policy, it sometimes discovers that the specific hazard it wanted to insure is not covered after all because of a technicality; or it learns that the insurer is able to offer a cheaper policy only by reducing services or following a niggardly claims policy. You should always attempt to see *why* you are saving money before you change insurers or policies.

7. Insure the correct exposure. One firm purchased coverage against equipment breakdown, but later found that defective design was the real cause of the trouble. Correcting the design removed the exposure. Another business bonded its employees who handled cash, but did not bond those who handled materials. One of the latter stole large amounts of merchandise, and the firm suffered an extensive and unrecoverable loss.

8. Investigate whether or not you can assume certain administrative duties required by your policies—such as reporting changing inventories for a

commercial property policy. Usually, the amount you will save in premiums will more than offset the expense you will have in performing the service.

9. Buy your insurance in as large a unit as possible. Thus you will be able to take advantage of the savings most insurers allow for large-unit policies. This is particularly true of life insurance and of many types of property insurance. Usually, the more property included in a single policy, the cheaper it is for the insurer to handle.

Source: Mark R. Greene, "Insurance and Risk Management for Small Business," *Small Business Management Series No. 30,* 2nd ed. (Washington, D.C.: Small Business Administration, 1970), pp. 63–64.

**FIGURE 5-8.   Purposes of business life insurance.**

Business life insurance can be written for numerous specific purposes. Chief among these are:

- A sole-proprietorship insurance plan to provide for maintenance of a business upon the death of the sole-proprietor.

- A partnership insurance plan to retire your partner's interest at death and vice versa.

- A corporation insurance plan to retire your shareholder's interest at death and vice versa.

- Key-man protection to reimburse for loss and to provide a replacement in the event of your key employee's death. Such insurance helps to prevent a setback that develops because of losing a vital employee.

- Group plan for employees. A group annuity or pension plan may be desirable where the number of employees is sufficiently large. Where only a few are involved, some form of individual retirement policy could be used, with the cost shared by employer and employees in any proportion desired.

- Reserve for emergencies. Most business life insurance plans utilize life insurance which has cash value. This cash value, growing over the years, provides the firm with a valuable reserve for emergencies in the event of any sharp dislocation in business conditions. When necessary, the policy cash value can be used as the basis for loans.

- Where your estate consists entirely of your interest in the business, insurance on your life, payable to your family on your death, provides them with ready cash and aids in liquidating your interest in the business.

**Source:** Institute of Life Insurance, "Business Life Insurance," *Management Aids No. 222* (Washington, D.C.: Small Business Administration, March 1975), p. 3.

The modern air-conditioned office, tastefully furbished and well equipped, is, indeed, a delight to behold and to work in. But you would be ill-advised to set your own sights so high at this time. Stifle the impulse to rent office space and furnish it with desk, swivel chair, electric self-correcting typewriter, and copying machine; not to speak

**SETTING UP YOUR "OPERATIONS CENTER"**

of filing cabinets, carpeting, pictures on the walls, and other refinements you might be tempted to install.

All this and more lies, it is hoped, in your future. But for today, and for next year as well, do not tie up any of your working capital in this fashion. You will probably need it for more important things.

One of the more attractive aspects of mail order selling is that it demands so very little in the way of capital investment at the outset. You need be concerned with little more than these basics:

- Modest amount of work space
- Table to work on
- Comfortable chair
- A few shelves (an old bookcase will do)
- Any kind of typewriter in good working condition, and a stand or table for it to rest on, at the proper height for you
- Inexpensive supplies
- An order-handling system
- A filing system

For many new mail order entrepreneurs, their first office begins at home—in the basement or garage, spare room, foyer, or the kitchen. If you start this way, you are already way ahead of the game. For even a small office has to cost several hundreds of dollars a month; that kind of rental easily amounts to $3,000 or $4,000 annually. If you are lucky enough to wind up your first year in the business with an exceptional bottom-line profit figure of, say, 15 percent of sales, you would have to reach something like $20,000 to $24,000 in sales that year just to pay for your office!

Here are the kinds of supplies you need for now:

- Writing tools—pens, pencils, a few marking pens
- Stationery—letterheads, envelopes, carbon paper, postcards (for quick messages), 3 x 5 index cards, ordinary paper clips, some rubber bands
- Advertising materials, as you develop them—circulars, folders, order forms, business reply envelopes
- Order handling materials—shipping labels (you can use stock labels available at your business stationer's), parcel post tape, postage stamps, several rubber stamps (name and address, variable dater) and a stamp pad, pad of standard purchase orders
- Filing cabinet—either a used one you can pick up for little money, or several heavy cardboard or corrugated cartons of the right sizes

Handling Your Mail

Shortly after your first classified or small space advertisement appears in print, or your first direct mail pieces reach their destinations, letters should begin to show up in your mailbox. Make sure you open and examine incoming mail daily. These letters will fall into one of two categories: orders (the majority) and inquiries (far fewer in number). Later on, of course, you may well expect an occasional letter of complaint, but you should be able to keep these to a minimum.

Staple all parts of each letter together, then make out an index card for each. On it print the name and address of the sender; enter all other details pertinent to the order or query. Clip the index card to the letter and separate orders from queries. Strive to fill and mail out every order within 48 hours. If you expect a serious delay, perhaps because you are temporarily out of stock on the item ordered, be certain to notify the customer and explain why the shipment may be delayed. (Ten days or more from the date of receipt might be considered a serious delay.)

After all orders have been processed for *that* particular day, answer your inquiries. Many require an original letter on your business stationery; some can be answered with a form letter or, perhaps, a note on a postcard. The reason for answering promptly is simple: when the prospective customer wrote to you, he or she was very interested in what you are offering, but as each day goes by, that interest wanes more and more—until it's too late to make a sale.

Your index cards can start a mailing list for the future. Purchase sheets of blank labels, gummed and perforated, and type the names and addresses from the cards on these sheets. (They come 33 labels to the sheet.) Type them in triplicate, using carbons. The original set of labels can be used for a first mailing, the duplicate and triplicate copies for follow-up mailings.

The letters can then be placed into your correspondence files (together with carbon copies of your responses, duplicate shipping labels, and other notes attached). File them by last names and in alphabetical order.

**SUGGESTED READING**

**Books**

AKERS, HERBERT, *Modern Mailroom Management*. New York: McGraw-Hill, 1979.

BECKMAN, GAIL MCKNIGHT, WALTER F. BERDAL, and DAVID G. BRAINARD, *Law for Business and Management*. New York: McGraw-Hill, 1975.

BETTS, P. W., *Office Management*. New York: David McKay, 1975.

BURSTINER, IRVING, *The Small Business Handbook: A Comprehensive Guide to Starting and Running Your Own Business*. Englewood Cliffs, N.J.: Prentice-Hall, Inc., 1979.

COLE, ROBERT H., *Consumer and Commercial Credit Management*, 6th ed. Homewood, Ill.: Irwin, 1980.

DORIS, LILLIAN, and BESSE M. MILLER, *Complete Secretary's Handbook*, 4th ed. Englewood Cliffs, N.J.: Prentice-Hall, Inc., 1977.

GETZ, G., *Business Law*, 5th ed. Englewood Cliffs, N.J.: Prentice-Hall, Inc., 1977.

GREENE, MARK R., *Risk and Insurance*, 4th ed. Cincinnati: South-Western, 1977.

HANCOCK, WILLIAM A., *Executive's Guide to Business Law*. New York: McGraw-Hill, 1979.

LANE, MARC J., *Legal Handbook for Small Business*. New York: AMACOM, 1977.

LITTLEFIELD, G. L., and others. *Management of Office Operations*. Englewood Cliffs, N.J.: Prentice-Hall, Inc., 1978.

NCR CORPORATION, *Credits and Collections*. Dayton, Ohio: NCR Corporation, 1972.

NICHOLAS, TED, *How to Form Your Own Corporation Without a Lawyer for Under $50.00*. Wilmington, Del.: Enterprise Publishing, 1978.

Terry, George R., and John J. Stallard, *Office Management and Control,* 8th ed. Homewood, Ill.: Irwin, 1980.

White, Edwin H., and Herbert Chasman, *Business Insurance,* 4th ed. Englewood Cliffs, N.J.: Prentice-Hall, Inc., 1974.

**Free Materials from the Small Business Administration**

*Management aids*

#201 Weber, Fred I., Jr., "Locating or Relocating Your Business," reprinted January 1974.

#222 Institute of Life Insurance, "Business Life Insurance," March 1975.

#232 O'Neal, Cooke, "Credit and Collections," May 1977.

#239 Baker, H. Kent, "Techniques of Time Management," January 1979.

*Small business bibliographies*

#31 Blake, Wm. Henry, "Retail Credit and Collections," revised April 1974.

#58 Carberry, Frank J., "Automation for Small Offices," reprinted July 1973.

*Small marketers aids*

#71 "Checklist for Going into Business," revised August 1970.

#104 Curtis, S. J. (Bob), "Preventing Accidents in Small Stores," reprinted April 1974.

#132 Murphy, Betty S., "The Federal Wage-Hour Law in Small Firms," revised December 1974.

#139 Kass, Benny L., "Understanding Truth in Lending," reprinted April 1974.

#148 Greene, Mark R., "Insurance Checklist for Small Business," July 1971.

**To Order from the Superintendent of Documents**

*Small business management series*

#21 Immer, John R., "Profitable Small Plant Layout," *Small Business Management Series No. 21,* 2nd ed. Washington, D.C.: Small Business Administration, 1964. (Stock #045-000-00029-1.)

#30 Greene, Mark R., "Insurance and Risk Management for Small Business," *Small Business Management Series No. 30,* 2nd ed. Washington, D.C.: Small Business Administration, 1970. (Stock #045-000-00037-1.)

*The starting and managing series*

#1 Metcalf, Wendell O., "Starting and Managing a Small Business of Your Own," *Starting and Managing Series Volume 1,* 3rd ed. Washington, D.C.: Small Business Administration, 1973. (Stock #045-000-00123-7.)

**6**

# PLANNING YOUR MAIL ORDER BUSINESS

Let's talk about planning. We are not taught how to plan in school. It is something we learn by doing. And it is an activity most of us tend to shy away from—and leave to others to do. This is partly because planning requires time, deep concentration, and lots of energy. It is also because we are more attuned to doing rather than thinking—and because we are intuitively suspicious about things beyond our control. Like the future. And luck.

So we avoid planning for the most part, except for really important issues—like going into your own business.

Before jumping into the water and risking the capital, hard work, and years of time needed to establish your mail order enterprise, doesn't it make sense to plan like mad (see Figure 6-1)? You need to examine why you are getting into business in the first place—and what your immediate and long-range goals are. You need to scan the entire field in which you plan to operate, so that you know what you're doing. For when you plan properly, you take in the whole picture: your own business, your competition, the media you will use, the state of the economy, government constraints, and so on. Not to do so exposes you to the danger of overlooking one or more major aspects, the absence of which may have a profound effect on your plan's outcome.

You cannot, of course, foresee all eventualities; no one can predict the future with any meaningful degree of certainty. Yet, by forcing yourself to think things through at the outset, and committing your thoughts to paper, you develop a guide that will see

**WHAT PLANNING IS**

**73**

you onto the pathway to success. It won't be infallible. Neither will it be, nor should it be, inflexible. Plans need to be adjusted all along the way.

---

**FIGURE 6-1.  Why make a business plan.**

You may be thinking: Why should I spend my time drawing up a business plan? What's in it for me? If you've never drawn up a plan, you are right in wanting to hear about the possible benefits *before* you do your work.

A business plan offers at least four benefits. You may find others as you make and use such a plan. The four are:

1. The first, and most important, benefit is that a plan gives you a path to follow. A plan makes the future what you want it to be. A plan with goals and action steps allows you to guide your business through turbulent economic seas and into harbors of your choice. The alternative is drifting into "any old port in a storm."

2. A plan makes it easy to let your banker in on the action. By reading, or hearing, the details of your plan the banker will have real insight into your situation if you are asking for a loan.

3. A plan can be a communications tool when you need to orient sales personnel, suppliers, and others about your operations and goals.

4. A plan can help you to develop as a manager. It can give you practice in thinking about competitive conditions, promotional opportunities, and situations that seem to be advantageous to your business. Such practice over a period of time can help increase an owner-manager's ability to make judgments.

---

**Source:** Office of Management Assistance, Small Business Administration, "Business Plan for Retailers," *Small Marketers Aid No. 150* (Washington, D.C.: Small Business Administration, reprinted March 1973), p. 3.

Planning itself is a three-step process. It consists of: (1) setting goals, (2) working out methods, techniques, programs, and time-tables to reach those goals, and (3) assessing progress being made and making the necessary adjustments. Planning your business will lead to the more efficient use of your resources and to improved operations.

It is helpful to adopt the systems approach when planning; this involves breaking the entire picture into segments. A good technique is to draw diagrams of these segments on paper, then study them—asking yourself the same one-word questions that the newspaper reporter uses to get at all the facts in a news story. They are the Five W's: Who? What? Where? When? Why? (and a sixth: How?).

The rest of this chapter contains what is in effect a mini planning workbook to assist you in planning. Answers to many of the questions or entries will require considerable attention on your part. It will be well worth it, however. Go at it slowly, in between your day-to-day activities, and when your head is clear. Seek a quiet room, with a good lamp and a table to work at. Take along several well-sharpened pencils and some extra sheets of writing paper for figuring, or for doodling, when you're temporarily stuck.

The planning workbook is divided into the following sections:

1. Preliminaries
2. My Customers
3. My Place of Business
4. My Merchandise Plan
5. My Selling Plan
6. My Personnel Plan
7. My Financial Plan

The last section will help you determine how much money you need to start up in business. It will also give you an overview of what your company's financial status should look like at the end of your first year of operation.

## THE PLANNING WORKBOOK

### 1. PRELIMINARIES

This is a brief description of my business:

My business name is:

The legal form I have chosen is:

Have I accomplished the necessary paperwork? (Filed certificate? Made partnership agreement? Set up corporation?)

Address from which I plan to operate:

Length and type of lease (if any):

Other principals involved in the business (if any):

Local regulations to comply with:

These are the names and addresses of the professionals I plan to work with:

Accountant:

Lawyer:

Insurance rep:

I intend to use this bank:

Number of my business checking account:

These are my objectives:

Immediate goals:

Goals to reach by end of the first year:

Long-term objectives (next five years):

## 2. MY CUSTOMERS

I will be selling directly to the consumer, rather than to other firms. This is a profile of my typical customer:

Sex:

Marital status:

Age (range):

Educational background:

Income level:

Number of children:

Type of residence:

Kind of automobile:

Sports, hobbies:

Other recreational activities:

Additional information:

These are some of the things my customers like:

These are some of the things my customers dislike:

When my customers shop by mail, they expect:

On the other hand, I plan to sell merchandise or services by mail to industry (manufacturers, wholesalers, retailers, service firms, or other types of companies). This is what my typical customer is like:

Type of firm (include all prospective types):

Sales volume of firm:

Size of firm (number of employees):

Titles of executives to be reached:

These are some of the things the executives like:

These are some of the things the executives dislike:

When this executive shops by mail, he or she expects:

## 3. MY PLACE OF BUSINESS

For my first year of operation, I will need:

_____ square feet for workroom space
_____ square feet for storage space

Other needs:

Lighting:

Ventilation:

Heating:

Air conditioning:

Remodeling:

Shelving:

Furniture and equipment needs:

| Description of item | Quantity Needed | Estimated Cost/Unit | Total Cost |
| --- | --- | --- | --- |

Supplies needed:

| Description of item | Quantity Needed | Estimated Cost/Unit | Total Cost |
| --- | --- | --- | --- |

Names, addresses, and other pertinent information of suppliers of needed furniture, equipment, and supplies:

## 4. MY MERCHANDISE PLAN

I plan to sell the following kinds of merchandise (or services):

These are the needs my merchandise will fulfill:

These are the sources I intend to check for new merchandise items:

I plan to read the following publications regularly in my search for items to sell:

This year I intend to visit the following trade shows:

Price ranges for my merchandise:

Quality levels I expect to maintain:

This is a description of my inventory control system:

My pricing and mark-up approaches will be:

My credit policy is:

I make some of the merchandise I sell. These are my sources for materials, components, supplies:

I plan to buy merchandise for resale. This is the pertinent information about my suppliers:

*Item*          *Name and Address*          *Terms and Conditions*

## 5. MY SELLING PLAN

These are my firm's strong points:

This is the kind of image I would like to project in my advertising and correspondence:

My customers will find the following advantages in buying from me rather than from competitors:

These are my approaches to customer credit:

This is a statement of my return policy:

My merchandise will be backed by the following guarantee(s):

These are my plans for handling (a) orders, (b) inquiries, (c) other correspondence:

(a)

(b)

(c)

This is how much I plan to spend on advertising:
  This year:
  Next year:
These are the media through which I can reach my customers most effectively:

These are the specific appeals I intend to build into my advertisements:

My advertising budget is as follows:

| Name of Medium | Audience Size | Approximate Date to Appear | Size of Advertisement | Estimated Cost |
|---|---|---|---|---|

These are my direct mail plans for the year:
  (a) Number of mailings I expect to make:

  (b) Quantities to be mailed each time:

  (c) Postal regulations to comply with:

  (d) Timetables for having mailing pieces printed:

  (e) Additional mailing list names to be rented:

| Source | Quantity |
|---|---|

## 6. MY PERSONNEL PLAN

Check one: ____ I need to hire people to fill these positions right away.

____ I don't need anyone now, but I anticipate the following job openings will develop in the near future (six months to one year).

____ I have no need for any employees for the first year of operation.

Job descriptions of the openings I foresee:

These are the job specifications I have outlined for these positions:

These are the methods and techniques I intend to use in selecting personnel:

I plan to pay these employees on the following basis:

These are the fringe benefits my employees may expect to receive:

This is how I plan to train my employees:

## 7. MY FINANCIAL PLAN

I believe the following sales projections for my new business are as sound as I can make them:

For my first three months of operation:    _____
For my second three months:    _____
For the third quarter:    _____
For the fourth quarter:    _____
Estimated sales for my first year:    _____

This is a summary of my planned insurance program:

This is how I have calculated the amount of initial capital I need to start this business:

(a) I worked with the aid of Worksheet No. 2 (Figure 6-2). This worksheet also appears in Appendix Figure A-1 with Worksheets No. 1 and 3.

(b) Where indicated at the top of Column 1 on the Worksheet, I entered my estimate of first-year sales volume.

(c) I completed all entries in Column 1, under "Estimated Monthly Expenses"—from "Salary of owner-manager" down to "Miscellaneous." (I used pencil, because I sometimes needed to rework a figure.)

(d) Using the suggestions given in Column 3, I came up with estimates for each expense—and then showed these in Column 2.

(e) I tackled the section that reads "Starting Costs You Only Have to Pay Once." I followed all suggestions provided in Column 3 for these "Starting Costs," and then completed Column 2.

(f) I added all entries in the second column; this yielded the figure I needed.

The "Total Estimated Cash" I need to start this business is:

My "Start-up" capital will come from these sources:

The money I have borrowed for my business operation will be paid back according to the following schedule:

I have calculated my breakeven point to be_____, by using the following formula:

$$\text{Breakeven (in dollars)} = \frac{\text{Total Fixed Costs}}{1 - \dfrac{\text{Total Variable Costs}}{\text{Sales Volume}}}$$

I have completed my proforma Profit and Loss Statement (expected for my first year of operation) on the form on p. 85

**FIGURE 6-2. Worksheet No. 2 (Small Business Administration).**

WORKSHEET NO. 2

| ESTIMATED MONTHLY EXPENSES | | | |
|---|---|---|---|
| Item | Your estimate of monthly expenses based on sales of $ _____ per year | Your estimate of how much cash you need to start your business (See column 3.) | What to put in column 2 (These figures are typical for one kind of business. You will have to decide how many months to allow for in your business.) |
| | Column 1 | Column 2 | Column 3 |
| Salary of owner-manager | $ | $ | 2 times column 1 |
| All other salaries and wages | | | 3 times column 1 |
| Rent | | | 3 times column 1 |
| Advertising | | | 3 times column 1 |
| Delivery expense | | | 3 times column 1 |
| Supplies | | | 3 times column 1 |
| Telephone and telegraph | | | 3 times column 1 |
| Other utilities | | | 3 times column 1 |
| Insurance | | | Payment required by insurance company |
| Taxes, including Social Security | | | 4 times column 1 |
| Interest | | | 3 times column 1 |
| Maintenance | | | 3 times column 1 |
| Legal and other professional fees | | | 3 times column 1 |
| Miscellaneous | | | 3 times column 1 |
| **STARTING COSTS YOU ONLY HAVE TO PAY ONCE** | | | Leave column 2 blank |
| Fixtures and equipment | | | Fill in worksheet 3 and put the total here |
| Decorating and remodeling | | | Talk it over with a contractor |
| Installation of fixtures and equipment | | | Talk to suppliers from whom you buy these |
| Starting inventory | | | Suppliers will probably help you estimate this |
| Deposits with public utilities | | | Find out from utilities companies |
| Legal and other professional fees | | | Lawyer, accountant, and so on |
| Licenses and permits | | | Find out from city offices what you have to have |
| Advertising and promotion for opening | | | Estimate what you'll use |
| Accounts receiveble | | | What you need to buy more stock until credit customers pay |
| Cash | | | For unexpected expenses or losses, special purchases, etc. |
| Other | | | Make a separate list and enter total |
| **TOTAL ESTIMATED CASH YOU NEED TO START WITH** | | $ | Add up all the numbers in column 2 |

**Source:** "Checklist for Going into Business," *Small Marketers Aid No. 71* (Washington, D.C.: Small Business Administration, 1975), pp. 6–7.

_____

(Firm's Name)

## PROFIT AND LOSS STATEMENT

For: Year Ended December 19XX

Net Sales. . . . . . . . . . . . . . . . . . . . . . . . . . . . . . . . . . . . . \_\_\_\_
Less cost of goods sold:
  Opening inventory         \_\_\_\_
  Purchases during year       \_\_\_\_
  Freight charges          \_\_\_\_
    Total goods handled. . . . . . . . . . . . . . . . . . . \_\_\_\_
    Less ending inventory, December 31   \_\_\_\_
      Total cost of goods sold. . . . . . . . . . . . . \_\_\_\_

Gross Margin                \_\_\_\_
Less Operating Expenses:
  Salaries and wages        \_\_\_\_
  Payroll taxes           \_\_\_\_
  Utilities              \_\_\_\_
  Telephone            \_\_\_\_
  Rent                \_\_\_\_
  Office supplies          \_\_\_\_
  Postage             \_\_\_\_
  Maintenance expense       \_\_\_\_
  Insurance            \_\_\_\_
  Interest expense         \_\_\_\_
  Depreciation           \_\_\_\_
  Delivery expense         \_\_\_\_
  Advertising           \_\_\_\_
  Dues and contributions      \_\_\_\_
  Miscellaneous expenses      \_\_\_\_
Total Operating Expenses. . . . . . . . . . . . . . . . . . . . . . . . . . . . . . . . . . \_\_\_\_

Operating Profit. . . . . . . . . . . . . . . . . . . . . . . . . . . . . . . . . . . . . . . . . \_\_\_\_
Other income:
  Dividends on stock        \_\_\_\_
  Interest on bank account     \_\_\_\_
  Other sources          \_\_\_\_
    Total other income . . . . . . . . . . . . . . . . . . . . . . . . \_\_\_\_

Total Income Before Income Taxes. . . . . . . . . . . . . . . . . . . . . . . \_\_\_\_
  Less provision for taxes. . . . . . . . . . . . . . . . . . . . . . . . . . . \_\_\_\_
  NET INCOME . . . . . . . . . . . . . . . . . . . . . . . . . . . . . . . . . \_\_\_\_

This is what I expect my first year's balance sheet to look like:

_____
(Firm's Name)

BALANCE SHEET

For: Year Ended December 19XX

ASSETS

Current Assets
    Cash on hand and in bank          _____
    Marketable securities          _____
    Accounts receivable (less allowance for
    bad debts)          _____
    Merchandise inventory          _____
    Inventory of supplies          _____
        Total current assets............................ _____

Fixed Assets
    Office machinery and equipment (less
    depreciation)          _____
    Furniture (less depreciation)          _____
    Leasehold improvements          _____
    Other fixed assets (list)          _____
        Total fixed assets.............................. _____
        TOTAL ASSETS     =====

LIABILITIES AND NET WORTH

Current Liabilities
    Accounts payable          _____
    Accrued expenses          _____
    Accrued taxes          _____
    Other current liabilities (list)          _____
        Total current liabilities........................ _____

Long-term Liabilities
    Loan payable, 19__          _____
    Loan payable, 19__          _____
    Mortgage          _____
        Total long-term liabilities...................... _____
        TOTAL LIABILITIES     _____
Net Worth     _____
        TOTAL LIABILITIES AND NET WORTH     _____

My projected cash forecast for the first year of operations follows on p. 87.

FIGURE 6-3. Form for making the cash forecast.

| | JAN | FEB | MAR | APR | MAY | JUN | JUL | AUG | SEP | OCT | NOV | DEC |
|---|---|---|---|---|---|---|---|---|---|---|---|---|
| (1) Cash in Bank (Start of Month) | | | | | | | | | | | | |
| (2) Petty Cash (Start of Month) | | | | | | | | | | | | |
| (3) Total Cash (add (1) and (2)) | | | | | | | | | | | | |
| (4) Expected Accounts Receivable | | | | | | | | | | | | |
| (5) Other Money Expected | | | | | | | | | | | | |
| (6) Total Receipts (add (4) and (5)) | | | | | | | | | | | | |
| (7) Total Cash and Receipts (add (3) and (6)) | | | | | | | | | | | | |
| (8) All Disbursements (for month) | | | | | | | | | | | | |
| (9) Cash Balance at End of Month in Bank Account and Petty Cash (subtract (8) from (7))* | | | | | | | | | | | | |

* This balance is your starting cash balance for the next month.

**Source:** Office of Management Assistance, Small Business Administration, "Business Plan for Small Manufacturers," *Management Aid #218* (Washington, D.C.: Small Business Administration, July 1973), p. 16.

87

These are my tax obligations:
(a) Federal taxes:


(b) State taxes:


(c) Local taxes:


**SUGGESTED READING**

**Books**

ALBRECHT, KARL, *Successful Management by Objectives*. Englewood Cliffs, N.J.: Prentice-Hall, Inc., 1977.

BURSTINER, IRVING, *The Small Business Handbook: A Comprehensive Guide to Starting and Running Your Own Business*. Englewood Cliffs, N.J.: Prentice-Hall, Inc., 1979.

COVENTRY, W. F. and IRVING BURSTINER, *Management: A Basic Handbook*. Englewood Cliffs, N.J.: Prentice-Hall, Inc., 1977.

MANCUSO, JOSEPH R., *How to Start, Finance, and Manage Your Own Small Business*. Englewood Cliffs, N.J.: Prentice Hall, Inc., 1978.

**Free Materials from the Small Business Administration**

*Management aids*

#179 GOLDE, ROGER A., "Breaking the Barriers to Small Business Planning," reprinted May 1977.

#218 Office of Management Assistance, Small Business Administration, "Business Plan for Small Manufacturers," July 1973.

*Small marketers aids*

#150 Office of Management Assistance, Small Business Administration, "Business Plan for Retailers," reprinted March 1973.

#153 Office of Management Assistance, Small Business Administration, "Business Plan for Small Service Firms," October 1973.

**7**

## BUILDING YOUR MAILING LIST

If you are like the typical newcomer to the mail order business, you have most likely found a product (or a service) that you believe will sell well by mail. And you have had the courage to test its potential by investing a few hundred dollars—or perhaps as much as a thousand dollars—in several small advertisements in the print media. Possibly, you have found that one or two of these earned a small profit and that the rest did not pull enough in the way of orders to cover your advertising cost.

Disheartened? You shouldn't be. You have accomplished something very important. You now "own" the names and addresses of a number of persons who have bought from your new mail order firm. These are worth money to you. They constitute the nucleus of your own mailing list.

I found this out many years ago, when I attempted to launch a part-time mail order business to supplement my regular income. My plans were to try to sell inexpensive novelty items through small space magazine and newspaper advertising in order to develop a good customer list which I would be able to use to send gift catalogs later on. One advertisement in particular brought in more than 100 orders for the novelty salt-and-pepper shaker set I had displayed. It sold for $1.25 at the time. After deducting my cost of merchandise and my packaging and postage expenses, I found I had lost nearly one-half of my advertising investment (let alone the work and time involved)! But, each set that was mailed out carried a "bounceback" in the form of a one-page circular containing photographs and descriptions of four other salt-and-pepper sets. This had cost me about $35 to have printed, for about 500 copies. But I received orders from more than 20 percent of my customers, and some ordered as many as 6 or 12 of the sets for holiday gifts. I hadn't realized, too, that some people collect these items as a hobby.

So, I finally earned a bit of profit, after all. *And* I had the start of a valuable mailing list for the future.

Just how important your own list will become may be difficult to perceive at the beginning. Yet, you cannot be successful in mail order selling without it—and without one that keeps growing and that you monitor zealously. Some worthwhile words on the subject come from mail order authority Ira Belth, of Belth Associates in East Meadow, New York.

When it comes to direct mail marketing, and mailing lists—the first thing to appreciate is that a mailing list is *not* a mailing list. It's an alignment of carefully selected people—people to whom you want to sell something. To achieve a high effectiveness quotient, your campaign has to be directed to the individual buyers, specifiers, influencers. If, in fact, you're dealing with "mailing lists," your energy and investment are being misdirected.[1]

One direct marketer began in business by selling office supplies to commercial firms. Advertisements in trade publications brought him hundreds of orders initially. Some of the offers he advertised were powerful enough to bring in enough sales to cover the advertising costs; others did not. Yet, all the names he obtained in this manner—customers and inquiries—went into building his house list. He followed his advertising with three mailings during the first year: a self-mailing folder and two small catalogs. His business prospered and grew.

**NAMES FOR YOUR HOUSE LIST**

Replies to your own advertising are, of course, a major approach to developing a mailing list, but there are other ways to go. For example, you can ask your own customers to recommend friends and neighbors who might be interested in your products. This is easily done by leaving room for one or more names and addresses on your mailing pieces and catalogs. You can also rent lists from mailing list houses (discussed later in this chapter).

Or you can do some research and compile your own mailing lists.

Here are some of the sources you can refer to:

　　Automobile registrations
　　Birth notices in newspapers
　　Business directories
　　Civic association memberships
　　College alumni groups
　　Contest entrants
　　Convention attendees

[1]Ira Belth, "Lists Are Not Just Lists: Some Audience Selection Basics," *Industrial Marketing,* (September 1980), pp. 90ff.

Fraternal order memberships

Industrial directories

Magazine advertisements

Marriage/engagement notices in newspapers

New business starts

Newspaper advertisements

Organization memberships

Professional group memberships

Social organizations and clubs

Tax rolls

Trade association memberships

Trade directories

Trade show attendees

Union memberships

Voter registrations

*Who's Who,* and similar reference works

Yellow Pages of the telephone directory

A helpful tactic is to separate your mailing list early in the game into three separate groups: (1) "active customer", for people who have purchased merchandise through your advertising efforts; (2) "prospective customer," persons who have requested information from you as well as those whom your customers have recommended; and (3) "catch-all" list, which should include all the names and addresses you are able to compile through your own research.

Keep these three lists separated while your names begin to mount into the thousands. Remember: the key to mail order success is to keep building your lists—and, all along, try to convert the names in lists 2 and 3 into "active customers." Since you do prepare a master index card for every entry, make certain you update these masters regularly, so that at all times they contain all vital information for ready reference. When you send out mailings, type the names and addresses directly on your outside envelopes, or use perforated gummed labels. Do not to invest in equipment, such as addressograph plates; you can't afford to automate until you are well established in your new business.

If you plan to sell to industry rather than to the individual consumer, a telephone call to the SBA's Texas headquarters (800-433-7212, or 800-792-8901 in Texas) will bring you a free copy of their Small Business Bibliography #13, "National Directories for Use in Marketing." This booklet lists the sources of a good number of directories, most published annually. It includes directories of manufacturers, retailers, wholesalers, exporters, physicians, manufacturers' representatives, and the like. A wonderful resource if you are trying to build up a mailing list!

**Industrial Mail Order Marketing**

You should also know about several useful directories that can be found in college and university libraries, and in many public libraries. (Of course, you can arrange to purchase them yourself if they contain the kinds of names you want.)

There is the two-volume *Million Dollar Directory,* put out by the Marketing Services Division of Dun and Bradstreet, Inc., 99 Church Street, New York, N.Y. 10007. Lists in this directory are arranged alphabetically, geographically, by product classification, and by line of business. All entries represent businesses with net worths of $1 million or more. The firm also issues the *Middle Market Directory,* which lists companies with net worths of between one-half and one million. Cumulative supplements to these books are issued during the year.

Another valuable source of information is the *Standard & Poor's Register of Corporations, Directors and Executives,* published by Standard & Poor, 25 Broadway, New York, N.Y. 10004. The first volume in this three-volume set lists corporations alphabetically, provides addresses and telephone numbers, and also gives the names, titles, and functions of officers, directors, and other principals. Also shown are the firms' SIC codes, annual sales volume, number of employees, and other data. Volume 2 contains individual listings of directors and executives. Volume 3 contains indexes to the directory, in six color-coded sections: SIC index, SIC codes, geographic (by states and major cities), obituary section, new individual additions, and new company additions. (See Figure 7-1 for a sample page from the *Register.*)

There is also the 16-volume *Thomas' Register of American Manufacturers—and Thomas' Register Catalog File,* a publication of the Thomas Publishing Company, 1 Penn Plaza, New York, N.Y. 10001. The first eight volumes list products and services of these companies alphabetically. Volumes 9 and 10 give such information as company names and addresses, telephone numbers, branch offices, capital ratings, names of company officials, brand names, and the like. The last six books contain company catalogs, bound alphabetically and cross referenced in the first 10 volumes.

Mail order firms frequently use this reference work to find products for resale.

**NAMES FROM OUTSIDE SOURCES**

You can expand your own mailings by renting, or occasionally buying, names and addresses from firms that offer other mailing lists. These list houses are often classified into general-line and limited-line companies. The latter specialize in specific list types, for example, older people, medical personnel (doctors, psychiatrists, and so on), lawyers, engineers, and other professionals. The general-line list house offers a far broader range. Commonly, these firms issue large catalogs that describe and indicate the rental costs for many hundreds, even thousands, of different lists. (See Figures 7-2 to 7-6 for sample catalog pages from several mailing houses.)

A more useful approach for the mail order operator is to identify such suppliers as either compilers or brokers. List compilers do just what the name implies. They collect—and put in order—names and addresses from a great many sources: from every conceivable type of directory, government publications, magazine subscriber lists, organization memberships, and other sources. The compiler will study your requirements and recommend available lists that might produce

**FIGURE 7-1. Sample page from Standard & Poor's Register.**

## AC AND S CORPORATION
120 N. Lime St., Lancaster, Pa. 17604
Tel. 717-397-3631

**ACandS**

*Pres—James W. Liddell
*Exec V-P—Hugh N. March
*Sr V-P—Charles W. Fowler, 1809 Liberty St., Kansas City, Mo.
*V-P—I. H. Greiff, 468 Park Ave., S., New York, N. Y.
*V-P—Alan L. Stokely, P.O. Box 946, Columbia, Md.
V-P—T. E. Decker, 180 W. Church St., King of Prussia, Pa.
V-P—J. S. Taylor, 6800 Odell St., St. Louis, Mo.
V-P—W. A. Jones, 501 Amsterdam Ave., N. E., Atlanta, Ga.
Treas—Alexander V. Stoycos
Secy—R. E. Fink
Cont—Donald S. Bowman
Accts—Arthur Andersen & Co.
Primary Bank—National Central Bank, Lancaster, Pa.
Primary Law Firm—Dechert, Price, Rhoades, Phila., Pa.
Sales: $58Mil    Employees: 2,500
       *Also DIRECTORS—Other Directors Are:
Kenneth W. Gemmill        R. Wesley Shope
Wilson D. Mc Elhinny      William J. Poorbaugh
PRODUCTS: Insulation contracting services, leisure homes
S.I.C. 1742

## ACS, INC.
2701 Pellissier Pl., Whittier, Cal. 90601
Tel. 213-692-7531
Pres—Charles Martin
Gen Mgr—Emile J. Petre
Chief Engr—Paul Letl
Primary Bank—United California Bank: El Sereno Branch, Los Angeles, Cal.
PRODUCTS: Wireless microphones high fidelity loudspeakers & sound systems & components, enclosures, cable condensor systems, calibration shakers
S.I.C. 3651

## ACS INDUSTRIES, INC.
P. O. Box 31, Woonsocket, R. I. 02895
Tel. 401-769-4700
*Chrm, Pres & Treas—George Botvin
V-P—Alfred S. Puccetti
Secy—Patricia Botvin
Accts—Ernst & Ernst, Providence, R. I.
Primary Bank—Citizens Trust Co!, Providence, R. I.
Primary Law Firm—Edwards & Angell, Providence, R. I.
Sales: $7.50Mil    Employees: 237
       *Also DIRECTORS—Other Directors Are:
George Forstot            Louis Handwerger
PRODUCTS: Wire, wire mesh products, entrainment separators, automotive catalytic converters, polypropylene yarns, staple( macrame' products, fibers & woven synthetic products
S.I.C. 3496; 2241; 2271; 2282; 3714

## AD-X CORP.
2329 W. Main St., Littleton, Colo. 80120
Tel. 303-794-1544
Pres—Max A. Romero
V-P—Wayne C. Canaga
Treas—Ruth B. Wehrly
Secy—Gregory G. Romero
Purch Agt—Max E. Romero
Accts—Gary A. Scofield, Littleton, Colo.
Primary Bank—The Littleton National Bank, Littleton, Colo.
Primary Law Firm—Richard W. Gillespie, Englewood, Colo.
Sales Range: $1—3Mil    Employees: 25
PRODUCTS: Fire extinguishing equipment
S.I.C. 3999

## ADM INDUSTRIES, INC.
212 S. Second St., Elkhart, Ind. 46514
Tel. 219-293-0404
*Pres & Treas—Richard E. Summers
Secy—Anthony J. Iemma
Accts—McGladrey, Hansen, Dunn & Co., Elkhart, Ind.
Primary Bank—First Pennsylvania Bank N.A., Phila., Pa.
Primary Law Firm—Iemma & Summers, Elkhart, Ind.
Revenue: $10Mil    Employees: 200
       *Also DIRECTORS—Other Directors Are:
Emerson Butts             Richard Littleton
Drexell Simpson
PRODUCTS: Manufacture, drapery & other hardware (whl.), sliding door hardware, by-pass door hardware, by-fold hardware, pocket door hardware, a variety of hardware products
S.I.C. 3429; 5072

## A & E MOBILE AIRE
(Subs. A & E Plastik Pak Co. Inc.)
200 W. 146th St., Gardena, Cal. 90248
Tel. 213-321-2245
Pres—Alexander Harkias
V-P—Kenneth K. Clissold
Prod & Plt Mgr—Lonnie Knauss
Accts—Arthur Anderden & Co., Los Angeles, Cal.
Primary Bank—Security Pacific, Los Angeles, Cal.
Primary Law Firm—O'Melvany & Myers, Los Angeles, Cal.
PRODUCTS: Plastic sliding drawers, refrigerators for rec. vehicles, ice boxes for rec. vehicles, custom vacuum forming
S.I.C. 3079; 3632

## A & E PLASTI-LINE/A & E TEXLITE
(Div. A&E Plastik Pak Co. Inc.)
P. O. Box 5066, Knoxville, Tenn. 37918
Tel. 615-947-1511
*Pres—James R. Martin
V-P (Installation)—Hum Hamelin
V-P (Oper)—Charles K. Rivard
V-P (Mktg)—Verne Spangenberg
V-P (Fin)—Bryan J. Collier
Accts—Arthur Andersen & Co., Chattanooga, Tenn.
Primary Bank—United American Bank, Knoxville, Tenn.
Primary Law Firm—Egerton, McAfee, Armisted & Davis, Knoxville, Tenn.
Sales: $20Mil    Employees: 450
       *Also DIRECTORS—Other Directors Are:
Nicholas H. Carlozzi      Yehockai Schneider
PRODUCTS: Plastic illuminated signs (mfg.); signs installation & maintenance
S.I.C. 3993

## A & E PLASTIK PAK CO., INC.
14505 E. Proctor Ave., City of Industry, Cal. 91749
Tel. 213-968-3801
*Chrm—Harry H. Lynch
*Pres & Chief Exec Officer—Yehochai Schneider
*Exec V-P—Nicholas H. Carlozzi
V-P—Keith A. Sharf
Secy—William R. Lindsay
Revenue: $66.41Mil    Employees: 1,460
       *Also DIRECTORS—Other Directors Are:
Melvin J. Erickson        Bruce I. Hochman
Harry G. Long             Robert B. Stobaugh
PRODUCTS: Plastic packaging (see-thru meat trays, thermosheet, plastic garment hangers, and berry baskets), outdoor signs, leisure products (plastic ice boxes, drawers, pumps and plumbing fixtures for recreational vehicles, plastic liners, domes for swimming pools)
S.I.C. 3079; 3993

## A & E TEXLITE
P.O. Box 5066, Knoxville, Tenn. 37919
Tel. 615-947-1511
Pres—James R. Martin
V-P (Fin)—B. Collier
V-P (Mktg)—E. Brown
V-P (Engr)—C. Ramsey
V-P (Mfg)—C. Rivard
V-P (I & M)—H. Hamelin
Employees: 125
PRODUCTS: Illuminated, nonilluminated plastic signs
S.I.C. 3993

## AEI CORP.
2260 Ave. A, Bethlehem, Pa. 18001
Tel. 215-865-2651
*Pres—Virginia Smith
*Treas—Jack Smith
Primary Bank—Union Bank & Trust Co., Bethlehem, Pa.
Primary Law Firm—Gross, McGinley & McGinley, Allentown, Pa.
Sales: Under $1Mil    Employees: 45
       *Also DIRECTORS—Other Directors Are:
Clemmens Suttinen         Donald Thompson
PRODUCTS: Portion packaged beverages; contract packaging.
S.I.C. 3551; 2086; 5149; 7399

## AEL INDUSTRIES INC.
P. O. Box 552, Lansdale, Pa. 19446
Tel. 215-822-2929
*Chrm & Exec V-P—Conrad J. Fowler
*Pres & Chief Exec Officer—Leon Riebman, Dr.
Group V-P & (Pres-AEL Service Corp)—Leon L. Berman
Group V-P & (Pres-Bernard S. Bernard
Group V-P & (Pres-AEL-Emtech Corp)—Harold Musnitsky
V-P—Raymond Markowitz
V-P—Iverson Korsen
V-P (Fin)—George King
Treas & Asst Secy—Jesse H. Riebman
Secy—Salvatore M. DeBunda
Per Dir—William R. Culp
Purch Agt—I. Gross
Accts—Arthur Young & Co, Philadelphia, Pa.
Primary Bank—American Bank & Trust Co. of Pennsylvania, Reading, Pa.
Primary Law Firm—Blank, Rome, Klaus & Comisky, Philadelphia, Pa.
Sales: $35.28Mil    Employees: 1,041

*Also DIRECTORS—Other Directors Are:
Nathan Cohen              Grinnell Morris
Donald H. Miller, Jr.     R. Victor Mosley
PRODUCTS: Microwave equip, antennas, counter measures equip, communications equip, electro-medical, biophysical & physiological test instruments, transmitters, CATV, equip. & systems, peripheral computer equip., chem. dispensing equip., hybrid microelectronics
S.I.C. 3662; 3559; 3573; 3679; 3841; 4833

## A. E. P. INDUSTRIES, INC.
20 Knickerbocker Rd., Moonachie, N. J. 07074
Tel. 201-955-6500
*Pres & Chief Exec Officer—Brendan Barba
*Exec V-P, Secy & Treas—David J. McFarland
V-P (Mfg)—Leroy Buskirk
Compt—Jack Emanuele
Gen Mgr (Southern Region)—Eddie Booth.
Natl Sales Mgr & Adv & Mktg Mgr—Robert Cron
Sales Mgr (Southern Region)—Bruce McClure
Per Dir—Arthur Buscemi
Purch Agt—David Heckman
Data Proc Mgr—William H. Cron
Product Mgr—Cesar Aliaga
Chief Engr—Robert Federkewicz
Traffic Mgr—Carlo Melia
Prod Mgr—Marwan Sholakh
Plt Mgr (Southern Region)—Rick Buskirk
Qual Con Mgr—Edward Anderson
Accts—Stephen P. Radics & Co., Haledon, N. J.
Primary Bank—Chemical Bank, New York, N. Y.
Primary Law Firm—Baldino & DeMaria, Hackensack, N. J.
Sales: $12Mil    Employees: 165
       *Also DIRECTORS
PRODUCTS: Polythylene products: bags, liners, tubing, sheeting, shrink film
S.I.C. 3079

## AFA PROTECTIVE SYSTEMS, INC.
519 Eighth Ave., New York, N. Y. 10018
Tel. 212-279-5000
*Chrm—Philip Kleinman
*Pres—R. C. Miller
*V-P & Treas—Alfred G. Seddon
V-P (Engr)—Howard L. Caretto
Secy—James H. Roberts
Sales Mgr—Reginald Miller
Purch Agt—F. Cerrato
Accts—Brout, Issacs, & Company
Revenue: $8.59Mil    Employees: 305
       *Also DIRECTORS—Other Directors Are:
Mervin J. Hartman         Richard D. Hausman
Robert S. Heller          Harvey Z. Shapiro
Harry Weyher
PRODUCTS: Central office automatic fire & sprinkler alarm serv.
S.I.C. 7393; 3569; 3662

## A.F.C CORP.
Westernreserve Rd., Canfield, Ohio 44406
Tel. 216-533-5581
*Pres & Treas—Alden D. Powers
*Secy—Eugene Passell
Purch Agt—Jack Northcott
Supt—Glenn Stack
Accts—Alexander Grant & Co., Youngstown, Ohio
Primary Bank—National City Bank Cleveland, Ohio, Cleveland, Ohio
Primary Law Firm—Manchester, Bennett, Powers Ullman, Youngstown, Ohio
Sales: Over $3Mil    Employees: 75
       *Also DIRECTORS—Other Directors Are:
G. B. Woodman             E. D. Powers
PRODUCTS: Refractory specialties, fire clays, wet & dry high temperature mortars tars, castables, refractory coatings & washes, ramming & casting mixes, blast furnace black magic, blast furnace & open hearth black glaze, fine grinding of materials for refractory & ceramic industry
S.I.C. 3255; 1453

## A. G. CO., INC.
309 E. Main St., Battle Ground, Wash. 98604
Tel. 206-687-3113
*Pres—James DeFrees
*V-P—Harlan Jones
*Treas—Art Kennedy
*Secy—Walter Andersen
Gen Mgr—Gilbert L. Kraus
Accts—E W Rector, Salem, Ore.
Primary Bank—First Independent Bank, Battle Ground, Wash.
Primary Law Firm—Earl Jackson, Battle Ground, Wash.
Sales Range: $5—7Mil    Employees: 60
       *Also DIRECTORS—Other Directors Are:
Jim Curtin                Walter Anderson
Art Kennedy               Ray Olsen
Alan Schumacher           Lawrence Jones
PRODUCTS: Dairy products (Whl. & retail), groceries, hardware, petroleum, feed (retail)
S.I.C. 5411; 5143; 5251; 5451

## AGA CORPORATION
(Subs. AGA AB)
550 County Ave., Secaucus, N. J. 07094
Tel. 201-866-3344
*Chrm—Curt Nystrom, 181 81, Lidingo, Sweden
*Pres—Dietrich Baeu
Treas—William Gnirrep
Geodimeter Product Mgr—Hans Edvardsson
Battery Product Mgr—William A. Washburn
Purch Agt—Lisa Haggis

**Source:** *Standard & Poor's Register of Corporations, Directors and Executives* (Standard & Poor's Corporation, 25 Broadway, New York, N.Y. 10003). Reprinted with permission.

93

good results for you. Lists may also be custom-compiled for special needs. For instance, National Business Lists distributes the *NBL List Directory,* a large catalog in which more than six million names, located in over 1,000 markets, are listed. (A letter or a telephone call will bring you a copy; their address, along with the names and addresses of other list houses, appears later in this section.) The same firm may also make available to you several other "idea guides" to assist the novice mail order entrepreneur, like "The Q Concept," "Maybe It Wasn't a Bad List," and others.

Like real estate brokers and their counterparts in other fields, list brokers act as go-betweens to bring together mail order companies with owners of lists. They are very knowledgeable people who are ready, willing, and usually able to give you their best thinking on the kinds of lists that will best match your needs. When you use these "brokered" lists, you are often required to submit your mailing package in advance to the list owner for approval.

Both compilers and brokers will counsel you on your list needs.

**How They Work**

The list house usually designates a minimum order size that will be accepted. It may be for $75 or $100, or more, or for a minimum of anywhere from 2,000 to 10,000 names. The names and addresses are rented customarily for one-time use. You may not use them for a second mailing. Indeed, dummy or "decoy" names are usually introduced into a rented list so that the compiler or list owner can readily discover any violation of this agreement, since your second mailing piece will arrive at one of these decoy addresses.

Lists, or parts of lists, are typically rented on a per thousand basis. Going rates with compiled lists may run from $25 to $45 per thousand or slightly higher, with the average running about $35 per thousand. There are additional charges for other selection factors. For instance, if you want particular states selected instead of a national selection, you might have to pay $2.50 or $3 extra per thousand. If telephone numbers are to be added to your labels, another $5 per thousand.

Lists are made available according to your needs on labels, on 3 x 5 index cards, on your mailing envelopes, and on magnetic tape. Ungummed Cheshire labels (for automatic machine affixing) are usually supplied free of extra charge, but gummed or pressure-sensitive labels command a premium of anywhere from $2.50 to $6 per thousand names. Names and addresses supplied on 3 x 5 index cards may cost you as much as $25 additional per thousand, and those typed on your #10 envelopes may run to $30 per thousand over and above the cost of the list.

Mailing list houses usually guarantee a high percentage of deliverability of their names, anywhere from 90 to 95 percent. This is because they clean their lists regularly. They will refund postage charges for pieces not delivered, if returned to them (see Figure 7-7, p. 102). Some companies may guarantee 100 percent deliverability; these firms update their lists constantly by telephone.

# FIGURE 7-2. Sample page from list catalog.

| Quantity | Category | Price |
|---|---|---|
| 3,657 | Banks with assets $50 Million or more | $35/M |
| 6,990 | Banks with assets $25 Million or more | $30/M |
| 11,000 | Banks with assets $10 Million or more | $30/M |
| 13,400 | Banks with assets $5 Million or more | $25/M |
| 1,203 | Banks with assets less than $5 Million | $30/M |
| 26,000 | Banks, Branches | $30/M |
| 15,000 | Banks, Cashiers | $25/M |
| 163,000 | Banks, Executives, Women | $25/M |
| 32,000 | Banks, Mutual Savings (HQ) | $30/M |
| 465 | Banks, National | $30/M |
| 4,280 | Banks, Savings & Loan | $25/M |
| 4,700 | Banks, State or Trust Companies | $30/M |
| 9,740 | Banks, Trust Officers | $25/M |
| 9,150 | Barber & Beauty Supplies | $30/M |
| 3,580 | Barber Shops | $30/M |
| 43,000 | Barge Lines | $25/M |
| 2,000 | Bars, Taverns, Cocktail Lounges | $35/M |
| 108,200 | Beauty Schools | $30/M |
| 1,800 | Beauty Shops | $35/M |
| 145,000 | Beer Brewers | $25/M |
| 165 | Beer Distributors | $35 |
| 6,300 | Behavioral Scientists | $30/M |
| 37,000 | Beverage Bottlers & Distributors | $30/M |
| 2,100 | Bicycle Dealers & Repairs | $30/M |
| 7,500 | Billiard Parlors & Poolrooms | $30/M |
| 3,900 | Biologists | $25/M |
| 15,000 | Blue Collar Workers | Inquire |
| 2,200,000 | Boat Basins (Marinas) | $30/M |
| 2,550 | Boat Dealers | $30/M |
| 9,200 | Boat & Marine Supplies | $30/M |
| 16,000 | Boat Owners | Inquire |
| 3,900,000 | Boat Yards, Building & Repairing | $35/M |
| 4,700 | Boards of Education | $25/M |
| 14,000 | Book Clubs | $25 |
| 85 | Book Publishers | $30/M |
| 3,600 | Book Publishers, Major | $35/M |
| 1,280 | Bookkeeping Services | $30/M |
| 11,500 | Bookstores | $30/M |
| 16,500 | Bookstores, College | $30/M |
| 3,400 | Bookstores, Religious | $30/M |
| 2,500 | Botanists | $30/M |
| 3,000 | Bottlers, Soft Drinks | $35/M |
| 2,100 | Boutiques | $30/M |
| 4,300 | Bowling Alleys | $35/M |
| 8,300 | Box & Container Mfrs. | $35/M |
| 2,200 | Boy Scout Councils | $30 |
| 380 | Boys Clubs | $30 |
| 950 | Branch Plants, Fortune 1,000 | $30 |
| 23,000 | Bread, Baked Goods Mfrs. | $30/M |
| 6,200 | Bricklayers, Stonemasons | $30/M |
| 13,450 | Bridal Shops | $30/M |
| 3,450 | Bridge Clubs | $30/M |
| 3,800 | Broadcasting Executives | $30/M |
| 31,000 | Broadcasting Stations—Radio AM | $25/M |
| 4,230 | Broadcasting Stations—Radio FM | $25/M |
| 3,380 | Broadcasting Stations—TV | $35 |
| 900 | Brokers & Agents, Insurance | $25/M |
| 210,000 | Brokers & Agents, Insurance (Offices) | $25/M |

| Quantity | Category | Price |
|---|---|---|
| 2,700 | Brokers, Business. | $30/M |
| 170,000 | Brokers, Real Estate. | $25/M |
| 15,600 | Brokers, Securities—Executives | $35/M |
| 9,100 | Brokers, Securities—Offices | $30/M |
| 175,000 | Building Contractors | $25/M |
| 49,600 | Building Materials & Supplies Dealers | $30/M |
| 21,100 | Building Materials & Supplies Wholesalers | $30/M |
| 10,500 | Building Specifications Officials. | $25/M |
| 8,800 | Burglar & Fire Alarm Installers. | $30/M |
| 3,200 | Burners (Oil) Dealers & Distributors | $30/M |
| 6,800 | Bus Companies (All) | $35/M |
| 3,000 | Bus Companies (Charter & Rental) | $35/M |
| 4,250 | Bus Companies (Inter-City) | $35/M |
| 9,000 | Bus Company Executives | $25/M |
| 2,000 | Business Brokers | $30/M |
| 2,000,000 | Business Executives | $25/M |
| 200,000 | Business Executives, Home Address | $30/M |
| 68,000 | Business Executives, Top Salaried, Home Address | $25/M |
| 8,200 | Business Machine Dealers | $30/M |
| 400,000 | Business Men, Small Town | $25/M |
| 1,000,000 | Business Owners, Home Address | Inquire |
| 585 | Business Schools (Collegiate) | $30 |
| 600 | Business, Secretarial Schools | $30/M |
| 3,300 | Business & Trade Organizations | $30/M |
| 3,400 | Business & Trade Publications | $35/M |
| 3,500 | Businesses, Minority Owned | $25/M |
| 2,500,000 | Businesses, One Man | $30/M |
| 22,600 | Butcher Shops | $30/M |
| 7,200 | Butchers, Wholesale | $30/M |
| 650 | Buyers, Resident, Offices | $40 |

**C**

| Quantity | Category | Price |
|---|---|---|
| 11,000 | Cabinet Makers | $30/M |
| 3,800 | Cable TV Operators | $35/M |
| 300,000 | Cafes, Restaurants, Eating Places | $30/M |
| 1,025 | Camera Clubs | $30/M |
| 3,300 | Camera Equipment Wholesalers | $30/M |
| 9,200 | Camera & Photo Stores. | $30/M |
| 3,400 | Camp Grounds | $35/M |
| 3,250 | Camper & Trailer Dealers | $35/M |
| 3,100 | Camping Equipment Retailers | $30/M |
| 7,100 | Camps, Children's, Summer. | $35/M |
| 13,500 | Camps, Trailer | $30/M |
| 3,400 | Campus Stores |  |

### CANADIAN

> Many categories shown in these pages can be supplied for CANADA. Prices and quantities will be supplied upon request.

| 4,400 | Candy, Confectionery Wholesalers | $30/M |
|---|---|---|

| Quantity | Category | Price |
|---|---|---|
| 860 | Candy Manufacturers | $35 |
| 22,400 | Candy, Tobacco, Stationery Stores | $30/M |
| 6,200 | Canners, Packers—Food | $30/M |
| 29,400 | Car Dealers, New. | $30/M |
| 59,000 | Car Dealers, Used. | $30/M |
| 36,000 | Car Dealers, Used, Independent | $30/M |
| 10,000 | Car Washes. | $30/M |
| 7,400 | Cards (Greeting) Shops. | $25/M |
| 155,000 | Career Women | $25/M |
| 51,000 | Carpenters (Individuals) | $50/M |
| 43,600 | Carpet, Rug, Floor Covering Dealers | $30/M |
| 20,250 | Carpet & Rug Cleaners | $30/M |
| 550 | Carpet & Rug Manufacturers | $40 |
| 4,600 | Casters (Foundries) | $30/M |
| 2,000 | Catalog, Mail Order Houses | $35/M |
| 24,500 | Caterers. | $30/M |
| 18,800 | Catholic Churches | $25/M |
| 57,500 | Catholic Clergymen | $25/M |
|  | Catholic Contributors. | Inquire |
| 3,000,000 | Catholic Families. | Inquire |
| 3,190 | Catholic Convents & Monasteries | $25/M |
| 8,970 | Catholic Elementary Schools | $25/M |
| 1,500 | Catholic High Schools | $25/M |
| 250 | Catholic Orphanages | $30 |
| 15,400 | Catholic Publications | $30 |
| 530 | Catholic Rosary Societies | $25/M |
| 4,700 | Catholic Seminaries | $30 |
| 7,350 | Cemeteries | $30/M |
|  | Ceramic Tile Contractors, Dealers | $30/M |

### CHAINS

| Quantity | Category | Price |
|---|---|---|
| 1,250 | Chains, Auto Supply | $30/M |
| 422 | Chains, Department Stores | $35 |
| 710 | Chains, Discount Stores | $30/M |
| 3,000 | Chains, Drugs | $30/M |
| 1,350 | Chains, Franchise Organizations | $35/M |
| 550 | Chains, Furniture, Home Furnishings | $35 |
| 4,585 | Chains, Grocery & Supermarket | $30/M |
| 2,250 | Chains, Hardware, Home Center | $30 |
| 333 | Chains, Hotel & Motel | $35 |
| 575 | Chains, Ladies Wear | $35 |
| 395 | Chains, Men's Wear | $30/M |
| 2,800 | Chains, Restaurant. | $35 |
| 470 | Chains, Shoes | $35 |
| 325 | Chains, Theater | $35 |
| 1,450 | Chains, Variety | $30/M |

### CHAINS, EXECUTIVES & BUYERS

| 50,000 | CHAINS, EXECUTIVES & BUYERS | Inquire |
|---|---|---|

| Quantity | Category | Price |
|---|---|---|
| 31,200 | Chairmen, Boards of Directors. | $30/M |
| 45,000 | Chairmen, Colleges & Universities, Departmental |  |
| 6,000 | Chambers of Commerce | $35/M |
| 610,000 | Chambers of Commerce Members | $25/M |
| 2,900 | Chambers of Commerce, Junior | $35/M |
| 235,000 | Charitable Organizations | $25/M |
| 3,900 | Charter Aircraft Operators | $30/M |
| 300 | Charter Flight Operators | $35 |

FIGURE 7-3. Sample page from list catalog.

# EDUCATION

| QUANT | LIST | SIC |
|---|---|---|
| 119,110 | 1st Grade Teachers | |
| 121,370 | 2nd Grade Teachers | |
| 113,800 | 3rd Grade Teachers | |
| 118,930 | 4th Grade Teachers | |
| 102,600 | 5th Grade Teachers | |
| 92,620 | 6th Grade Teachers | |
| 2,920 | 6th Grade Social Studies Teachers | |
| 8,020 | 6th Grade Math/Science Teachers | |
| 13,360 | 7th Grade Teachers | |
| 13,870 | 8th Grade Teachers | |
| 74,750 | K-6 Special Education Teachers | |
| 18,090 | K-6 Music Teachers | |

*Personal names can be selected by expenditures, enrollments, and special facilities at no additional charge.

96,210 ADMINISTRATORS BY NAME

Principals

| | Public | Catholic | Private | Total |
|---|---|---|---|---|
| Elementary | 61,960 | 8,060 | 5,100 | 5,120 |
| Grades K-12 | 1,630 | 90 | 2,560 | 4,280 |
| Total | 63,590 | 8,150 | 7,660 | 9,400 |

Librarians

16,810 Elementary, Public

39,740 **Junior High Schools** (At Schools With 7-8 Grades)

By Grade Span

| | Public (8212 & 15) | Catholic (8213 & 16) | Private (8218) |
|---|---|---|---|
| K-1 thru 8 | 14,640 | 7,880 | 100 |
| 4-5-6 thru 8 | 2,670 | 70 | 10 |
| 7-8 only | 2,260 | 10 | |
| K-1 thru 9 | 400 | 70 | 60 |
| K-1 thru 12 | 4,040 | 350 | 360 |
| 7 thru 9 | 3,860 | 20 | 5 |
| 7-8 thru 12 | 2,610 | 120 | 210 |
| Total | 30,480 | 8,520 | 750 |

By Enrollment

| | Public (8212) | Catholic (8213) | Private (8218) |
|---|---|---|---|
| (R6) under 250 | 5,650 | 2,610 | 420 |
| (R5) 250 to 500 | 8,080 | 3,220 | 180 |
| (R4) 500 to 1,000 | 9,260 | 2,130 | 90 |
| (R 1/3) over 1,000 | 2,750 | 480 | 10 |
| (R7) Unknown | 4,740 | 80 | 50 |
| Total | 30,480 | 8,520 | 750 |

By Expenditure Per Student*

| | | SIC |
|---|---|---|
| 690 | Small, Low-Spending Schools | J1 |
| 1,250 | Small, Moderate-Spending Schools | J2 |
| 1,410 | Small, High-Spending Schools | J3 |
| 1,210 | Medium, Low-Spending Schools | J4 |
| 2,190 | Medium, Moderate-Spending Schools | J5 |
| 1,830 | Medium, High-Spending Schools | J6 |
| 600 | Large, Low-Spending Schools | J7 |
| 760 | Large, Moderate-Spending Schools | J8 |
| 580 | Large, High-Spending Schools | J9 |

*Spending: Low = Under $34.99; Moderate = $35.00 to $49.99; High = $50.00+
Size: Small = Under 500; Medium = 500 to 999; Large = 1000+

| QUANT | LIST | SIC |
|---|---|---|
| 320,900 | TEACHERS BY NAME* | |
| 3,680 | French Teachers | |
| 5,510 | Spanish Teachers | |
| 2,760 | Other Foreign Language Teachers | |
| 86,910 | English Teachers | |
| 50,270 | Science Teachers | |
| 58,310 | Social Studies Teachers | |
| 12,060 | Music Teachers | |
| 53,880 | Special Education K-12, 7-12 | |
| 47,530 | Home Economics Teachers 7-12 | |

*Personal names can be selected by expenditures, enrollments, and special facilities at no additional charge.

36,900 ADMINISTRATORS BY NAME

Principals

| | Public | Catholic | Private | Total |
|---|---|---|---|---|
| 6-8, 7-9 | 10,480 | 40 | 40 | 10,560 |
| 7-12 | 4,100 | 160 | 340 | 4,600 |
| K-12 | 1,630 | 90 | 2,560 | 4,280 |
| Total | 16,210 | 290 | 2,940 | 19,440 |

Librarians

17,460 Grades 7-12, Public

25,630 **Senior High Schools**

By Grade Span

| | Public (8215) | Catholic (8216) | Private (8218) |
|---|---|---|---|
| K-1 thru 9 | 400 | 70 | 60 |
| K-1 thru 12 | 4,040 | 350 | 360 |
| 7 thru 9 | 3,860 | 20 | 5 |
| 7-8 thru 12 | 2,610 | 120 | 210 |
| 9-10 thru 12 | 9,800 | 1,620 | 270 |
| Mis. Grades | 1,090 | 70 | 500 |
| Total | 21,810 | 2,240 | 1,580 |

By Enrollment

| | Public (8215) | Catholic (8216) | Private (8218) |
|---|---|---|---|
| (R6) Under 250 | 2,400 | 540 | 890 |
| (R5) 250-500 | 3,770 | 690 | 380 |
| (R4) 500-1,000 | 7,180 | 710 | 190 |
| (R 1/3) Over 1,000 | 5,680 | 260 | 20 |
| (R7) Unknown | 2,770 | 40 | 100 |
| Total | 21,810 | 2,240 | 1,580 |

By Expenditure Per Student*

| | | SIC |
|---|---|---|
| 1,190 | Small- Low-Spending Schools | S1 |
| 2,190 | Small, Moderate-Spending Schools | S2 |
| 3,530 | Small, High-Spending Schools | S3 |
| 1,150 | Medium, Low-Spending Schools | S4 |
| 1,520 | Medium, Moderate-Spending Schools | S5 |
| 1,450 | Medium, High-Spending Schools | S6 |
| 1,270 | Large, Low-Spending Schools | S7 |
| 2,160 | Large, Moderate-Spending Schools | S8 |
| 1,840 | Large, High-Spending Schools | S9 |

*Spending: Low = Under $34.99; Moderate = $35.00 to $49.99; High = $50.00+
Size: Small = Under 300; Medium =

| QUANT | LIST | SIC |
|---|---|---|
| 316,500 | TEACHERS BY NAME* | |
| 5,300 | French Teachers | |
| 7,630 | Spanish Teachers | |
| 6,900 | Other Foreign Language Teachers | |
| 79,460 | English Teachers | |
| 46,230 | Science Teachers | |
| 57,260 | Social Studies Teachers | |
| 12,310 | Music Teachers | |
| 53,880 | Special Education K-12, 7-12 | |
| 47,530 | Home Economics Teachers | |
| 151,330 | Athletic Coaches | |

*Personal names can be selected by expenditures, enrollments, and special facilities at no additional charge.

39,380 ADMINISTRATORS BY NAME

| | Public | Catholic | Private | Total |
|---|---|---|---|---|
| 9-12, 10-12 | 11,040 | 1,400 | 600 | 13,040 |
| 7-12 | 4,100 | 160 | 340 | 4,600 |
| K-12 | 1,630 | 90 | 2,560 | 4,280 |
| Total | 16,770 | 1,650 | 3,500 | 21,920 |

Librarians

17,460 Grades 7-12, Public

**Special Facilities in Public Schools**

| | |
|---|---|
| 28,450 | Media Centers |
| 20,550 | Elementary Schools |
| 2,720 | Junior High Schools |
| 5,180 | Senior High Schools |
| 9,810 | Vocational Education |
| 1,770 | Junior High Schools |
| 8,040 | Senior High Schools |
| 44,530 | Special Education |
| 29,880 | Elementary Schools |
| 5,780 | Junior High Schools |
| 8,870 | Senior High Schools |

Teachers Who Buy Through the Mail *Please Inquire For More Information*

**Coaches & Athletic Directors**

| | |
|---|---|
| 28,250 | High School |
| 14,630 | Athletic Director |
| 13,080 | Baseball |
| 25,620 | Basketball |
| 8,630 | Cheerleading |
| 8,300 | Cross Country |
| 12,710 | Football |
| 9,160 | Golf |
| 4,090 | Gymnastics |
| 3,290 | Soccer |
| 5,910 | Softball |
| 4,630 | Swimming |

**Source:** "The Source: Directory of List Markets," Ed Burnett Consultants, Inc., 2 Park Avenue, New York, N.Y. 10016. Reprinted with permission.

## FIGURE 7-4. Sample page from list catalog.

**DEPENDABLE LISTS INC**
THE LIST INFORMATION RESOURCE

257 Park Avenue South, New York, N.Y. 10010 ● (212) 677-6760
1025 Vermont Avenue, N.W., Washington, D.C. 20005 ● (202) 347-8311
333 North Michigan Avenue, Chicago, Ill. 60601 ● (312) 263-3566

| | | |
|---|---|---|
| 115,000 | Fraternal Orders | $30 M |
| | (Also See Clubs) | |
| 4,400 | Fraternities, College | $30 M |
| 3,500 | Fraternities, Professional | $30 M |
| 26,000 | Freezer Dealers | $30 M |
| 4,500 | Freight Forwarders | $30 M |
| 7,400 | Freight Transport Services | $30 M |
| 16,000 | Frozen Custard Stands | $30 M |
| 4,000 | Frozen Food Executives | $30 M |
| 2,500 | Frozen Food Lockers | $30 M |
| 2,100 | Frozen Food Processors | $30 M |
| 2,800 | Frozen Food Wholesalers | $30 M |
| 2,000 | Fruit Canneries | $30 M |
| 2,000 | Fruit and Nut Farms | $30 M |
| 7,000 | Fruit Stores | $30 M |
| 6,500 | Fruit Wholesalers* | $30 M |
| 21,000 | Fuel Oil Dealers* | $30 M |
| 13,000 | Fumigating Companies | $30 M |

**FUND RAISING—
SEE CONTRIBUTORS**

| | | |
|---|---|---|
| 175,000 | Fund Raising Individuals | $30 M |
| 155,000 | Fund Raising Organizations | $30 M |
| 750,000 | Fund Raising Prospects | $30 M |
| 85,000 | Fund Raising Women | $30 M |
| 24,000 | Funeral Parlors | $30 M |
| 500 | Funeral Directors Supplies | $50 L |
| 500 | Fur Manufacturers | $50 L |
| 2,300 | Fur Shops | $30 M |
| 37,000 | Furnace Contractors | $30 M |
| 400 | Furnance Manufacturers | $50 L |
| 14,000 | Furnace Wholesalers | $30 M |

# Furniture

| | | |
|---|---|---|
| 600 | Chains | $50 L |
| 2,700 | Custom Made | $30 M |
| 63,000 | Dealers* | $30 M |
| 36,000 | Dealers, Household | $30 M |
| 950 | Dealers, Juvenile | $50 L |
| 9,500 | Dealers, Office | $30 M |
| 11,000 | Dealers, Used | $30 M |
| 14,000 | Industry Executives | $30 M |
| 10,000 | Manufacturers* | $30 M |
| 13,000 | Movers | $30 M |
| 6,300 | Refinishers | $30 M |
| 7,000 | Repair | $30 M |
| 16,000 | Wholesalers | $30 M |

# G

| | | |
|---|---|---|
| 9,300 | Galleries and Art Dealers | $30 M |
| 3,000 | Game Manufacturers | $30 M |
| 118,000 | Garage and Auto Repair* | $30 M |
| 9,500 | Garbage Collectors | $30 M |
| 10,500 | Garden Centers | $30 M |
| 225,000 | Garden Club Members | $30 M |
| 400 | Garden Editors | $50 L |
| 33,000 | Garden Stores* | $30 M |
| 4,800 | Garden Wholesalers | $30 M |

| | | |
|---|---|---|
| 17,000 | Gardeners, Landscape | $30 M |
| 2,300 | Gas Companies | $30 M |
| 3,600 | Gas Companies, Natural | $30 M |
| 8,000 | Gas Company Executives | $30 M |
| 10,600 | Gas Dealers, Bottled | $30 M |
| 11,200 | Gasoline Distributors | $30 M |
| 1,000 | Gasoline Station Chains | $50 L |
| 203,000 | Gas Stations* | $30 M |
| | By Brand | Inq. |
| 54,000 | Gem Collectors | $30 M |
| 175,000 | General Contractors* | $30 M |
| 33,000 | Gen. Merchandise Stores* | $30 M |
| 2,000 | Geneticists | $30 M |
| 5,400 | Geographers | $30 M |
| 1,100 | Geological Engineers | $60 L |
| 11,000 | Geologists | $30 M |
| 12,000 | Geologists, Petroleum | $30 M |
| 14,000 | Geophysicists | $30 M |
| 1,100,000 | Georgia Residents | Inq. |
| 37,000 | Georgia Wealthies | $30 M |
| 3,700 | Geriatric Doctors | $30 M |
| 4,000 | Gift Boutiques | $30 M |
| 29,000 | Gift Buying Executives | $30 M |
| 165,000 | Gift Giving Firms | $30 M |
| 64,000 | Gift Shops* | $30 M |
| 14,000 | Gift Shops, Better | $30 M |
| 5,200 | Gift Shops, Hospital | $30 M |
| 138,000 | Gift Show Attendees | $35 M |
| 3,000 | Gift Novelty Wholesalers | $30 M |
| 925 | Girl Scout Councils | $50 L |
| 10,000 | Glass Dealers, Auto | $30 M |
| 16,000 | Glass Dealers, Window, Etc. | $30 M |
| 1,400 | Glass Products Mfrs. | $60 L |
| 2,000 | Glass Wholesalers | $30 M |
| 2,500 | Glassware Shops | $30 M |
| 675 | Glove Manufacturers | $50 L |
| 500 | Glue Manufacturers | $50 L |
| 5,300 | Golf Club Managers | $30 M |
| 145,000 | Golf Club Members | $30 M |
| 7,500 | Golf Club Professionals | $30 M |
| 9,200 | Golf and Country Clubs | $30 M |
| 950 | Golf Driving Ranges | $50 L |
| 2,000 | Golf Equipment Dealers | $30 M |
| | GOLFERS | INQ. |
| 1,300 | Gourmet Shops | $60 L |
| 245,000 | Gourmets and Epicures | $30 M |

**GOVERNMENT**

| | | |
|---|---|---|
| 17,000 | Contractors | $30 M |
| 850,000 | Employees | $30 M |
| 110,000 | Offices | $30 M |
| 75,000 | Officials, City | $30 M |
| 43,000 | Officials, County | $30 M |
| 15,000 | Officials, Federal, Top | $30 M |
| 3,300 | Officials, State | $30 M |
| 7,100 | Officials, Welfare | $30 M |
| 10,500 | Officials, Women | $30 M |
| 11,000 | Purchasing Depts. | $30 M |
| 7,800 | State Legislators | $30 M |
| 2,500 | Top Aides, Federal | $30 M |
| 15,000 | Who's Important In | $30 M |

| | | |
|---|---|---|
| 1,100 | Graduate Schools | $60 L |
| 23,000 | Grain & Feed Dealers | $30 M |
| 4,600 | Grain Elevators | $30 M |

| | | |
|---|---|---|
| 8,400 | Grain Wholesalers* | $30 M |
| 375,000 | Grandparents | $30 M |
| 35,000 | Graphic Arts Experts | $30 M |
| 5,000 | Gravel and Sand Producers | $30 M |
| 8,300 | Gravel and Sand Dealers | $30 M |
| 1,400 | Gray Iron Foundries | $60 L |
| 33,000 | Greenhouses & Nurseries | $30 M |
| 170 | Greeting Card Mfrs. | $50 L |
| 11,700 | Greeting Card Shops | $30 M |
| 8,000 | Greeting Card Wholesalers | $30 M |
| 4,000 | Grocery Brokers | $30 M |
| 5,000 | Grocery Chains | $30 M |
| 21,000 | Grocery Store Executives | $30 M |
| 176,000 | Grocery Stores* | $30 M |
| 5,000 | Grocery Supermarket Chains | $30 M |
| 16,000 | Grocery Wholesalers | $30 M |
| 3,700 | Guard Services | $30 M |
| 31,000 | Guidance Counselors | $30 M |
| 3,200 | Gun and Rod Clubs | $30 M |
| 7,100 | Gun Dealers | $30 M |
| 76,000 | Gun Sportsmen | $30 M |
| 1,500 | Gymnasiums | $60 L |
| 17,000 | Gynecologists | $30 M |

# H

| | | |
|---|---|---|
| 2,680 | Halls and Auditoriums | $30 M |
| 360,000 | Ham Operators | $30 M |
| 5,100 | Ham Radio Clubs | $30 M |
| 1,900 | Hand Stamp Manufacturers | $60 L |
| 360 | Handbag Manufacturers | $50 L |
| 1,900 | Handbag Shops | $60 L |
| 135,000 | Handicapped Appeal Donors | $30 M |
| 2,200 | Hardware Chains | $30 M |
| 2,100 | Hardware Manufacturers | $30 M |
| 5,700 | Hardware Wholesalers* | $30 M |
| 600 | Hardwood Mills | $50 L |
| 2,500 | Harness Shops | $30 M |
| 65,000 | Harvard Grads in Business | $30 M |
| 2,000 | Hatcheries | $30 M |
| 11,000 | Hawaiian Businesses | $30 M |
| 20,000 | Hawaiian Executives | $30 M |
| 3,500 | Hawaiian Professionals | $30 M |
| 185,000 | Hawaiian Residents | Inq. |
| 8,400 | Hawaiian Wealthies | $30 M |
| 23,000 | Hay Dealers | $30 M |
| 2,300 | Health Agencies | $30 M |
| 8,000 | Health Care Officials | $30 M |
| 3,100 | Health Clubs | $30 M |
| 182,000 | Health Conscious Individuals | $30 M |
| 21,000 | Health Education Teachers | $30 M |
| 57,000 | Health Ed. Teachers, H.S. | $30 M |
| 5,800 | Health Food Stores | $30 M |
| 7,600 | Health Officers, Public | $30 M |
| 525 | Health Publications | $50 L |
| 145,000 | Health and Welfare Donors | $30 M |
| 9,200 | Health and Welfare Groups | $30 M |
| 4,700 | Hearing Aid Dealers | $30 M |
| 13,000 | Heat Transfer Engineers | $30 M |
| 37,000 | Heating Contractors* | $30 M |
| 21,000 | Heating Engineers | $30 M |
| 550 | Heating Equipment Mfrs. | $50 L |
| 4,300 | Heating Equipment Whlse. | $30 M |

**List Explanations:** M—per thousand. L—complete list.
Names are provided on Cheshire labels—4 up or 1 up.
12    *Available by rating.

Surcharges for gummed labels $ 2.50 M
Pressure sensitive labels $ 6.00 M
3 x 5 cards $15.00 M
State selection $ 2.50 M

**Source:** "Guide to the Multi-Billion Direct Marketing Business," Dependable Lists Inc., 257 Park Avenue South, New York, N.Y. 10010. Reprinted with permission.

## FIGURE 7-5. Sample page from list catalog.

| SIC | DESCRIPTION | MARKET GPS. | COUNT |
|---|---|---|---|
| 2065 | Candy & confectionery products mfrs. | G10 | 831 |
| 5441 | Candy, nut & confectionery stores | G12 | 8,005 |
| 2032 | Canned specialties producers | G10 | 184 |
| | Canners see Fruit | | |
| 2394 | Canvas & related products mfrs. | | 1,083 |
| | Cap mfrs. see Hat | | |
| 5521 | Car dealers - used | A54 | 57,885 |
| 7542 | Car washes | | 10,041 |
| 3624 | Carbon & graphite products mfrs. | | 79 |
| 2895 | Carbon black mfrs. | | 39 |
| 3955 | Carbon paper & inked ribbon mfrs. | O05 | 96 |
| | Carbonated water mfrs. see Soft drink | | |
| 7539B | Carburetor repair shops | A55 | 1,975 |
| 3592 | Carburetor, piston, ring & valve mfrs. | A53 | 90 |
| | Cargo service see Air or Marine | | |
| 1751 | Carpentry contractors | C20 | 23,947 |
| 5023A | Carpet & floor covering whls. | C05,F24 | 413 |
| | Carpet & Rugs | C05 | |
| 5713A | Carpet & rug dealers | C05,F25 | 36,323 |
| 1752B | Carpet & rug laying contractors | C05 | 4,509 |
| 2272 | Carpet & rug mills - tufted | C05,F23 | 399 |
| 2279 | Carpet & rug mills, n.e.c. | C05,F23 | 2,145 |
| 2271 | Carpet & rug mills - woven | C05,F23 | 128 |
| 7217B | Carpet & rug repairing | C05,L10,R10 | 2,127 |
| 7217A | Carpet & upholstery cleaners | C05,F26,L10 | 22,018 |
| 7394B | Carpet & upholstery cleaning equipment rentals | C05,L10 | 4,923 |
| | Carpet rentals see Furniture | | |
| | Carting companies see Trucking | | |
| 0110 | Cash grain farms | F05 | 247 |
| 3995 | Casket mfrs. - burial | | 304 |
| 3369 | Casting foundries (nonferrous), n.e.c. | F12 | 499 |
| | Casualty insurance companies see Fire | | |
| | Cat kennels see Kennels | | |
| 5812A | Caterers | P22 | 22,889 |
| 3672 | Cathode ray TV picture tube mfrs. | T05 | 112 |
| 8662A | Catholic churches | C10 | 12,425 |
| 8213 | Catholic elementary schools | S10 | 8,100 |
| | Cellulosic see Fiber | | |
| 5039C | Cement & concrete dealers - whl. | B10 | 4,159 |
| 3241 | Cement mfrs. - hydraulic | B10 | 239 |
| 6553 | Cemeteries | | 5,193 |
| 3253 | Ceramic tile mfrs. - wall & floor | B10 | 1,154 |
| 2043 | Cereal breakfast food mfrs. | G10 | 60 |
| 8931B | Certified public accountants | A05,F08,P20 | 33,054 |
| 1771G | Cesspool construction contractors | C20 | 343 |
| 5251A | Chain saw & electric tool dealers | B10,T15 | 21,254 |
| | Chairmen of The Board see Executives | | |
| 8611D | Chambers of Commerce | A45 | 3,499 |
| 4140 | Charter service passenger transportation | | 108 |
| | Check cashing services see Money order | | |
| 2022 | Cheese mfrs. - natural & processed | G10 | 546 |
| 5451A | Cheese stores | G12 | 3,380 |
| 8911C | Chemical engineers | E10 | 464 |
| 2819 | Chemical mfrs. (ind'l inorganic), n.e.c. | | 1,434 |
| 2899 | Chemical preparation mfrs., n.e.c. | | 1,405 |
| 5161 | Chemicals & allied products whls. | | 6,890 |
| 8999B | Chemists & scientists | P20 | 852 |
| | Chief financial officers see Executives | | |
| | Children's clothing mfrs. see Apparel | | |
| 7349C | Chimney cleaning service & repair | B15 | 1,679 |
| 7699C | China & glassware repairing | R10 | 114 |
| 5719A | China & glassware stores | F25 | 3,212 |
| 5023B | China & glassware whls. | F24 | 1,111 |
| 8041 | Chiropractors | M25 | 16,415 |
| | Chlorine mfrs. see Alkali | | |
| 2066 | Chocolate & cocoa products mfrs. | G10 | 79 |
| 8663H | Christian/Disciples of Christ churches | C10 | 4,851 |
| 8663J | Christian reformed churches | C10 | 1,292 |
| 8663K | Christian Science churches | C10 | 1,658 |
| 8663I | Church of Christ - Christian | C10 | 226 |
| 8663M | Church of God | C10 | 5,870 |
| 8663G | Church of the Brethren | C10 | 886 |

| SIC | DESCRIPTION | MARKET GPS. | COUNT |
|---|---|---|---|
| 8663O | Church of the Covenant | C10 | 392 |
| 8663T | Church of the Nazarene | C10 | 2,804 |
| 5086B | Church supplies whl. | C10 | 2,904 |
| 8662 | Churches - Catholic | C10 | 13,280 |
| 8664X | Churches - other | C10 | 20,448 |
| 8664 | Churches - misc. | C10 | 29,064 |
| 8663 | Churches - Protestant | C10 | 120,836 |
| | Church organizations see Religious | | |
| | Churches | C10 | |
| 2121 | Cigar mfrs. | | 63 |
| 5993 | Cigar stores & stands | | 319 |
| 2111 | Cigarette mfrs. | | 21 |
| 7392B | City & town planners | A40,C20 | 2,042 |
| 9111A | City halls | G08 | 14,555 |
| 8911D | Civil engineers | E10 | 6,843 |
| 3259 | Clay products mfrs. (structural), n.e.c. | B10 | 98 |
| 3255 | Clay refractories | | 143 |
| 7212 | Cleaners & dyers | L10 | 38,835 |
| 5087C | Cleaners & launderers equipment whls. | L10 | 3,321 |
| 7215B | Cleaners - self-service | L10 | 2,342 |
| 2842 | Cleaning (specialty) mfrs. | | 1,198 |
| 7349 | Cleaning/maintenance svc. - home & bldg | | 24,626 |
| 8081A | Clinics | M25 | 17,662 |
| | Clock repair services see Watch | | |
| | Clock mfrs. see Watch | | |
| 5065F | Closed circuit television system whl. | T05 | 1,632 |
| | Closure plants see Crown | | |
| 5621 | Clothing (ready to wear) stores - women's | | 71,922 |
| 5641 | Clothing/furnishing stores - children's | A30 | 9,289 |
| 5611 | Clothing/furnishing stores - men's & boys' | A30 | 31,784 |
| 5136 | Clothing/furnishing whls. - men's & boys' | A29 | 5,244 |
| 5931C | Clothing dealers - secondhand | A30 | 1,639 |
| 5699F | Clothing designers | | 155 |
| 2329 | Clothing mfrs. (men's & boys'), n.e.c. | A28 | 1,197 |
| 5611B | Clothing stores - boys' | | 1,675 |
| 5651 | Clothing stores - family | A30 | 4,195 |
| 5137 | Clothing whls. - women's & children's | A29 | 13,600 |
| 8641B | Clubs & social associations | A45 | 30,729 |
| 5982A | Coal & coke dealers | F20 | 2,267 |
| 5052 | Coal & coke whls. | F20 | 1,009 |
| 1100 | Coal mining - anthracite | F20,M30 | 230 |
| 1200 | Coal mining - bituminous & lignite | F20,M30 | 4,850 |
| | Coal products mfrs. see Petroleum | | |
| 2363 | Coat & suit mfrs. - children's | A28 | 91 |
| | Coat mfrs. see Suit | | |
| | Cocoa products mfrs. see Chocolate | | |
| 5963A | Coffee brewing services | | 2,433 |
| 5499A | Coffee dealers | G12 | 1,249 |
| 2095 | Coffee mfrs. - roasted | G10 | 98 |
| | Coin dealers see Stamp | | |
| 7215 | Coin operated laundries & dry cleaners | | 16,617 |
| 7321 | Collection agencies | | 6,146 |
| 8221 | Colleges & universities | S11 | 1,855 |
| 8222 | Colleges - junior | S11 | 1,301 |
| | Colleges & Universities | S11 | |
| 2752 | Commercial & lithographic printing | P15 | 14,513 |
| 5081 | Commercial machine & equipment whls. | | 35,314 |
| 7333 | Commercial photography, art & graphics | | 26,060 |
| | Commercial testing see Testing | | |
| 6221 | Commodity brokers & dealers | F08 | 2,140 |
| 4899 | Communication services, n.e.c. | | 3,401 |
| 7392C | Communications consultants | C15 | 2,873 |
| 8663N | Community & Congregational churches | C10 | 2,349 |
| 5084I | Compressor (air & gas) whls. | M10,G05 | 4,183 |
| 7699A | Compressor & pump repair services | G05 | 4,595 |
| 3563 | Compressor mfrs. - air & gas | G05 | 154 |
| 7372 | Computer programming & software services | | 701 |
| 5211C | Concrete and ready mixed cement dealers | B10 | 2,918 |
| 3271 | Concrete block & brick mfrs. | B10 | 1,250 |
| 5039E | Concrete block & shape dealers - whl. | B10,T10 | 12,306 |
| 1771A | Concrete contractors | C20 | 13,149 |
| 3273 | Concrete mfrs. - ready mixed | | 3,763 |
| 3272 | Concrete products mfrs. - ex. block/brick | B10 | 3,045 |

**Source:** "Business List Directory," Market Data Retrieval, Ketchum Place, Westport, Conn. 06880. Reprinted with permission.

## FIGURE 7-6.  Sample page from list catalog.

| | | |
|---|---|---|
| 2,827 | Brokers, motor transportation | 4723+ |
| 605 | Bronze, brass & copper foundries | 3362 |
| 6,046 | Bronze tablet, plaque & trophy shops | 5999E+ |
| 336 | Brush & broom mfrs. | 3991 |
| 203 | Buddhist Temples | 8660R |
| 196,570 | Building contractors | 1500+ |
| 20,444 | Building & dwelling services | 7349+ |

### BUILDING MATERIALS & HARDWARE

#### -Manufacturers-

| | | |
|---|---|---|
| 213 | Building paper & board mills | 2661 |
| 201 | Cement - hydraulic | 3241 |
| 706 | Clay products - structural | 3250 |
| 12,659 | Concrete, gypsum & plaster prod. | 3270+ |
| 15,356 | Fabricated structural metal prod. | 3440+ |
| 137 | Flat glass | 3211 |
| 2,114 | Hdwe., cutlery & hand tool mfrs. | 3420 |
| 34,259 | Lumber & wood products | 2400+ |
| 22,223 | Millwork, veneer, plywood & wood members | 2430+ |
| 165 | Mineral wool | 3296 |
| 100 | Nonclay refractories | 3297 |
| 20 | Particleboard plants | 2492 |
| 449 | Prefabricated metal buildings | 3448 |
| 607 | Prefabricated wood buildings | 2452 |
| 763 | Roofing & paving materials | 2950 |
| 4,694 | Saw mills & planing mills | 2420 |
| 18,457 | Stone, clay, glass & concrete prod. | 3200+ |
| 886 | Stone (cut) & stone products | 3281 |

#### -Retailers-

| | | |
|---|---|---|
| 37,301 | Hardware stores | 5251+ |
| 9,576 | Lawn mower dealers | 5261C+ |
| 52,743 | Lumber & other bldg. mat'l. dlrs. | 5211+ |
| 46,817 | Paint, glass & wallpaper dealers | 5231+ |
| 33,030 | Paint dealers | 5231A+ |
| 25,696 | Plywood, lumber&bldg. mat'l. dlrs. | 5211A+ |
| 6,411 | Roofing & siding material dlrs. | 5211B+ |
| 16,165 | Wallpaper stores | 5231B+ |
| 12,708 | Window, jalousie & door dealers | 5211C+ |

#### -Wholesalers-

| | | |
|---|---|---|
| 1,602 | Building materials | 5039A+ |
| 1,127 | Ceramic tile | 5039B+ |
| 1,168 | Concrete blocks & shapes | 5039C+ |
| 23,482 | Construction materials | 5039+ |
| 3,733 | Crushed & natural stone | 5039D+ |
| 6,206 | Hardware | 5072+ |
| 9,915 | Lumber, plywood & millwork | 5031+ |
| 148 | Non-ceramic tile | 5039E+ |
| 6,945 | Paints & varnishes & supplies | 5198+ |
| 20,812 | Plumbing & hydronic heating supls. | 5074+ |
| 9,123 | Sand & gravel | 5039F+ |
| 1,079 | Wallpaper | 5198B+ |

### BUILDING SERVICES

| | | |
|---|---|---|
| 1,023 | Construction consultants | 8911G+ |
| 14,270 | Disinfecting & exterminating | 7342+ |
| 56,361 | Engineering & arch. - all types | 8911+ |
| 17,643 | Janitorial | 7349A+ |
| 5,855 | Office building management firms | 6512A+ |
| 5,081 | Window cleaning | 7341+ |
| 8,513 | Burglar alarm systems wholesalers | 5063A+ |
| 345 | Burlap wholesalers | 5199B+ |
| 1,015 | Bus companies, school | 4151 |
| 3,384 | Bus cos. - charter, rental & tours | 4142+ |
| 4,493 | Bus lines, intercity | 4131+ |
| 694 | Bus & truck body mfrs. | 3713 |
| 2,712 | Business brokers | 7399C+ |
| 2,718 | Business form mfrs. - manifold | 2761+ |
| 20,369 | Business form & stationery stores | 5943+ |
| 9,371 | Business form & stationery whls. | 5112+ |
| 37,472 | Business machine & equip. whls. | 5081+ |
| 1,397 | Business machine mfrs. | 3570 |
| 16,021 | Business management consultants | 7392D+ |
| 1,935 | Business & secretarial schools | 8244 |
| 71,846 | Business services, n.e.c. | 7399+ |
| 13,831 | Business supply stores | 5943A+ |
| 10,435 | Business & trade organizations | 8611 |
| 1,656,969 | BUSINESSES IN MOTION | Page 53 |
| 175 | Butter mfrs. | 2021 |
| 110 | Button mfrs. | 3963 |
| 571 | Buttonhole makers | 2395 |

## C

| | | SIC or Page No. |
|---|---|---|
| 14,112 | Cabinet makers, kitchen | 2434+ |

| | | |
|---|---|---|
| 55 | Cabinet mfrs., wood, TV & radio | 2517 |
| 13,773 | Cabinet stores, kitchen | 5712D+ |
| 103,171 | Cafes, bars & drinking places | 5823+ |
| 2,192 | Cafeterias | 5815A+ |
| 68 | Calculating & acctg. mach. mfrs. | 3574 |
| 250 | Calculating & statistical services | 8931C+ |
| 3,263 | Calking contractors | 1799C+ |
| 1,298 | Calling, paging&signal equip. whls. | 5065A+ |
| 731 | Camera equipment & supls. mfrs. | 3861 |
| 3,813 | Camera equipment wholesalers | 5043+ |
| 10,121 | Camera & photo. supply stores | 5946+ |
| 4,286 | Campgrounds | 7033 |
| 6,093 | Camper & pick-up coach dealers | 5561A+ |
| 408 | Camper & pick-up coach whls. | 5012C+ |
| 1,018 | Camper & travel trailer mfrs. | 3792 |
| 3,082 | Camping equipment stores | 5941B+ |
| 3,290 | Camping & travel trailer dealers | 5561B+ |
| 386 | Can manufacturers, metal | 3411 |
| 622,907 | CANADIAN BUSINESS LISTS | Page 55 |
| 749 | Candy & confectionery mfrs. | 2065 |
| 4,913 | Candy & confectionery whls. | 5145+ |
| 8,103 | Candy, nut & confectionery stores | 5441+ |
| 181 | Canned specialties producers | 2032 |
| 762 | Canners, fruit & vegetable | 2033 |
| 973 | Canvas products manufacturers | 2394 |
| 345 | Canvas wholesalers | 5199B+ |
| 17,187 | Car rental & leasing | 7512+ |
| 69,227 | Car & self-service restaurants | 5815+ |
| 11,504 | Car washes | 7542+ |
| 34 | Carbon black mfrs. | 2895 |
| 76 | Carbon & graphite products mfrs. | 3624 |
| 94 | Carbon paper & inked ribbon mfrs. | 3955 |
| 1,784 | Carbonated water&soft drink mfrs. | 2086 |
| 100 | Carb., piston, ring & valve mfrs. | 3592 |
| 2,827 | Cargo & freight transp. agencies | 4723+ |
| 4,071 | Cargo services, air | 4712C+ |
| 588 | Carnival supplies wholesalers | 5199C+ |
| 7,906 | Carpentry work contractors | 1751+ |

### CARPETS & RUGS

| | | |
|---|---|---|
| 22,372 | Cleaners | 7217+ |
| 3,221 | Cleaning equip. rental agencies | 7394A+ |
| 8,101 | Cleaning equip. & supplies whls. | 5087C+ |
| 33,368 | Dealers (retail) | 5713A+ |
| 4,189 | Laying contractors | 1752C+ |
| 560 | Mills | 2270 |
| 1,694 | Repairing services | 7699M+ |
| 2,320 | Wholesalers | 5023A+ |
| 2,896 | Cash register & supplies whls. | 5081D+ |
| 315 | Casket manufacturers | 3995 |
| 1,437 | Castings, ferrous metal fndry. | 3321 |
| 605 | Castings, nonferrous metal fndry. | 0752A+ |
| 6,485 | Cat & dog kennels | 2047 |
| 190 | Cat, dog & other pet food mfrs. | 5999M+ |
| 8,037 | Cat, dog & other pet shops | 5816+ |
| 24,507 | Caterers | 3672 |
| 60 | Cathode ray picture tube mfrs. | 8660C |
| 12,200 | Catholic Churches | 8213 |
| 8,233 | Catholic elementary schools | 8216 |
| 1,695 | Catholic secondary schools | 2823 |
| 61 | Cellulosic man-made fiber mfrs. | 3241 |
| 201 | Cement mfrs., hydraulic | 6553+ |
| 5,428 | Cemeteries | 6553A+ |
| 4,930 | Cemeteries, human | 6553B+ |
| 315 | Cemeteries, pet | 5713B+ |
| 2,139 | Ceramic tile dealers | 3253 |
| 99 | Ceramic tile manufacturers | 5039B+ |
| 1,127 | Ceramic tile wholesalers | 2043 |
| 58 | Cereal breakfast food mfrs. | |

### CHAIN HEADQUARTERS & BUYING OFFICES

| | | |
|---|---|---|
| 924 | Department stores | 5311BD |
| 361 | Discount department stores | 5311AD |
| 1,274 | Drug stores | 5912/D |
| 1,171 | Grocery stores | 5411/D |
| 277 | Hotels & motels | 7011/V |
| 844 | Variety stores | 5331/D |

### CHAIN OUTLETS

| | | |
|---|---|---|
| 9,546 | Department stores | 5311BO |
| 5,967 | Discount department stores | 5311AO |
| 7,235 | Drug stores | 5912/O |
| 33,668 | Grocery stores | 5411/O |
| 8,125 | Shoe stores | 5661/O |
| 9,793 | Variety stores | 5331/O |
| 4,243 | Chambers of Commerce | 8611A |
| 753 | Chambers of Commerce, Jr. | 8611B |
| 419 | Charm & modeling schools | 8299E |
| 4,467 | Charter services - air | 4521+ |

| | | |
|---|---|---|
| 3,614 | Charter services - pass., ground | 4140+ |
| 1,141 | Check cashing services | 6059A |
| 632 | Cheese manufacturers | 2022 |
| 3,129 | Cheese stores | 5451A+ |
| 12,068 | Chemical & allied products mfrs. | 2800 |
| 11,970 | Chemical & allied products whls. | 5161+ |
| 21 | Chewing gum manufacturers | 2067 |
| 1,232 | Chemists, analytical & consulting | 8999B+ |
| 112,987 | Chief executive officers in leading firms | Page 5₄ |
| 67,661 | Chief financial officers in leading firms | Page 5₄ |
| | Children's & inf. wear See Apparel | |
| 699 | Children's veh., game & toy mfrs. | 3944 |
| 3,036 | China & glassware stores | 5719A+ |
| 697 | China & glassware wholesalers | 5023B+ |
| 38 | China table & kitchenware mfrs. | 3262 |
| 7,241 | Chinese & other oriental food rest. | 5814B+ |
| 16,853 | Chiropractors offices | 8041 |
| 95 | Chlorine & alkali manufacturers | 2812 |
| 91 | Chocolate & cocoa products mfrs. | 2066 |
| 7,178 | Christ, Churches of | 8660Q |
| 4,880 | Christian & Christian Ref. Chs. | 8660J |
| 1,687 | Christian Science Churches | 8660D |
| 4,585 | Church & religious goods whls. | 5086F+ |
| 7,731 | Church organizations | 8661A |

### CHURCHES

| | | |
|---|---|---|
| 173,986 | All denominations combined | 8660 |
| 5,364 | Assemblies of God | 8660A |
| 42,128 | Baptist | 8660B |
| 203 | Buddhist | 8660R |
| 12,200 | Catholic | 8660C |
| 4,880 | Christian & Christian Reformed | 8660J |
| 1,687 | Christian Science | 8660D |
| 978 | Churches of the Brethren | 8660U |
| 7,178 | Churches of Christ | 8660Q |
| 6,300 | Churches of God | 8660S |
| 3,104 | Churches of the Nazarene | 8660V |
| 1,554 | Community | 8660W |
| 4,111 | Congregational | 8660E |
| 1,462 | Covenant & Evangelical | 8660H |
| 1,195 | Disciples of Christ | 8660F |
| 5,423 | Episcopal | 8660G |
| 1,184 | Greek Orthodox | 8660X |
| 2,565 | Jewish | 8660I |
| 13,115 | Lutheran | 8660K |
| 713 | Mennonite | 8660L |
| 20,026 | Methodist | 8660M |
| 5,177 | Pentecostal | 8660Y |
| 8,699 | Presbyterian | 8660N |
| 2,119 | Seventh Day Adventist | 8660P |
| 553 | Unitarians & Universalists | 8660T |
| 21,183 | Other denominations, n.e.c. | 8660Z |
| 138 | Cigar & cigarette mfrs. | 2100 |
| 4,155 | Cigar & cigarette stores & stands | 5993+ |
| 2,509 | Cigar & cigarette wholesalers | 5194+ |
| 12,899 | City halls | 9111A |
| 2,007 | City & town planners | 7392A+ |
| 48,852 | Civic, social & fraternal orgns. | 8641 |
| 706 | Clay products manufacturers | 3250 |
| 39,392 | Cleaners & dyers | 7212+ |
| 8,101 | Cleaners, dyers&lndry equip. whls | 5087C+ |
| 2,198 | Cleaners, self-service | 7215B+ |
| 8,510 | Cleaning & dyeing plants | 7216+ |
| 1,056 | Cleaning, polishing & sanitation goods manufacturers | 2842 |
| 19,687 | Clinics, medical & dental | 8081+ |
| 16,328 | Clock, watch & jewelry repr. shops | 7631+ |
| 221 | Clock, watch & watchcase mfrs. | 3873 |
| 7,787 | Clock, watch and jewelry whls. | 5094 |
| • | Clothing mfrs. See Apparel | |
| | Clothing rental excl. formalwear | 7299F+ |
| | Clothing retailers See Apparel | |
| | Clothing wholesalers See Apparel | |
| 4,668 | Closed circuit TV system whls. | 5065B+ |
| | Clubs See Associations | |
| 1,816 | Coal & coke dealers | 5982A+ |
| 1,590 | Coal, mineral & ore wholesalers | 5052+ |
| 123 | Coal mining firms - anthracite | 1100 |
| 3,151 | Coal mining firms - bituminous & lignite | 1200 |
| 55 | Coal & petrol. prod. mfrs., n.e.c. | 2999 |
| | Coat & suit mfrs. See Apparel | |
| 2,101 | Coating (metal) & allied services | 3479+ |
| 103,171 | Cocktail lounges, drinking places | 5823+ |
| 91 | Cocoa & chocolate products mfrs. | 2066 |
| 95 | Coffee roasters | 2095 |
| 138 | Coil & transformer mfrs. | 3677 |
| 3,434 | Coin & stamp dealers | 5999N |
| 14,989 | Coin-operated laundries & cleaners | 7215+ |
| 5,428 | Collection agencies | 7321B+ |
| 1,222 | Colleges, Junior | 8222A |

16

For more detailed description of lists, see page 28.

**Source:** "Directory," National Business Lists Inc., 295 Madison Avenue, New York, N.Y. 10017. Reprinted with permission.

## List Testing

You rent additional names to supplement your own in-house mailing list so that you can find new customers for the products or services you offer through the mails. An outside list may run to tens or even hundreds of thousands of names—and there are literally thousands of lists to select from. It thus makes good sense to rent segments of a number of different lists, and test these out for results, instead of renting an entire single list. For example, should you want to add 10,000 names for your next mailing, you would be better off choosing a 5,000-name segment from each of two lists instead of the entire lot from one. Or even better, smaller amounts from four or five different lists. Some direct mail people suggest that you should never test fewer than 3,000 names from a list; others feel more comfortable assessing the results from a test of at least 5,000. What you would be looking for, of course, are those list segments that bring enough responses to be able to break even, or earn some profit, on your mailing.

You need to make sure you are testing the lists, not one or more of ten or twenty variables that have nothing to do with the lists themselves. This means you must send the identical mailing piece (or "package") to all names and addresses on all list segments. It also means that you need to drop all mail at the same time, to rule out possible effects of time variations. Further, since differences in geographical areas can produce varying results, you need to make sure the lists you are comparing go to the same parts of the country, same states, and so on.

Each list you sample will pull differently. Even three or four samples from the same list will show different results. (Probability theory tells us that samples of a large "universe"—such as a list of 200,000 names—will show different "mean" results, and that these means will themselves be distributed over a range. However, without getting into the finer nuances of the "normal curve," you will be able to observe which samples outpull the others rather readily.) Some will not pay off at all; others will. And you will add the names and addresses of these new customers to your house list, for future mailings.

## SAMPLING OF LIST HOUSES

In this section, you will find names, addresses, and telephone numbers of some mailing list companies. Some are compilers; others are list brokers; still others combine both activities and can also act as list managers for you when your list has grown substantially. A few of these firms offer complete in-house printing services and have automated mail-processing equipment. Included are firms with specialized lists, such as Senior Citizens Unlimited of Tuckahoe, New York, and the Farmer/Data Bank of St. Paul, Minnesota. The Lifestyle Selector (Denver, Colorado) stores information in forty-nine interest areas on their names in addition to demographic data. Every name represents a buyer of consumer goods or equipment; interests range from collecting antiques and bicycling through raising horses and racquetball, to science fiction, snowmobiles, wines, and the like.

ADDRESSES UNLIMITED
14621 Titus Street
Van Nuys, CA 91402
(213) 787-1414

BELTH ASSOCIATES, INC.
971 Richmond Road
East Meadow, NY 11554
(516) 483-3030

ED BURNETT CONSULTANTS,
  INC.
2 Park Avenue
New York, N.Y. 10016
(212) 679-0630

CAHNERS PUBLISHING
  COMPANY
5 South Wabash Avenue
Chicago, IL 60603
(312) 372-6880

COMPILERS PLUS INC.
2 Penn Place
Pelham Manor, N.Y. 10803
(914) 738-1520

CONSUMERS MARKETING
  RESEARCH, INC.
600 Huyler Street
South Hackensack, N.J. 07606
(201) 440-8900

THE COOLIDGE COMPANY, INC.
25 West 43rd Street
New York, N.Y. 10036
(212) 730-5660

CUSTOMIZED MAILING LISTS,
  INC.
158–23 Grand Central Parkway
Jamaica Estates, N.Y. 11432
(212) 969-8800

DEPENDABLE LISTS INC.
257 Park Avenue South
New York, N.Y. 10010
(212) 677-6760

DUNHILL INTERNATIONAL LIST
  COMPANY, INC.
2430 West Oakland Park Boulevard
Ft. Lauderdale, FL 33311
(305) 484-8300

DUN'S MARKETING SERVICES
99 Church Street
New York, N.Y. 10007
(212) 285-7136

FARMER/DATA BANK
The Webb Company
199 Shepard Boulevard
St. Paul, MN 55116
(612) 647-7237

GEORGE-MANN ASSOCIATES,
  INC.
6 Old Cranbury Road
Cranbury, N.J. 08512
(609) 443-1330

FRITZ S. HOFHEIMER INC.
88 Third Avenue
Mineola, N.Y. 11501
(516) 248-4600

CEIL LEVINE SCREENED
  MAILING LISTS, INC.
250 West 57th Street
New York, N.Y. 10019
(212) 586-2086

THE LIFESTYLE SELECTOR
A Division of National Demographics
  Ltd.
1624 Market Street
Denver, CO 80202
(303) 534-5231

MAILING LISTS, INC.
675 Third Avenue
New York, N.Y. 10017
(212) 867-8990

MARKET DATA RETRIEVAL
Ketchum Place
Westport, CT 06880
(203) 226-8941

NATIONAL BUSINESS LISTS, INC.
2 North Franklin Street
Chicago, IL 60606
(312) 236-0350

SENIOR CITIZENS UNLIMITED
273 Columbus Avenue
Tuckahoe, N.Y. 10707
(914) 632-1595

ANGELO R. VENEZIAN, INC.
10–64 Jackson Avenue
Long Island City, N.Y. 11101
(212) 784-0500

ALVIN B. ZELLER, INC.
475 Park Avenue South
New York, N.Y. 10016
(212) 689-4900

One day, you will discover that your mailing list has become your most valuable asset. You will want to protect it, to keep it current. You will also find that lists are dynamic; about one out of every five Americans moves to another address every year. Some estimates

**MAINTAINING YOUR LIST**

**FIGURE 7-7. Example of guarantee and terms.**

GUARANTEE: Deliverability of 95% is guaranteed on all lists, except retailers and contractors, which are guaranteed 92%. We will refund at the rate of the current minimum third class postage for undeliverable pieces in excess of the guarantee, if such pieces are returned to us within 45 days of our shipping date. Mail returned by the post office with a forwarding address shown is not included in the guarantee. If more than one copy of a list is purchased at one time, guarantee applies only to the first mailing. Maximum liability shall not exceed the total amount of the specific order involved.

TERMS: Net 30 days. Minimum order: $75.00, plus shipping charges and sales tax where applicable, except for specific categories where minimums vary.

ORDERS must be submitted in writing or USE THE HANDY ORDER FORMS IN THE BACK OF THIS CATALOG. Payment in full must accompany orders from new accounts. Credit and open account can be established for future orders. Lists cannot be returned or exchanged after delivery, and cancellations for work in progress will be charged on basis of amount of work completed.

COMMISSIONS: 20% to qualified mailing lists brokers, 15% to recognized advertising agencies and lettershops.

ADDITIONAL CHARGES:
Cheshire labels (ungummed) ....................... No charge
Pressure sensitive labels ........................ $ 7.00 per M
Gummed, perforated labels .................... $ 2.50 per M
3x5 cards........................................Inquire
State selection ................................. $ 2.50 per M
SCF Zip Code (3 digit) selection ................. $ 2.50 per M
Title addressing .............................. $ 2.50 per M
Key coding ..................................... $ 1.00 per M
Telephone Numbers...............................Inquire
Magnetic tape ............................. $25.00 per tape
Additional copies ...............................Inquire
Sales Tax ................................... As applicable
Shipping/Handling ............... $5.00 minimum per order

All prices and quantities subject to change without notice.

**Source:** Catalog of Alvin B. Zeller, Inc.. 475 Park Avenue South, New York, N.Y. 10016. Reprinted with permission.

range up to 25 percent of the population. What this means is that, out of a list of 5,000 names, over 1,000 may well become worthless *unless* you are able to locate their new addresses.

Many mail order firms see to it that the statement "Address Correction Requested" is printed, along with their company names and addresses, in the "corner cards" of their mailing envelopes. The post office will inform you of the new address for each individual that has moved in the interim—for a small charge, of course. It is also a good idea to "clean" your list at least once each year by sending out a first-class mailing, since such letters will be forwarded automatically to new addresses. Be sure you enclose a note somewhere in the mailing package, asking whether the addressee has moved and requesting that he or she write down the new address and return the information (perhaps on a postage-free return card or on the order form enclosed).

Despite your every precaution, however, some pieces out of every mailing you make will be returned to you as undeliverable. In mail order jargon, these pieces are referred to as "nixies." Take pains to check each nixie against your master list. Perhaps the name was misspelled on the label or envelope, the numbers transposed in the address, or the ZIP code was wrong. And, of course, enter any change of address on your master cards, too.

## RENTING YOUR HOUSE LIST

Although this aspect of list management probably lies several years in the future for you, it won't hurt to know something about it now. Granted continued success in your mail order enterprise, you will keep building your own mailing list through a combination of media advertising, direct mail, and the testing of outside lists. Eventually, you will wind up with several thousand names and addresses of people to whom you have sold merchandise. This is when you can start thinking about list rental as an additional source of income for your business.

You can try on your own to offer your house list to other mail order companies that you think may be able to sell their wares to your customers. Some will be interested in renting your names. They may pay you as much as $40 to $50 per thousand, for a one-time use. If you have the time, you can arrange to type your names on their envelopes for an extra fee. Although the per-thousand rate may not seem to amount to much, bear in mind that you might be able to rent your list as many as ten or twenty times a year. Even at the $40 per thousand rate, your list of 5,000 names could bring you anywhere from $2,000 to $4,000 and more of extra income, actually extra *profit*, because there is no cost of merchandise involved here as there is when you sell your goods through the mails.

Of course, it is not easy for the small mail order operator to find companies interested in renting his or her list. You would be better off, especially when your list has grown some more, contacting a list broker or list management company to handle such arrangements. You will have to pay this representative perhaps 20 percent of what you earn, but it will be worth it. You may also think about computerizing the list when it gets big enough (see Figure 7-8). Dependable Lists Inc., of New York City, recommends that you look to the computer when you have accumulated 20,000 names, as a rough rule of thumb. (Incidentally, this firm offers some valuable little booklets at token cost to the mail order operator. Among their mail order guides are such titles as "How to Test a Mailing List," "How to Computerize and Maintain Your Mailing List for Greater Profit," "Psychographics: The Life Style of the Mail Order Buyer," and others.)

**FIGURE 7-8. Advantages of having your list computerized.**

Putting your list on computer offers you the following advantages:

1. It provides easy access to a wide range of information about the customers and prospects on your list. In a matter of seconds, you can have *counts by zip code,* by *sectional center,* by *state,* by *product type,* and by *media source.*

2. You can have *demographic and/or psychographic information* about your customers and prospects: sex, where they live, what they buy, how they bought (cash, credit), etc.

3. You can have the vital "RFM" of your customers—meaning the *recency, frequency,* and *monetary value* of your customer's purchase. This is the basic formula of his [or her] past behavior which sheds the most light on the likelihood of his [or her] future performance.

4. You can avail yourself of many of the computer applications available to increase your marketing efforts.

**Source:** From the mail marketing guide, "How to Computerize and Maintain Your Mailing List for Greater Profit," © 1978 by Dependable Lists Inc., New York, N.Y. 10010, pp. 3–4. Reprinted with permission.

**TABLE 7-1. State abbreviations.**

| | | | |
|---|---|---|---|
| Alabama | AL | Montana | MT |
| Alaska | AK | Nebraska | NE |
| Arizona | AZ | Nevada | NV |
| Arkansas | AR | New Hampshire | NH |
| California | CA | New Jersey | NJ |
| Colorado | CO | New Mexico | NM |
| Connecticut | CT | New York | NY |
| Delaware | DE | North Carolina | NC |
| Florida | FL | North Dakota | ND |
| Georgia | GA | Ohio | OH |
| Hawaii | HI | Oklahoma | OK |
| Idaho | ID | Oregon | OR |
| Illinois | IL | Pennsylvania | PA |
| Indiana | IN | Rhode Island | RI |
| Iowa | IA | South Carolina | SC |
| Kansas | KS | South Dakota | SD |
| Kentucky | KY | Tennessee | TN |
| Louisiana | LA | Texas | TX |
| Maine | ME | Utah | UT |
| Maryland | MD | Vermont | VT |
| Massachusetts | MA | Virginia | VA |
| Michigan | MI | Washington | WA |
| Minnesota | MN | West Virginia | WV |
| Mississippi | MS | Wisconsin | WI |
| Missouri | MO | Wyoming | WY |

CROWN, PAUL, *What You Should Know About Building Your Mailing Lists.* Dobbs Ferry, N.Y.: Oceana Publications, 1973.

*Directory of Mailing List Houses,* 1977. Coral Springs, Fla.: B. Klein Publications, 1977.

FOSTER, ROBERT L., *Business Mailer's Handbook.* Englewood Cliffs, N.J.: Prentice-Hall, Inc., 1977.

HODGSON, RICHARD S., *Direct Mail and Mail Order Handbook,* 3rd ed. Chicago: Dartnell Corporation, 1980.

STONE, BOB, *Successful Direct Marketing Methods,* 2nd ed. Chicago: Crain Books, 1979.

### *Small business bibliographies*

#13 DEBOER, DR. LLOYD M., "National Directories for Use in Marketing," revised March 1980.

#29 MILLICAN, RICHARD D., "National Mailing-List Houses," revised January 1973.

Free Materials from the Small Business Administration

# 8

## THE PERSONAL SELLING PROCESS

It is imperative that you try to learn all you can about the art of selling itself, for skill in this area can ensure success in mail order marketing. Direct, person-to-person selling is the most effective way known of persuading people to buy. Happily, it is also something we have all had experience with, if only at the other end. We have shopped in many stores; by now, we can certainly distinguish between the capable salesclerk and the uninspired one. Many of us have also been exposed to the sales presentations of house-to-house canvassers, who sell everything from Avon and Amway products to vacuum cleaners, encyclopedias, and household utensils.

Like all advertising, mail order selling operates under a serious handicap—the lack of personal contact. There is no salesperson present; no chance to project a positive personality, vary the pitch and tone of the voice, take cues from the prospect, and modify the sales presentation accordingly. Printed matter replaces the salesperson's visit; you must depend on it to do the entire selling job, which is all the more reason why you need to understand the selling process itself. You need to know what your advertising (or direct mail) must accomplish to make that sale.

**THE SALESPERSON**

A popular vocation, selling is vital to the nation's economy. Estimates of the number of people employed in sales positions range between six and nine million. Some of them sell goods and services to the wholesale and retail trades; others sell raw materials, machinery,

107

equipment, and supplies to manufacturing plants. Still others supply schools, hospitals, utilities, government agencies, and other nonprofit organizations. Some selling jobs, like that of the route salesperson or the clerk in a fast food operation, require almost no real selling ability. Others call for a great deal of ingenuity and creativity, commonly found among salespersons who sell real estate or life insurance.

Traditionally, the salesperson has always needed to be familiar with the company's history, products, and prices, as well as those of the competition. In addition, he or she had to be an effective communicator. Today, that isn't enough. Today's salesperson must be sincerely interested in—and acquainted with—the needs, wants, and problems of prospective customers, must be an effective problem-solver, and must have a practical, working knowledge of psychology.

## THE "AIDA CONCEPT"

For decades, students in marketing and sales courses have been taught how to sell "by formula" to the tune of "AIDA"—not the opera, but a simple mnemonic designed to help the student remember what the salesperson must do in order to accomplish the sale, or, for that matter, what an advertisement or direct mail "package" must do.

The letters in AIDA stand for:

A—Attention
I—Interest
D—Desire
A—Action

To make the sale, the sales representative needs to: (1) get the prospect's attention, (2) arouse interest in the product or service being presented, (3) build desire on the part of the prospect to have what is being offered, and (4) get action in the form of an order.

## THE SELLING PROCESS

In applying the AIDA concept to an actual selling situation, the salesperson follows certain steps. These steps describe the selling process in effect, and they are discussed in this section. The steps are:

Prospecting
Qualifying prospects
Making the presentation
Meeting objections
Closing the sale
Following up the sale

### Prospecting

Career salespersons face an ongoing challenge; they need to keep locating likely candidates for the goods and services they sell. Without a continuous pool of these "prospects," salespeople cannot put their selling expertise to the test. So, they must use their intuition, insight, know-how, and creative ability to ferret out these individuals.

Here are some of the sources they tap:

- Advertising in the media for leads
- Business directories
- Cold canvassing (door-to-door)
- Company records
- Conventions
- Customers
- Direct mail efforts
- Family, friends, and acquaintances
- Government records of all kinds
- Magazines
- Mailing lists
- Newspapers
- Organization memberships
- Other salespersons
- Radio
- Recommendations
- Reference works
- Telephone directories
- Telephone solicitation
- Television
- Trade publications
- Trade shows

**Qualifying Prospects**

You might think that, having developed a lengthy list of prospects, the salesperson's next logical move would be to contact them for appointments. In effect, however, this would cost far too much in the salesperson's time and effort; and time and effort are what translate to income. A distinction first must be drawn between the *real* prospects on the list and the more numerous *suspects*, as they are often referred to by sales representatives. In reality, prospects are prospective buyers; suspects are those who *may* be buyers but need first to be converted into prospects. This is accomplished by *qualifying* them, involving a procedure whereby each person (or firm) on the list is queried directly, or checked on indirectly, to ascertain two vital points: (1) that the suspect needs or could use the product or service, and (2) that the suspect can afford or is in a position to buy it.

There is more to the qualifying process than this, however. The salesperson should also attempt to gain insights into what the prospect is like: background, likes and dislikes, interests, and so on. This is the time for researching; the better the salesperson understands the prospective buyer, the more effectively he or she can shape the sales presentation so that the interview will most likely culminate with a signed purchase order. If a firm is the targeted prospect, the sales representative needs to become thoroughly familiar with the kind of business it is in, what the problems may be and where they lie, the company's approximate sales volume, its credit history, the size of the organization, and so on. Moreover, there is a need to know as much as possible about the purchasing agent as well.

Some authors of textbooks on selling and sales management label this the "preapproach" phase. They consider it a separate step in the selling process, following that of qualifying. I cannot see separating one from the other; both are essential preparation for the sales visit.

## Making the Presentation

Experienced salespersons enter the prospect's office with determination, confident in the knowledge that they have prepared thoroughly for the interview. They are determined to quickly gain the prospect's attention and confidence, establish rapport immediately, then use their selling skills to interest, woo, and convince the individual to make the purchase. Along the way, they know that objections will most likely be raised, and they are prepared to meet and resolve them readily.

A good sales presentation usually starts with a hook or opening designed to enable the salesperson to caputre the prospect's interest and, at the same time, make a smooth transition into the presentation itself. As an example, there is the "question" or "benefit" opening: "Good morning, Mr. Barr. Would you be interested in saving your company $1,600 a month?" Now, there is just no way that Mr. Barr will say "I'm not interested" to that kind of beginning.
Naturally, a claim of this sort must be both truthful and supportable by evidence.

Many other openings are possible. You will discover some of those more frequently used in any of the books on selling. They have even been given descriptive names.[1] Here are four of them:

- Product approach
- Referral approach
- Premium approach
- Introductory approach

During the presentation, salespeople use everything at their command to lead the prospect to the final placement of an order. Sure to be covered are the major selling points about the product or service and the benefits the prospect may expect. Charts, photographs, and other visual aids may help the process. Involving the prospect in the presentation, through appealing to the various senses and/or emotions, makes for increased interest and more conviction. The use of testimonials may really tie things up nicely so that all claims made are believable. Finally, the salesperson's ability to meet and counter objections that are raised will make (or break) the sale.

## Meeting Objections

Nearly everyone will harbor doubts or misgivings during a sales presentation. Perhaps we are a little too suspicious of strangers, especially those who seem intent on getting money from us. Perhaps it is only natural to expect that, if we are not wary, we may be taken

---

[1]For example, see: Frederic A. Russell, Frank H. Beach, and Richard H. Buskirk, *Textbook of Salesmanship*, 10th ed. (New York: McGraw-Hill, 1978), pp. 181–90.

advantage of. But it also makes sense to ask questions, to seek further information before making the commitment to spend.

The experienced salesperson also knows these things and is prepared, indeed trained, to handle objections that may be raised during the interview. Because certain types of objections recur time and again, sales trainers usually teach their students how to forestall them or how to overcome them. Most common are those that have to do with either the price or the quality of the product or service. There may be other kinds of objections as well, to the company, to its service, or to the salesperson.

As is the case with the many kinds of openings to a presentation, there are a variety of techniques for handling objections—and they, too, carry popular labels. (The reader can easily learn how to apply half a dozen or more of these by reading through the appropriate sections in several of the sales texts listed at the end of this chapter.) Some of the techniques are:

- Direct rebuttal (or direct denial) method.
- Boomerang (or conversion) method.
- "Yes, but.." (or indirect denial) method.
- Compensation method.

**Closing the Sale**

After the salesperson has satisfactorily resolved all of the prospect's objections and questions, he or she will then strive to bring the sales interview to its hoped-for end, the writing of the order. This is the *close* or the *closing;* both terms are used in selling. It may involve as simple a technique as the "assumptive close," where the salesperson starts to write up the order, confident that the prospect is ready to become a customer. Of all closes, this is the one most frequently used.

Often, however, things do not run quite so smoothly. Good salespeople learn how to use other kinds of closes; these may be brought into play to handle different situations. There are literally dozens of practical closing techniques available. Thompson,[2] for example, lists and describes eight:

- Compliment technique
- Continuous-yes technique
- Summary close
- Emotional close
- T-account close
- Assumptive close
- SRO (Standing Room Only) technique
- Closing on a minor point

One or two examples should suffice at this point. In the SRO close, the salesperson suggests to the prospect the urgency of ordering today, implying that demand for the product is so heavy that should there be any delay, "we may not be able to fill your order." In the T-account method, the sales representative will draw a line down

[2]Joseph W. Thompson, *Selling: A Managerial and Behavioral Science Analysis,* 2nd ed. (New York: McGraw-Hill, 1973), pp. 525–31.

the center of a blank sheet of paper, then write the word "Yes" at the top of one half and "No" at the top of the other. Reasons why the prospect should buy are listed in the affirmative column; points against the decision to buy are shown in the negative column. The prospect—it is hoped—easily sees on this "balance sheet" the weight of the arguments in favor of making the purchase.

## Following Up the Sale

The "follow up" is a term commonly applied to what takes place after the sale has been concluded and the salesperson has a signed copy of the buyer's order. In the retail store, the salesclerk "follows up" by: (1) thanking the customer, (2) assuring the customer that he or she has made a wise decision, and (3) suggesting that the customer "come back to visit us soon."

Selling to organizations is not much different. The same things are done, but the sales representative goes even further. There is need to check back with the customer later on, after the order has been delivered, to make sure that the buyer is thoroughly satisfied with both the goods and the service. Any complaints are taken care of at once, for the salesperson looks to establish a sound, lasting relationship, one that will ensure additional future orders.

## SUGGESTED READING

### Books

BODLE, YVONNE and JOSEPH COREY, *Retail Selling,* 2nd ed. New York: McGraw-Hill, 1977.

BUSKIRK, RICHARD H., *Retail Selling: A Vital Approach.* San Francisco: Canfield Press, 1975.

ENIS, BEN M., *Personal Selling: Foundations, Process, and Management.* Santa Monica, Calif.: Goodyear Publishing, 1979.

KIRKPATRICK, C. A. and FREDERICK A. RUSS, *Salesmanship,* 7th ed. Cincinnati: South-Western, 1981.

KURTZ, DAVID L., H. ROBERT DODGE, and JAY E. KLOMPMAKER, *Professional Selling.* Dallas, Tex.: Business Publications, 1976.

PEDERSON, CARLTON A., and MILBURN D. WRIGHT, *Selling: Principles and Methods,* 6th ed. Homewood, Ill.: Irwin, 1978.

REID, ALLAN L., *Modern Applied Selling,* 3rd ed. Santa Monica, Calif.: Goodyear Publishing, 1981.

ROBESON, JAMES F., H. LEE MATHEWS, and CARL G. STEVENS, *Selling.* Homewood, Ill.: Irwin, 1978.

RUSSELL, FREDERIC A., FRANK H. BEACH, and RICHARD H. BUSKIRK, *Textbook of Salesmanship,* 10th ed. New York: McGraw-Hill, 1978.

THOMPSON, JOSEPH W., *Selling: A Managerial and Behavioral Science Anaylsis,* 2nd ed. New York: McGraw-Hill, 1973.

### Free Materials from the Small Business Administration

*Small marketers aids*

#95 GRUBB, KENNETH, "Are Your Salespeople Missing Opportunities?" September 1963.

#114 LAWS, DWAYNE, "Pleasing Your Boss, the Customer," June 1965.

Mail Order Selling

# 9

## CREATING PRINT ADVERTISEMENTS

With the sole exception of personal selling, direct mail marketing is your most effective and most personal means of persuading people to buy. It is, of course, the mainstay of most mail order companies' sales efforts. Direct mail is used in two ways: (1) to sell merchandise or services directly, and (2) to accomplish precisely the same aim *after* having advertised in some other medium to generate names and addresses of prospective buyers.

The most likely candidates among the various media for reaching that second goal, at least so far as the smaller mail order merchant is concerned, are magazines and newspapers. (The whys and wherefores for this are treated in later chapters.) Not that the print media cannot profitably be used to sell goods and services directly. Of course, they can! Both can be worthwhile vehicles for you.

**THE CHALLENGE OF PRINT ADVERTISING**

It is easy to see that the preparation of newspaper and magazine advertisements has much in common with the creation of folders, broadsides, brochures, or other direct mail formats. Either approach calls for careful planning, ideation, the organization of elements, and execution in print. Both require writing persuasive copy, selecting headlines that stimulate reader interest and accent the highlights of your proposition, and introducing the kinds of illustrations that will help sell the item. Yet the challenge of preparing a print advertisement is more difficult than the problem of devising a typical mail order piece. Why? Basically because of space constraints. In writing and laying out a circular or brochure, you can be as expansive as you wish to be. If you decide you need additional space, you can tack on a second, or even a third, sheet to your first one. Or, perhaps, use a larger page, and make another flap or fold. Usually, your only added cost is for the paper.

On the other hand, the newspapers and magazines you use will charge you for every column inch and for every agate line of space you purchase. And space costs can be substantial! Smaller mail order organizations, for instance, seldom will contact for full-page advertisements. More likely, they think in terms of small space advertisements, perhaps 10 or 12 inches in size (5 or 6 inches by two columns across), or, perhaps, one-twelfth of a page in the mail order section of a magazine. (More on space costs and other details are found in Chapters 12 and 13.)

This means you will have to tell the whole story, effectively, within a relatively small area. And this is where your "expertise" will come in handy.

**Start to Develop Your Skills**

Even before starting up in your new business, you owe it to yourself to spend some time studying your new field. You need to do lots of homework to familiarize yourself with typical print advertising in mail order.

Visit the local branch of your public library. In the reading room, you will find displayed current issues of several dozen magazines. Leaf through each one, checking for any advertisements that may call for immediate *reader response by mail*. Some magazines—as, for example, *Good Housekeeping, House Beautiful,* and other "shelter" publications—contain mail order sections toward the back of the book. Most magazines, of course, do not. Still, in many of these books, you will occasionally come across one or more mail-order advertisements.

You might also consider adding to your studies the magazine section (and, possibly, the comics) of your own Sunday newspapers each week. These editions often carry some mail order advertising.

Only part way into your preparation, you may conclude that most such advertising—whether designed to elicit inquiries, distribute catalogs or other literature, or sell merchandise directly—has these components in common:

- A headline and maybe one or two subheadlines
- An illustration
- Words and sentences that tell the story (the "copy")
- The advertiser's name and address
- A coupon (in many cases) to be filled out, clipped, and mailed by the interested reader

You will also become sensitive to other characteristics of the mail order advertisement: the frequent use of borders of different types around the ad; how the major elements, such as headlines, illustrations, and copy blocks, are arranged within the confines of the space; the interesting (or, perhaps, uninteresting) choice of objects or subjects used as illustrations; and how white space can be cleverly used to make an advertisement stand out from other surrounding ads.

Be sure to photostat some of the advertisements that seem to attract your attention smartly and make you want to read all of the finer print. Keep these for further study and analysis.

In Chapter 8, we discussed personal selling and the AIDA concept. If you intend to sell through newspaper or magazine advertising, keep those same elements in mind: attention, interest, desire, and action. But in these media, you must rely on your ingenuity far more, for you are limited to "touching" your audience only through the reader's sense of sight. No spoken communication can take place, unless, of course, you resort to a technique that inserts a recorded message—on a prepared phonograph disc—into the publication. The problem with this approach, however, is that you usually have to pay heavily for the insertion (*and* the discs themselves), and take a full-page advertisement in the magazine as well.

**Procedure for Ad Creation**

For the novice ad maker, it is recommended that you start out by consciously following the simple approach outlined below. When you have made a dozen or so advertisements entirely on your own, the process will be second nature to you and you will no longer think of the steps in 1–2–3 fashion.

1. Clarify your perception of the persons with whom you will be communicating. What are they like? (Think in terms of sex, age, income level, education, and other demographics.)

2. Attempt to describe the product (or service) you want to sell—in writing. Be as detailed as you can. Ask yourself questions such as: Of what value is this item? What satisfactions would it bring to the purchaser? Why would consumers buy it? How can it be used? How is it different from what is now available in stores?

3. Study what you have written down. Then try to write one paragraph, however lengthy, that summarizes your thinking to this point about the product. Write as if you are speaking directly to one of your prospective customers. Keep your mental picture of that person in front of you; you must first try to pique his or her interest, then spark the desire to buy.

4. Make a list of *all* the customer benefits to be expected from the product. Then select the two or three that you judge most important to the potential customer. Describe each in one or two sentences, and integrate the results with the paragraph you wrote in step 3.

5. Think about an illustration. Ask yourself what kind of artwork would be most likely to grab the reader's attention, best convey the meaning of the story you would like to tell, or best complement the copy you plan to use. Should you use a line cut, a wash drawing, a photograph? (Do not attempt this step and those that follow until you have read—and thoroughly digested—the material in the rest of this chapter.)

6. Sketch a rough, but pleasing, layout for your advertisement.

7. Build in a "mail-back" coupon for your reader. (Study all the print mail order advertisements you can; clip samples of coupons that seem interesting to use as models, using your own creativity to make changes.)

8. Go back to the rough copy you wrote in steps 3 and 4. Begin to cut and polish it in accordance with the copywriting suggestions in this chapter.

9. Select an appropriate headline (or headlines) to use with the advertisement.

10. Put everything aside. Look at what you've done in two or three days. Does it seem to accomplish what you want? Can you make any improvements in the advertisement? If you can, do so.

Preparing an actual mechanical of the advertisement is something that only a professional should do. What you have accomplished to this point is only a rough, which serves as direction for the newspaper or magazine production department.

Every time you finish an advertisement, look over your production and ask yourself these four questions:

Will it stop the reader?
If the reader does stop, will the ad reward that behavior?
Does the excitement come directly from the product?
Does it meet the overall advertising objectives?[1]

## THE ELEMENTS OF ADVERTISING LAYOUT

When a store designer starts to lay out the interior of a new store, he or she first draws a diagram of the space and then proceeds to sketch in all the elements: ceiling, walls, flooring, fixtures, aisles, bins, shelves, and so on. The designer anticipates the customer traffic that will be flowing in and out, and the need for behind-the-counter space so that salesclerks may pass back and forth freely. All of the details must be so arranged that the resulting total package will be as attractive as it will be serviceable; that is to say, it will accomplish the store's objectives.

In direct mail advertising, you follow essentially the same sort of process in laying out a print advertisement, a circular, or a brochure. All the necessary elements must be incorporated into it, in proper position and arranged so as to accomplish the desired effect. The advertisement or printed piece must be functional (get the reader to act) and attractive.

### Rough Layouts: Thinking on Paper

The process calls for getting one's thoughts down on paper, in what generally turns out to be a series of little drawings, one after the other, called thumbnail sketches. The professional layout artist draws them rapidly with charcoal or soft pencil, indicating the position of the artwork by a blob or mass of black, copy by straight or wavy lines, a coupon by a dotted horizontal line and scribbling below, and so on.

When you are making your own layouts, you may discard quite a few of these thumbnails, just as the artist does, as you wrestle with the problem of coordination. You need to coordinate headlines and subheads, photograph or art, body copy, and other elements—all according to the basic principles of design—into an attractive unit. The result must be a total package that will stop the reader and cause him or her to look and read on.

[1]Christopher Gilson and Harold W. Berkman, *Advertising: Concepts and Strategies* (New York: Random House, 1980), pp. 404–5.

Once you are at the point of prefering a particular thumbnail, your next step is to outline the advertisement (or printed piece) on your paper, preferably drawing it to the exact size the finished piece is to be. Sketch in all elements, following up on what you did in the thumbnail. But this new rough layout will be more finished. For example, you put in the actual headline drawn to scale. You write (or type in) the actual body copy. Thus, it will contain enough information for the newspaper or your printer to follow easily in setting up the advertisement or circular.

The layout artist, in addition to worrying about incorporating the parts of an advertisement (headlines and so on), must think in terms of good design. An attractive advertisement, for example, reflects proper balance, unity, interesting contrast, and other characteristics. These are briefly described below; read appropriate sections of the relevant books listed at the end of the chapter for further information.

**Design Principles**

### Balance

An advertisement can be mentally split down the center into two halves as you look at it. Using *formal* balance, there is an equal distribution of sizes and shapes (and deep to light tones of black as well) on both sides. With *informal* balance the distribution is unequal. (The former is more conservative; the latter, perhaps, somewhat more interesting.)

### Contrast

This applies to varying the shapes and sizes of the ad elements—copy, artwork, and so on. Contrasting elements produce more reader interest.

### Movement

This is a sense of rhythm or flow to the advertisement where the eye will follow a route intended by the layout artist.

### Proportion

An advertisement is pleasing when no element is out of proportion to the others, and only one dominates. Again, shapes and sizes are important here.

### Unity

The layout artist seeks one unified effect—a complete package of the advertisement that blends all elements into one presentation.

**ILLUSTRATIONS**

In checking through magazines and newspapers, you may come across mail order advertisements that rely entirely on the printed word to sell products or services. This is especially true of small scale display (and, of course, classified) advertising because of cost constraints. In fact, to reduce the monotony of having to read through large blocks of copy, as well as to gain the attention of more readers, different techniques are often used: the introduction of a catchy headline, the use of subheadings on occasion, the use of white space to set off paragraphs or special phrases, and so on.

Such approaches do help, of course. But reader interest level can drop quite rapidly if there is just too much copy in the ad, no matter how artfully it has been arranged.

An illustration will break up the mass of "cold copy." More importantly, it can call the reader's attention to the advertisement in the first place. And, at the same time, it can inform the reader as to what the ad is all about. An illustration can be used to set a mood, act as a hook to get the reader to read the copy, highlight a product benefit or show an item being used, demonstrate how a product is made, and for many other purposes.

People like to see what they are being offered. They want to understand what a product or service is all about, what it can do for them, how it is to be used, and the like. Artwork, if not worth 1,000 words, is certainly the equivalent of at least several hundred. *If* it is appropriate artwork!

A look through current issues of publications produced a list of these illustrations:

| | | |
|---|---|---|
| banknotes | ladies' handbags | shirts |
| books | lamps | shoes |
| bracelets | magazines | slacks |
| burglar alarms | mittens | slippers |
| calculators | nameplates | stamps (foreign) |
| calendars | necklaces | suitcases |
| cheeses | neckties | sunglasses |
| clocks | nutmeats | toys |
| copiers | pendants | T-shirts |
| correspondence courses | perfume bottles | TV antennas |
| free catalogs | rare coins | vases |
| fuel-saving devices | records and tapes | vitamins |
| games | rings | watches |
| how-to-reports | self-defense courses | weathervanes |

**Kinds of Illustrations**

Several different types of illustrations are used in printing. These include line and wash drawings and halftones. The line drawing consists of solid lines, drawn in black ink for best reproduction, or filled-in masses of black. It is a simple drawing that shows no shadings or tones, being characterized by the contrast of black on white. A wash drawing, on the other hand, does show variation. It is drawn in different color paints. Often, the most productive artwork you can use in mail order is an actual glossy photograph of the merchandise from which a halftone is made.

**HEADLINES**

The headline in an advertisement is like a traffic signal, like a blinking red light or stop sign. It signals the reader to stop, then look attentively. It is also much like the title of a short story or a magazine article. Not only must it catch the reader's attention, but it must also act as a hook or cue that stimulates the reader to read on—and to find out more about what is "promised" in the headline.

This is why the headline is typically set apart from the body copy, and why it appears in larger (and often bolder) type.

But in mail order advertising, there is more to the headline of an advertisement than just being a signal device. It is probably far easier (and quicker) for the mind to grasp the significance of a headline than to understand an illustration or make out the intent behind a photograph. Often, the headline is used to instantly inform the reader about the product or service, or about its benefits, or to arouse his or her curiosity and lead into the copy below it.

In the mail order game, if all other elements in the advertisement remain the same, a change of headline alone can make a drastic difference in the number of responses. One headline can draw three, four, five, or more times the numbers of returns that an alternate headline pulls, or one-fifth of the number.

For this reason, each time you prepare a print ad or direct mail piece, devote considerable energy and time to playing around with alternative headlines. It is wise to work up a list of 10 or more appropriate headlines for each advertisement, then select the one you feel will best do the job. These must be completely relevant; keep both your objective and your customer clearly in mind while "ideating." And it is a good idea to limit the number of words in the headlines. Most of the time, the shorter the better!

Headlines may be couched in simple declarative statements or in question form. They may also be positive or negative in tone, although the latter type is seldom used. The declarative statement is popular. Here are some examples from current mail order advertising:

**Types of Headlines**

- Desk Organizer
- Electric Television Antenna
- Extra Income Can Be Yours
- Hand-engraved Jewelry
- Income Tax Organizer
- Original Mexican Paintings
- Stops Leaks Instantly
- Thousands in Profit through the Mail

Here are questions used as headlines:

- Are You a Back Sufferer?
- Ever Wonder Where Your Money Goes?
- Gas Prices Too High?
- Need Energy?
- Overweight?
- What Are Your Chances of Success?

Also used is the phrase or sentence that is a command, or imperative, such as:

- Be an Electrician!
- Be Your Own Boss!
- Borrow By Mail!
- Control Paperwork Expense!
- Learn Accounting at Home!
- Quit Smoking!
- Remove Unwanted Hair Forever!
- Win at Poker!

Headlines may also fall into a number of categories depending on their purpose or effect—the benefit headline, the how-to headline, the news or announcement headline, and so on. Here are examples:

*Benefit*

- Buy Direct and Save
- Cut Your Electric Bills in Half
- Get Your Promotion Fast
- Reduce Without Dieting
- Save on Perfumes
- Spare Time Cash at Home
- Win on Slot Machines
- You Can Look Prettier

*"How to"*

- How to Build Your Own Gun Cabinet
- How to Cut Your Income Tax
- How to Earn Big Money
- How to Make a Résumé
- How to Prepare Your Own Will
- How to Save on Grocery Bills
- How to Start Your Own Part-time Business
- How to Survive During Inflation
- How to Win at Blackjack

*News or Announcement*

- Amazing New Calculator
- Get This Free, Money-Saving Report
- Good News for Back Sufferers
- Here's the Fishing Rod You Always Wanted
- Just Out! Our New Spring Catalog
- New Treatment for Itch
- Now, Free Yourself of Debt
- Pre-Holiday Sale
- Special Introductory Offer

**WRITING COPY THAT SELLS**

Even if you do have an excellent command of the language, remember that copywriting is both a skill and an art that takes a great deal of time and practice to develop. Indeed, it is probably wise, especially if you plan to advertise frequently in the media or use direct mail regularly, to tie up with a small advertising agency, especially for the first year or two in the mail order business.

Nevertheless, you will want to write your own copy sooner or later. Read all you can on the subject. Play with writing copy for your own needs as often as you can, even though you leave the "finalization" to the agency. Along the way, study and analyze advertisements that have been placed by other direct marketing firms, especially those that are repeated time and again.

Later in this section, you will find a list of suggestions for writing effective copy. But first, heed well the next few sentences. They will help to set the boundaries and the guidelines more clearly for you.

When you first tackle the job of writing copy for an advertisement, be sure to think *economy*. Remember that you will be paying the print medium for every agate line or column inch of space you decide to use. Therefore, each word you choose for an advertisement costs you *money*. Be frugal. Save your money. Make every word and sentence count. Every word and sentence must contribute to the total purpose. This means you must write, rewrite, and rewrite again—always trying to convey your thoughts more concisely and in less and less space.

Before you start out to write a piece of advertising copy, build a firm picture of your reader in your mind. Holding that vision before you, list all the important points you would want to get across if you had the opportunity to speak directly with that person on a one-to-one basis. Write them down, freely using the second person "you" form of address, with the language you would use in conversation. Think in terms of interesting, exciting, involving, motivating, and persuading your reader. Appeal to emotions, capitalize on the news value of your offer (if it does contain newsworthiness), explain all benefits, add a testimonial or two if you feel these would help, and offer a guarantee.

Your print advertisement (or mailing piece) is as much a real-life sales presentation that you would make to a prospective customer as if you were there in person.

No one develops overnight into a capable copywriter. So, to repeat, read several of the books at the end of this chapter and others you may locate at the library. And then practice, for practice (eventually) makes perfect, or, at least, near perfect.

These copy suggestions will help to develop your skill.

**Hints for More
Effective Copy**

Don't write to impress your reader with your superior knowledge of English.

Good communication implies reader understanding. Present your information clearly.

Short words do the job far better than long words, especially those of three and four syllables.

Sentences should be short and to the point.

Every word must contribute toward your objective and toward the kind of impression you want to make.

Be as brief (but clear) as possible. Don't write more, or less, than is necessary.

Be specific. Avoid generalities.

Bear in mind the reader's natural skepticism, especially when it comes to a sales pitch.

Be honest. Never stretch the truth.

Work on the reader's feelings and emotions.

Select words and phrases your reader will be familiar with.

Use active, fresh words and phrases.

Build reader interest and involvement.

Tie your copy to the reader's needs and wants. Show him or her how your product or service will satisfy.

Specify the benefits of what you are offering.

Write in an enthusiastic, personal style.

Try to be convincing. Offer proof, if this is needed.

Make sure your proposition is clear.

State the price. Point out why your offer is a good value.

Show the reader how to order or respond to your advertisement.

## SUGGESTED READING

### Books

BOCKUS, H. WILLIAM, JR., *Advertising Graphics,* 3rd ed. New York: Macmillan, 1979.

BURKE, JOHN D., *Advertising in the Marketplace,* 2nd ed. New York: McGraw-Hill, 1980.

BURTON, PHILIP WARD, *Advertising Copywriting,* 4th ed. Columbus, Ohio: Grid Publishing, 1978.

CAPLES, JOHN, *Tested Advertising Methods,* 4th ed. Englewood Cliffs, N.J.: Prentice-Hall, Inc., 1974.

DIRKSEN, CHARLES J., ARTHUR KROEGER, and FRANCESCO M. NICOSIA, *Advertising Principles: Problems and Cases,* 5th ed. Homewood, Ill.: Irwin, 1977.

ERNST, SANDRA B., *The Creative Package: A Working Text for Advertising Copy and Layout.* Columbus, Ohio: Grid Publishing, 1979.

GILSON, CHRISTOPHER, and HAROLD W. BERKMAN, *Advertising: Concepts and Strategies.* New York: Random House, 1980.

HAFER, W. KEITH and GORDON WHITE, *Advertising Writing.* St. Paul, Minn.: West Publishing, 1977.

HAIGHT, WILLIAM, *Retail Advertising: Management and Technique.* Glenview, Ill.: Scott, Foresman, 1976.

KLEPPNER, OTTO, and NORMAN A. P. GOVONI, collaborator. *Advertising Procedure,* 7th ed. Englewood Cliffs, N.J.: Prentice-Hall, Inc., 1979.

MALICKSON, DAVID L., and JOHN W. NASON, *Advertising: How to Write the Kind that Works.* New York: Scribner's, 1977.

MILTON, SHIRLEY F., *What You Should Know About Advertising Copywriting.* Dobbs Ferry, N.Y.: Oceania Press, 1969.

NORINS, HANLEY, *The Complete Copywriter,* 2nd ed. Huntington, N.Y.: Robert E. Krieger Publishing, 1980.

NYLEN, DAVID W., *Advertising: Planning, Implementation, and Control,* 2nd ed. Cincinnati: South-Western, 1980.

OIKO, JUDY Y., *Retail Advertising Copy: The How, the What, the Why.* New York: National Retail Merchants Association, 1977.

*Small marketers aids*

#160 RISO, OVID, "Advertising Guidelines for Small Retail Firms," 1977.

Free Materials from the Small Business Administration

# 10

## BASICS
## OF PRINT
## PRODUCTION

So much promotional activity in a mail order business revolves around printed pieces that you need to learn a good deal about printing itself. You should also learn, by doing, the necessity for scheduling all your print jobs well in advance, and how to solicit quotations and compare prices before placing your orders for such material.

Expertise in the more technical aspects of printing will be acquired as you go along. You will learn how and why to select different types of paper for each situation, according to weight, texture, color, and other characteristics. You will be introduced to composition and to how typographers choose the type best suited to your presentation and your purposes. You will understand more and more about how illustrations and photographs are reproduced in finished mailing pieces, and you will become familiar with such terms as Bodoni, sans-serif, halftones, and mechanicals.

**PRINTING AND COPYING**

A printer is a technician skilled in reproducing images of words, artwork, photographs, and the like, usually through a transfer of ink onto paper. Such images can, of course, be imprinted on the surfaces of other materials; glass, plastics, metals, and silk are some examples. It is also possible to print without using ink at all. A studio photographer may "print" —or make prints from—a film negative; these prints are also called "positives."

For the most part, printing in mail order applies to inked images reproduced on paper stock. Whatever the method, some type of printing mechanism is needed. Paper is fed to or through the machine; printing plates make contact with the paper (either directly or through an intermediate roller); printing ink is transferred to the paper, and impressions are deposited on the paper's surface.

Office Copiers

It is important to distinguish between ordinary office copying machines and professional printing methods. Most offices have one or more copiers. For the most part, these machines are used for making copies of memoranda, documents, correspondence, and internal forms needed in small quantities. Most do not require trained operators. There are modern and efficient desk-top copiers and larger, free-standing floor types. Some firms rent these machines instead of purchasing them outright. This type of machine is mainly used to make small numbers of copies at one time; if larger amounts are needed, there are cheaper ways of duplicating.

In fact, earlier types of duplicating machines are still extensively used. Two kinds in particular are worth considering here, spirit duplicators and mimeograph machines.

### Spirit duplicators

Many years ago, the spirit duplicator (often referred to as the "ditto") enjoyed tremendous popularity. Practically every elementary and secondary school building across the country had one or more. Teachers used them to reproduce quizzes and handout materials for their pupils; administrators used them to run off bulletins and memoranda for internal distribution. Even these days in the business world, small offices still profitably rely on these machines because they are relatively inexpensive to purchase, operate, and maintain.

With the ditto, you can run off up to a few hundred copies from a single original, or master, before the printing becomes too blurred to be readable. The master is a carbon-backed sheet. You type, write, print, or draw directly on it; what you inscribe shows up on the back of the sheet, in reverse. You remove the carbon backing; the master is attached to the machine's drum; a special fluid dissolves tiny particles of the carbon as the drum revolves; and the images are transferred to sheets of paper. By substituting different colored carbon backings on the same master, it is easy to reproduce two, three, or even more colors simultaneously on the same sheet of paper.

### Mimeographs

These machines work on a different principle. You also use an original master sheet, just as you do with the spirit duplicator. However, there is no carbon backing. The sheet is called a "stencil"; you "cut" the stencil by typing matter directly onto it, or by using a hand tool known as a "stylus." That is to say, the letters of your typewriter or the point of the stylus, when pressed against the thin but somewhat tough material of the stencil, cut into it. The backing—paper with smooth hard finish that makes for good, clear impressions—is removed from the stencil, which is then hooked onto the drum of the machine. The drum is then made to revolve; as it does, ink is forced through the openings cut into the stencil and pressed against the sheets of paper being carried through the machine.

Large quantities of copies can be made from a single stencil—as many as 8,000 or 10,000.

Three different printing methods are in use today: letterpress, lithography, and rotogravure. Basically, the three approaches differ according to the surface from which the printing is done—whether that surface is raised, level or flat, or depressed.

### Letterpress

This is the oldest of the three printing processes. Images are transferred to paper from a raised, or "relief," surface. The printer sets metal type into a printing plate, fastens the plate to the press, and then inks the plate. As the press operates, only the raised surfaces on the plate contact the paper; the result is printing of generally excellent quality. Metal plates may also be prepared from drawings and photographs through an etching of the metal by chemical means.

Letterpress is still used to print stationery, wedding invitations, and other jobs where not much typesetting is involved. Some magazines are still printed by this method.

### Lithography

This printing method is now the most popular. While letterpress involves the reproduction of images from raised surfaces, lithography works from a completely flat surface. (Hence the equivalent term *planography;* the prefix *plano-* means "having a flat surface.")

There are two lithographic processes, direct and indirect. In the direct form, both printing plate and paper come in direct contact with each other. But the indirect form, popularly known as "offset" or "offset lithography," is by far the more commonly used. There is no direct contact between plate and paper. Instead, the printing plate deposits the image to be reproduced onto a "blanket" (a cylinder covered with thin rubber), and the image is transferred to the paper from the blanket.

This method of printing works on a rather simple principle: grease does not mix with water. The area of the printing plate that is *not* to be printed is so treated as to repel printing ink, and the image scheduled for reproduction will take the ink.

An offset press turns out many thousands of copies at exceptional speeds and at relatively low cost.

### Rotogravure

This is a fairly uncommon printing process today, except perhaps, for its use by newspapers in putting out Sunday supplements. Rotogravure printing is done on a rotary press, the word *rotary* carrying connotations of something that is wheellike and turns on an axis. And "gravure" comes from the same root as the word *engraving.* Indeed, the printing plate that is used is engraved— impressions being carved into it—through a chemical etching process.

This method is also known as "intaglio printing," a term derived from the Italian verb *intagliare,* meaning "to carve" or "to engrave."

## COMPOSITION

Copy to be reproduced by any of the printing methods must be properly prepared so that it can be transferred to printing plates. Words and sentences must be broken down into individual characters: letters, numbers, and punctuation marks. These need to be prepared with an eye to legibility, appropriate style, size, spacing, and other considerations. Thus, composition becomes an area of substantial expertise in print production.

A compositor is a person who "composes" type; that is to say, he or she sorts, assembles, and readies the type according to instructions for use in printing. A compositor is also referred to as a "typesetter."

An even more skilled craftsperson is the typographer. This technician analyzes the requirements of the print job, creates a mental picture of what the finished work ought to look like, then selects the ideal type (shape, style, size, and so on) for accomplishing the communication objectives.

### Methods of Composition

Type can be composed by hand (using ready-made foundry type), by machine, or by photographic methods.

#### Typesetting by hand

Printers stock different styles and sizes of type. These are generally of metal and purchased from foundries that specialize in casting type. When a print order comes in to be worked on, the printer selects the type to be used from stock—or orders it, if he or she does not stock it, then sets it by hand into the printing plate for letterpress printing.

#### Machine composition

Machines such as the Linotype and the Monotype are used to fabricate type for printing. Hot, molten metal is poured into forms; as the metal cools, it hardens, forming letters and other type characters, and even words, as in the case of the Linotype (formed as slugs of metal).

Machines like the Varityper and the standard office typewriter are also used to "set type." Actually, they produce finished copy on sheets of paper, which are then used to produce the printing plates.

#### Setting type photographically

Keeping pace all along with the rapid growth in popularity of offset lithography, typesetting for print production is often arranged for today by a process known as photocomposition. Letters and words are filmed; the film is then linked to a phototypesetting machine, which can manufacture the type itself at tremendous speed. A computer may even be linked to this system.

Most of us are familiar with those little rubber stamps, or stampers, you can order through your local stationery store—the name-and-address stamp, the first-class-mail stamp, the paid stamp, the variable date stamp, and many other varieties. With the aid of an inked stamp pad, you can "print" whatever is carried on the stamp literally thousands of times. You will, of course, recognize this as a "letterpress" process, pure and simple, for the characters on the stamp, usually of rubber, are raised.

In printing, the word *type* refers to a little block of metal that bears a character on its face, set off in relief. Here are some other printing terms:

- Blueprint (or vandyke)—a print or proof from an offset negative, to be checked for possible errors
- Boldface—typefaces that produce heavier and darker impressions than usual type
- Copyfitting—fitting the copy to the required space
- Font (of type)—a complete assortment of letters, numbers, and punctuation marks in one size of a typeface
- Leading—the space between lines of type (pronounced "ledding")
- Points—this has to do with the size of type; there are 72 points to the inch
- Sans-serif—see serifs below. (*Sans* is French for "without.")
- Serifs—little lines, bars, or flourishes that extend from the ends of strokes in letters
- Typeface—the shape and design of the type; the printing surface of type
- Type family—a complete set of typefaces (all with the same design) in various sizes and widths
- Type style—regular (copy) italics, script, light face, and boldface are examples

Many hundreds of type families are available, although never all from one printer. Here are a few of them:

| | |
|---|---|
| Baskerville | Garamond |
| Bodoni | Helvetica |
| Caledonia | Korinna |
| Caslon | News Gothic |
| Cheltenham | Old English |
| Cloister | Optima |
| Franklin Gothic | Serif Gothic |
| Futura | Times Roman |

## ILLUSTRATIONS

The technical aspects involved in preparing both artwork and photographs for print production are, of course, dependent to an extent on the printing method chosen. You will recall that the surfaces of the printing plates may be flat, depressed, or raised (for lithography, rotogravure, or letterpress printing).

More about Type

Drawings are photographed and the film negative is then used to reproduce the image on the printing plate through a chemical process. In letterpress, a "line cut" is produced. With photographs, reproduction generally involves converting the original print into a halftone first (see Chapter 9).

## Color Printing

Mail order companies frequently resort to color in their direct mail and occasionally in their print media advertising. Color is added to provide more attention-getting capability for the advertisement or printed piece, and also for several other purposes: to create a desired mood or atmosphere, to take advantage of the psychological associations people carry with certain colors, for contrast, or to highlight certain aspects of the advertisement.

On the average, a two-color circular or brochure, for example, will generate more responses than a monotone piece. A full, four-color process job will be even more successful.

Printing an additional color can add considerably to your costs. Often, you can accomplish much the same effect at modest cost by printing your mailing piece in one color, such as black, on paper of a second color, instead of white paper. Naturally, you must watch the legibility factor.

In a true, two-color print job, where, for example, the copy is to appear in black and the headline and illustration in green, two separate impressions usually must be made on the printing press. First, the black plate is printed. The press is then stopped and washed, the second color (green) is added along with the second plate, and the partially printed paper—in sheets or rolls—is then run through the press again. Because of the two impressions needed, this is a costly process. A two-color press, one that can do both parts of the job simultaneously, can save money for you. However, such presses are usually used only for long runs.

## Process Color

To reproduce material in full color, the printer must use a special four-color printing process. Four separate printing plates must be prepared, and, in the actual printing, the impressions made on the paper by each of the plates must register in perfect accordance with those of the other plates. In addition to the one plate necessary for reproducing black, three others are needed—one for each of the three primary colors—red, yellow, and blue. When these colored inks are mixed in the right proportions, they can yield all possible desired colors.

Negatives called color separations are made by photographing the original (artwork or photographs) four different times. Each time a special filter is used, which permits only the one color to pass through. From the separations, halftones are then made. In turn, these are used for preparing the printing plates.

## PRINTING PAPERS

An exceptionally wide range of paper stocks is available to the direct mail advertiser for print production. Papers range in weight from ultralight, tissuelike paper to newsprint, parchment, and kraft (used for wrapping packages) to cardboards and book cover stocks. Most of the paper used by the mail order firm falls into the book stock classification, although writing papers constitute an important secondary genre. This latter group is used for such purposes as sales letters (in direct mail), company stationery, business forms, records, and other purposes that require paper to be typed or written on. Bond paper is a prime example. It comes in varying finishes and with varying contents of wood pulp and rag.

Papers in the book paper family run from the soft, somewhat rough, and uncoated antique paper to the English finish and machine-finished papers. Indeed, paper can be coated on one or both sides, with either a dull or a glossy finish, or can be left uncoated. It can also be textured or have a variety of different finishes, such as cockle, coral, leather, and so on.

In selecting the right paper for the print job, a printer will think in terms of cost, the size of the standard sheet (and its weight), the impression it will receive at the hands of the reader, and how well it will "take" the ink used in printing.

**WORKING WITH YOUR PRINTER**

In your new mail order operation, you will quickly discover what a vital asset a good print shop can be to your business. Early in the game, search for a local printer who is not too big or too busy to devote full attention to servicing your initial needs, and one who is willing, even anxious, to work closely with you as your activity begins to expand. Seek to cultivate a friendly, mutually satisfying, long-term relationship with this important supplier.

The printer is a prime source of good advice, and a good friend. Printers know where to go for the kinds of assistance you may need along the way: artists, layout people, compositors, mailing houses, and the like. They are familiar with the many different types, weights, and finishes of paper. They know the proper inks to use on papers that are selected; they are able to convert your copy, illustrations, and photographs into finished printing that is attractive and will do the job. They can show you how to save money on your mailings; for example, they may suggest the use of a lighter weight paper (and envelope) so that you avoid paying for additional postage on each piece you mail; or how to cut your printing costs by running two print jobs of yours on the same press at the same time, instead of a single job. This saves money for you by halving the number of impressions required by the press, and it avoids "paper waste." Sometimes, the printer can offer you the chance to have your circular or brochure "ride along" with another firm's printing, thus saving you money.

Often, the key to a profitable advertiser-printer relationship is early, thorough planning and giving the printer lots of lead time.

**SUGGESTED READING**

**Books**

FAUX, IAN, *Modern Lithography,* 2nd ed. Central Islip, N.Y.: Transatlantic Arts, 1979.

GROSS, EDMUND J., *One-Hundred-One Ways to Save Money on All Your Printing.* No. Hollywood, Calif.: Halls of Ivy Press, 1971.

TURNBULL, ARTHUR T., and RUSSEL N. BAIRD, *The Graphics of Communication: Typography, Layout, Design, Production,* 4th ed. New York: Holt, Rinehart & Winston, 1980.

WALKER, JOHN R., *Graphic Arts Fundamentals.* South Holland, Ill.: Goodheart-Wilcox, 1980.

**11**

## SELLING DIRECT BY MAIL

Among the advertising media, direct mail occupies a unique position. It is in a class by itself, for through no other medium are you able to focus on specific types of prospects with such unerring accuracy. Furthermore, it is the most personal and most intimate of all. It can carry your messages directly into the home or workplace with the strict confidentiality of private correspondence, and without the clutter of competing advertisements surrounding them.

Today, direct mail is big business. More and more companies that are not ordinarily involved in mail order selling are getting into it every month. It is now in third place among the media in the amount of billions spent annually, behind only newspapers and television. In fact, more than twice as much money goes into direct mail than into radio. Manufacturers use it to obtain leads for their sales forces and to get orders directly. Retailers use it to generate traffic in their stores and to sell more merchandise to their charge account customers. But these are only a few of the ways organizations use direct mail. (Figure 11-1 lists some more—by no means, all—possibilities.)

Direct mail usage has been growing rapidly, especially since the advent of the computer (and despite the increasing costs of postage, materials, and printing). Today, the names and addresses of mailing lists can be segmented not only by age group, sex, income level, and other customary demographics, but also by geographical location, personal life-style, range of interests, recency of purchase, and other factors.

**DIRECT MAIL
A MEDIUM
OF MANY USES**

**133**

But direct mail is a highly specialized field, calling for specific talents. If you plan to make money with it, you will need professional counsel and lots of practice. Proper timing, for example, can be vital to success. Some months, like November and January, are excellent for mailings, at least for the majority of merchandise items. On the other hand, summers can produce poor results. Even the days of the week on which mail arrives can affect the number of replies.

Of course, the list you work from is a significant factor. Customer lists pull better than the names and addresses you may have collected from incoming inquiries. Rented lists pull even less than inquiries, and pieces you mail out in a cooperative venture with other firms will probably show still poorer results.

In the consumer goods field, some areas of the country are more productive of sales than others. A lot, of course, depends on what you are offering. You are not likely to sell too many winter parkas to residents of Georgia or Florida through the mail. Neither can you count on many sales of tractors and other farm equipment if you target in on people living in metropolitan areas.

---

**FIGURE 11-1. Uses of direct mail advertising.**

Direct-mail advertising has many uses for manufacturers, retailers, and service businesses. Here are a few of them:

To solicit mail-order or phone-order business.

To presell prospects before a salesman's call—to soften up the buyer by acquainting him with your company and your products.

To announce new models, new designs, new lines, new items, or changes in your products, services, or equipment.

To notify your customers of price increases or decreases.

To substitute for a salesman's call on a regular customer.

To follow up on salesmen's calls to prospects.

To welcome new customers.

To help regain lost customers.

To increase the full-line selling of your salesmen.

To thank all customers for their business at least once a year.

To create an image for your business.

To remind customers and prospects of seasonal or periodic needs.

To make the most of special events such as feature sales.

To take advantage of printed advertising materials supplied by manufacturers.

---

**Source:** Harvey C. Cook, "Selecting Advertising Media: A Guide for Small Business," *Small Business Management Series No. 34* (Washington, D.C.: Small Business Administration, 1969), p. 17.

Why is direct mail so attractive? To the customer, it offers an exceptionally easy means of shopping from one's home. There is no need to hop into a car, travel a few blocks or perhaps a few miles, and spend time shopping around in stores; let alone the wear and tear on your car and the high price of gasoline. And there is usually a good variety of items to choose from when ordering by mail, often far broader a selection than most stores carry, besides merchandise that just cannot be found in stores at all!

From the firm's point of view, let us look at some of the major benefits of selling through this medium.

### Selectivity

You decide who is to receive your advertising. You send your advertising material only to people who presumably can use (and have the money to pay for) the merchandise or service you sell. You can confine your efforts to a small area anywhere in the country, or expand them to cover the entire nation. You can tailor your messages deliberately to accountants, dentists, social science or language teachers, people who earn upward of $75,000 or $100,000 a year, motorcyclists, numismatists, or any other group or segment of the population you choose to go after.

### Flexibility

Outstanding flexibility characterizes the direct mail medium. You may use the simplest kind of presentation, or the most elaborate. You can mail an entire "package" or a one-sheet self-mailer. You are not required to fit into the constraints of a typical magazine mail order advertisement that would cost anywhere from several hundred to a thousand dollars or more. You can get your mailing out within a week or so after preparing it, rather than wait for 6 to 10 weeks before you see your advertisement in print. With little expense and effort, you can test all sorts of minor changes in your mailing pieces that might result in increased sales.

### Control

Direct mail offers near-perfect control of your advertising effort. With newspapers and magazines, your advertisement generally appears where the publishers think best (except where you pay for a preferred position). And there is lots of competition from other advertisements in those publications, along with news, stories, and editorial matter. Your mailing piece arrives intact. You can schedule your mailings during optimum times of the year, so that you obtain the best results. Moreover, you have the space to tell the entire story and to back up your statements with illustrations, testimonials, and guarantees.

### Knowledge of results

It is easy to record every sale made from each mailing so that at all times you can appraise the success or failure of your advertising. You code each mailing in some manner so that when the orders arrive, you are able to identify their source and assign them to the proper mailing. To code, you may use mechanical methods such as notching or clipping the corners of order forms. Or add tiny distinguishing marks to the form, or to the return envelope, with pen or crayon. Many mail order companies place their codes directly on the mailing labels. Often, these codes are quite complex in format, so they yield far more information than simply the source.

**Drawbacks to the Medium**

As with all other things human, not all is happiness and bliss in direct mail. It has its disadvantages, too. The biggest drawback is cost in relation to other media. It is by far the costliest way to reach quantities of people. For example, you can place a classified advertisement in newspapers and some magazines for as little as $2 to $5 per word; or insert a small display advertisement in such periodicals for several hundred dollars. With either, you are able to reach a few hundred thousand readers; this means your "cost per thousand" breaks down in actuality to only a few pennies per person, or less. By contrast, direct mail, even at the lower third class rate, will run you much more for just the postage alone. Then there are the printing costs, the cost of the envelopes, the charges you pay for collating, folding, and inserting the enclosures, the rental fee for an outside mailing list, and so on. Even at a per unit cost of 30¢, your cost per thousand would be $300.

The other disadvantages are not too disheartening: the "junk mail" attitude, the fact that you will need professional help in preparing your mailings, and the dependency of results on the quality of the mailing list.

**TOOLS OF THE TRADE**

No medium is more challenging to the exercise of one's creativity than direct mail. You have an astounding variety of "tools of the trade" to draw from. These range from the simple government postcard through self-mailing circulars or folders to the mail order catalog. Probably the most frequently used tool is the so-called classic mailing piece. This consists of a cover envelope and a number of enclosures: a sales letter, a main advertising piece, an order form, and a return envelope.

Advertising pieces themselves come in every conceivable shape and size, printed in many different colors of ink on an almost infinite selection of papers. They may be miniatures or giant-sized pieces. They may be diecut into round, square, oblong, triangular, diamond-shaped, or dozens of other geometric patterns. They may even be made to pop up when unfolded. They may be designed to look like:

| | | |
|---|---|---|
| banknotes | invoices | photographs |
| book pages | licenses | posters |
| boxtops | newspaper pages | sheets of music |
| checks | oversized coins | and a hundred |
| documents | package labels | other formats |
| invitations | paper bags | |

They may carry messages written in invisible ink, or revealed when you rub off a carbon coat with a damp cloth. They can be used as package inserts, as statement stuffers, in cooperative mailings with other mail order houses, or even hand-delivered door-to-door.

You will have no problem whatsoever identifying those parts of a mailing known as the order form, the sales letter, or the return envelope. But there are a number of other terms commonly used to refer to the different types of printed advertising pieces, such as: booklets, broadsides, brochures, and so on.

**Major Types of Advertising Enclosures**

### Booklets

This word literally translates to "little books." A booklet is meant to be read; most of its contents consist of typed matter. Examples include little books of instruction on how to play chess, build an outdoor barbecue, or repair clocks. It is generally not bound like a regular book, may have a paper cover, or may lack a cover page entirely. Booklets are also called pamphlets.

### Broadsides

These are large, often impressive-looking printed pieces that contain artwork (halftones, drawings) and printed matter. Actually, they are extralarge circulars, printed on both sides of the paper, then folded for delivery to prospective buyers. When unfolded, some of the printing (or art) runs across the folds of the broadside. This is the characteristic that distinguishes it from other advertising formats.

### Brochures

More select or fancier mailing pieces than the circular or folder, these carry a feeling of quality. Brochures are usually folded two or more times before use as enclosures in a mailing piece or being used directly as a self-mailer.

### Catalogs

These are the powerhouses of the mail order companies (discussed later in more detail). They carry a quantity of halftones or illustrations of different merchandise, along with descriptions, prices, details regarding special promotions, and other information. An order form, along with shipping instructions, may appear as one of the catalog pages or may be attached to the catalog. Often, a return envelope is also bound in. Catalogs come in various sizes; 6 x 9, 8 x 11, and 9 x 12 inches are quite common. They may run from as few as six or eight pages to many hundreds of pages, like the big catalogs of companies such as Alden's and Sears, Roebuck and Company.

### Circulars

These are often used by smaller mail order firms when first starting in business. They are inexpensive print jobs, consisting usually of a single sheet of paper carrying advertising matter in the form of one or two halftones and descriptive copy. Printing may be on one or on both sides of the paper. An order coupon may appear on the circular itself, or a separate order form may accompany the circular. Circulars are also useful as package inserts to be enclosed in each package you mail out, to bring in extra sales. They may also be profitably used as bill enclosures, if you extend credit to any of your customers. You mail them along with your monthly statements.

### Folders

This is a term often used by the public to denote printed pieces, like circulars, broadsides, and others, which need to be folded for insertion into mailing envelopes, or for use as self-mailers. Actually this is a catch-all type of name.

### Leaflets

These are circulars, too. A leaflet, however, refers to a single sheet of paper (a circular can be, although ordinarily is not, composed of more than one sheet). In addition, a leaflet may not carry any illustration or other art at all, but simply typed matter.

## The Cover Envelope

It is obvious to all that the main purpose of a cover envelope—also referred to as an outside or mailing envelope—is to see to it that the contents it holds get to their destination via the U. S. Postal Service. Yet, there is so much more purpose to it in direct mail than this mechanical aspect. Because many people dislike receiving "junk mail," there is a good chance that an uninteresting-looking envelope will wind up in the trash can, unopened. For this reason, mail order companies will occasionally depart from using the standard #10 white envelope, even to the point of substituting brown paper bags, little cloth sacks, cardboard tubes, and other variations.

More often, they choose more acceptable varieties from the extraordinary selection of papers, sizes, shapes, and colors available. Cover envelopes come with both covered or uncovered "windows," or are completely windowless. They can be diecut or cut out in a thousand ways or made to command attention through what is printed on them. There can be one or more lines of catchy copy, line drawings or bendays, even photo reproductions. The printing may be on the envelope face, on the reverse side, or on both sides.

Still, the most popular cover envelope seems to be the #10 size mentioned earlier, with the firm's "corner card" (name and address) neatly printed in the upper left-hand corner.

### Avoiding the impersonal third-class mail look

To get away from the unwanted advertising mail image, the names and addresses of your prospective customers may be typed, or even handwritten, directly on the envelopes, instead of appearing on labels or being imprinted by addressograph. Most often, mail order houses use printed indicia or metered stamps (see Figures 11-2 and 11-3). You may prefer affixing postage stamps for more attention-getting value, especially new issues or commemoratives. Precanceled stamps may also be used for such purposes; these have the added value of reducing the time and costs of mail handling. There are, however, certain restrictions on their use, so it would be wise to contact your postmaster for complete information.

You will need a license to use a postage meter. Submit Form 3601-A, "Application for a Postage Meter License," to the post office where your metered mail will be deposited. No fee is charged.

**FIGURE 11-2.  Form of permit imprints.**

Permit imprints must be prepared in one of the forms illustrated. The addition of extraneous matter is not permitted.

a. FIRST-CLASS MAIL

b. SECOND-, THIRD-, AND FOURTH-CLASS MAIL
   (*Date and First-Class Mail omitted*)

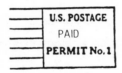

**Source:** United States Postal Service, "Mailing Permits," *Publication 13* (Washington, D.C.: U. S. Government Printing Office, 1977), section 145.4.

The Sales Letter

Of all the tools available to the direct mailer, the sales letter is the most widely used. No other printed piece approaches its versatility or possesses its power to persuade and convince the reader to act. Its possibilities are endless; it can be adapted to almost every conceivable type of sales objective. Representing a one-to-one contact, seller with buyer, it replaces both the personal visit and the sales presentation.

Although most often accompanied by other enclosures—folders, brochures, order forms, it is frequently used by itself. In its simplest form, you can even print your sales letter on a simple postcard, or on a double or three-part card.

---

**FIGURE 11-3.  Postage meters and meter stamps**

Postage meters are made to print single, several or all denominations of postage. They contain in one sealed unit the printing die or dies and two recording counters. One adds and keeps a total of all postage printed by the meter. The other subtracts and shows the balance of postage remaining in the meter. When the amount runs out, the meter will lock automatically.

Meter stamps may be used on any class of mail. Metered mail is entitled to all privileges and subject to all conditions applying to the various classes of mail.

You may obtain a license to use a postage meter by submitting an *Application for a Postage Meter License,* Form 3601-A (or a form supplied by the manufacturer), to the post office where your metered mail will be deposited. No fee is charged. On approval, the postmaster will issue a license.

There are certain responsibilities that a meter licensee must assume. These are outlined in the material given to you when you receive your meter.

There are also certain advantages to having a postage meter:

☐ You can use advertising matter or slogans printed with your meter stamps.

☐ Your mail bypasses postal cancellation equipment and goes directly to distribution. This could mean faster service.

☐ You can obtain on-site meter setting at a fee.

Requirements of the mailer are that he:

☐ Bundle, box or otherwise package mailings of five or more letter-type pieces with the addresses facing in one direction.

☐ Mail the metered letters on the dates shown in the meter indicia.

☐ Deposit metered mail in any receptacle or at any place under the jurisdiction of the post office shown in the meter stamp.

Mailers are requested to change their meter dates to the following day if they know the mail will be deposited after the last daily collection.

You may obtain a refund of 90 percent of the face value of unused meter impressions when submitted within one year from the date shown on the postmark. Envelopes or wrappers bearing metered stamps must be submitted intact. Metered stamps printed on tape, which have not been affixed to wrappers or envelopes, must be submitted loose.

Refunds of 100 percent of face value of meter postage are made when the Postal Service is at fault or when meter malfunctions cause errors in printing postage.

If the meter malfunctions in any way, you are responsible for seeing that no more postage is imprinted until the machine is again operable.

**Source:** United States Postal Service, *Mailers Guide*, pp. 32–33.

I prefer not to use postcards in place of actual letters neatly clothed in quality envelopes. The postcard should be relegated to its proper place in the scheme of things, at least in the mail order business. It ought to be restricted, in the main, to these two "mechanical" areas: notifying people of delays in shipment or responding to brief queries. Once in a great while, postcards may be used effectively for something a bit more creative, like sending out an informal, friendly announcement about an upcoming promotion.

Letters are inexpensive to reproduce, too. Once you have prepared the original, thousands of offset copies can be run off at a very low cost.

A sales letter may run less than a page in length, or it may be as long as three, four, or more pages. It may be printed on only one side of the paper or on both. Often, it appears on both sides of a single sheet of paper, measuring 11 by 17 inches, then folded into a four-page booklet.

How long should a sales letter be? As long, or as short, as is needed to do an effective job of selling the reader.

### Contents

The format of most direct mail letters is much like that of an ordinary piece of business correspondence. They are printed on regular business stationery, usually with the company's name, address, and telephone number appearing at the top and centered. Some firms have letterheads printed with this information running along one side or along the bottom of the sheet. Often, a line cut or some other form of artwork accompanies the name and address. The typing is neatly done; ample margins surround the typed matter on all sides; and the typical "parts" of a letter are readily seen: date, name and address of the prospect, greeting (salutation), body of the letter, closing and signature, and occasionally a postscript.

There are differences, however. In the direct mail letter, there are problems in inserting the customer's name and address properly—in the correct space and in the exact typeface and color that match the printed page (unless, of course, you do it all by computer). Frequently, a headline is used instead of personalizing the sales letter, or a general greeting, such as "Dear Worried Home-Owner" or "Dear Stamp Collector."

Then, too, the postscript is often made to play a significant role in the sales letter. It can be used to hammer home one more time an important point already stressed in the body copy. Or to furnish additional support for the claim. Or to add a sense of urgency, so the reader responds more quickly.

But over and above these and other relatively minor details, there are two major keys to writing successful sales letters: the copy and the offer. The former need not be discussed here, for the skill (and art) of copywriting are treated elsewhere in this book. But the second item, the offer, merits attention at this juncture.

It is what you have to sell that clinches the sale, not just how you describe the item or service. This includes, of course, the terms or conditions under which the offer is made, as well as the guarantee you back it up with. Direct mail authority Jim Kobs points out that "the offer is one of the simplest and most dramatic ways to improve direct marketing results." In his article in *Direct Marketing*, he groups many types of mail offers in categories, such as free gift, discount, sample, time limit, and other offers.[1]

A sincere and unequivocal statement of your guarantee should appear in your letter. However it is worded, it must convey clearly your willingness to refund the customer's money fully and promptly if he or she is not completely satisfied.

**The Order Form**

Experience strongly suggests that you send along a separate order form with every mailing piece. This is preferable to having your order coupon printed on the piece itself, one that the shopper-by-mail has to clip out with a pair of scissors. That is perfectly sensible in your newspaper or magazine advertisements; it does help increase the number of replies. But using a separate order blank generally results in a minimum 10 percent jump in orders, and often much more.

The form itself may be a single sheet of paper (5 x 8 inches, or 6 x 9, or whatever), or it can be printed directly on the back of a business reply card if no payment is required with the order. Mailers often also resort to a combination order form and return envelope, printed in one piece.

Here are the items for which you may have to leave space on the form:

Customer's name and address
Account number (with *your* company)
Credit card number and necessary data (for MasterCard, Visa, and others)
Name and address the merchandise is to be shipped to, if not destined for the customer
Item number, name, color, size, quantity, unit price, total price
Page number (if items selected are from your catalog)
Instructions regarding postage, shipping, and handling charges
Sales tax, where applicable
Names and addresses of friends and others who might be interested in receiving your catalogs or mailings (Space for this item can be left to the back of your business reply envelope. Note that some companies affix peel-off labels to their mailing pieces and catalogs. The customer is asked to peel these off and place them in the space allotted to the customer's name and address, to save time and trouble.)

**The Return Envelope**

You would be wise to include a return envelope with most of your mailings; or, if no money must be enclosed with the order, a return

[1]Jim Kobs, "99 Direct Response Offers That Can Improve Results," *Direct Marketing* (October 1975), pp. 24ff.

postcard. This tactic will increase the number of returns. Why permit the customer's interest to wane for three or four minutes while he or she searches for an envelope, and then has to write your firm's name and address on it? In fact, anything you can do to make the ordering process simpler for your shopper is bound to help your sales. (An exception might be where your budget absolutely precludes the use of any kind of mailing piece but a self-mailer. But even in this situation, you might consider using a folder with a detachable return envelope or card.)

It is even more pleasurable for the customer not to have to pay any postage when placing an order. This does not mean, of course, that you should affix postage stamps to all of these envelopes. What a criminal waste of your funds! But consider the business reply envelope. You order them from your printer or envelope house by the thousands at relatively low cost; there is no additional cost to you if they are not used by your customer (see Figure 11-4 for the appropriate form of imprint). When you do receive orders in these envelopes, you pay the appropriate first-class postage plus a small fee (currently, five cents per piece, if you maintain a BRM advance deposit trust account at the post office).

Apply at your post office for a permit; ask for Form 3614, "Application to Distribute Business Reply Cards, Envelopes and Labels." You pay an annual fee for this privilege.

**CATALOGS: THOSE FORMIDABLE SALES PRODUCERS**

Sooner or later, you will want to try out your first catalog. It may not be much more ambitious than a small six- or eight-pager, printed in one color on white paper, but if your first effort brings in any profit at all, you have arrived, and you are probably well on your way to a healthy and successful mail order business. Eventually, you can expect your catalogs to generate the largest share of your sales, with most of the balance derived from your direct mail and the rest from media advertising.

However, do not attempt to put out a catalog until you have acquired an extensive list of customers to mail to. Although some direct marketing experts maintain that a list of at least 10,000 names and addresses is needed to tackle catalog selling, you can probably make a go of it with as few as 2,500, provided, of course, that these are all people who have already bought merchandise from you and that you have maintained your house list in top order. Given these conditions, you can anticipate as much as a 10-percent return much of the time, and occasionally, you might reach as high as 20 percent. (This depends very much on your catalog merchandise, the quality of your list, your pricing policies, and the time of year.) This means you can expect several hundred orders, and the profit margin on those orders may be more than enough to cover your printing and distribution costs, especially if you start out with an inexpensive catalog.

**Rented Lists**

As is the case with most print jobs, the more catalogs you order at one time, the cheaper an individual catalog becomes. Many mail order concerns expand their mailings by renting additional thousands of

**FIGURE 11-4.  Form for business reply envelopes.**

.235 *Form of Imprint and Address*

Any photographic, mechanical, or electronic process, or any combination of such processes, other than handwriting, typewriting, or handstamping, may be used to prepare the address side of business reply cards, envelopes, cartons, or labels. The address side must be prepared both as to style and content in one of the following forms without the addition of any matter other than a return address.

a. *Alternate Style and Content for Domestic Mail*

.236 *Form of Imprint and Address*

Business reply cards, envelopes, cartons, and labels may be distributed:

a. In any quantity for return to any post office in the United States and its Territories and possessions, including military post offices overseas; except in the Canal Zone, where they may not be returned without prepayment of postage. They should not be sent to any foreign country.

b. In any manner except by depositing in receptacles provided by customers for receipt of mail.

.237 *Responsibility of Distributor*

The distributor guarantees payment on delivery of postage on returned business reply mail. Any concern distributing business reply cards, envelopes, cartons, or labels under one permit for return to its branches or dealers guarantees to pay postage on any returns refused by any authorized addressees.

**Source:** United States Postal Service, "Mailing Permits," *Publication 13.* (Washington, D.C.: U.S. Government Printing Office, 1977), section 131.235–7.

names from compilers or through list brokers. Such rented lists, of course, never are as productive as your own house list, but they do pull orders nevertheless. Often, the percentage of orders is sufficiently high, not only to compensate for the rental fee, but also to reflect an attractive profit picture on the merchandise sold.

Catalogs are heavily used by department and specialty stores; among the media these retailers use, they are strongly entrenched in third place, behind newspapers and radio. The biggest catalogs are, of course, aimed at the Fall-Winter (Christmas) season, but today's Spring-Summer books are not that much smaller. In addition to the catalogs of the big department stores, you have most likely come across those put out by the major mail order houses, like Alden's Spiegel's, and Sears, or those of specialty mail order firms, such as Foster and Gallagher, Sunset House, Spencer Gifts, Hanover House, and the like.

**What Catalogs Are Like**

Well in advance of trying your own hand at catalog making, you should send for and analyze as many catalogs as you can get your hands on. Write for a copy of every catalog offered free in the magazine ads. And it would be worth your while, several times over, if you have to part occasionally with a dollar bill, where the firm has put a price tag on their catalog. The education will pay for itself. But even after that, you will need a capable catalog consultant, or an advertising agency experienced in catalog sales, to develop your catalogs for you. Highly specialized skills are required to design and produce these "showrooms in print."

A catalog is never a simple, haphazard collection of pictures and descriptions. All of the following elements—and more—must be taken into consideration and handled with extreme care:

Physical dimensions of the book
Format
Merchandise to be displayed
Positioning of merchandise items within the catalog
Artwork: drawings, illustrations, halftones, and the like
Typography
Headlines, subheadlines, and selling copy
Prices of the merchandise shown
Promotional information
Instructions for ordering from the book
Order form and return envelope
Printing method to be used

**Ready-Made "Drop-Ship" Catalogs**

A number of companies advertise their own "professionally made" catalogs for use by mail order operators. These firms will offer to sell catalogs on a per hundred or per thousand basis, usually at a price you could not duplicate yourself (unless you print a couple of hundred thousand at a time). For a nominal charge, they will imprint your firm's name and address on the cover page, and they are prepared to "drop-ship" most of the items in the catalog for you. This means that when you get orders, you send your own labels to the firm with your customers' names and addresses properly typed out, and they will mail the merchandise for you. You pay them the wholesale price for the items.

This is the kind of thing you might want to test for yourself to see if it pays (experience says that it seldom does). But you might want to try these catalogs out as "stuffers" along with the merchandise you ship. This way, you have no additional postage costs, and you might get in enough orders to make it worthwhile (see Figure 11-5).

---

**FIGURE 11-5.   Direct mail: no easy road to riches.**

Probably the most damaging shibboleth is that *"direct mail is easy to enter, anyone can make a go of it."* The truth is this is a business for pros, who know products, markets, media, the mathematics of marketing, the mystique of computers, and back room control. And the beginner needs a good deal of luck, a great deal of stick-to-it-ivity, and a number of helping hands to keep him from initial or continuous disaster.

The purveyors of "How to Make Money Easy in Direct Mail" entice a new batch of hopeful suckers each year—and with the exception perhaps of 2 in 1,000, the only ones who profit are the sellers of the service. For years a few catalog houses have sold copies of their mail order catalog to neophytes— telling them all they had to do was find a good list—and make a mint. Their pitch includes the time honored "nothing to stock, nothing to buy in advance, we dropship for you at 50% of the retail price." What the neophyte doesn't know is that the owner of the catalog makes a profit on the sale of the catalogues, plus a profit on the merchandise—and if the owner knew of a list which could pull a profit on the catalog he would use it or has already used it himself.

---

**Source:** From a report on "Shibboleths" by direct mail pioneer Ed Burnett, of Ed Burnett Consultants, Inc., 2 Park Avenue, New York N.Y. 10016. Reprinted with permission.

**COOPERATIVE MAILINGS AND SYNDICATION**

These two areas have been growing rapidly since about 1965. Some mail order companies will permit your enclosures to be mailed along with theirs and those of other firms under an arrangement by which postage and handling costs are shared. The names and addresses of such companies frequently appear in *Direct Marketing* and other mail order publications, and are available from some mailing list houses that handle such arrangements. You must submit your proposed material to these "co-ops" well in advance of their shipping dates, for their approval; and, of course, pay the required fee.

Syndicators invite mail order firms with sizable mailing lists to use their professionally prepared direct mail materials. These companies prepare complete mailing packages for you. You send them out to your house list; they supply the merchandise you are able to sell at a wholesale cost. You may decide to maintain some of their stock on hand, or you can have the syndicator drop-ship the items for you to your customers.

It is also possible, with some mail order firms, to arrange for your catalogs or brochures to be inserted in the packages they ship out to their customers. A useful little guide— "How to Profit from Co-ops, Inserts and Specialized Response Media"—that describes this kind of operation, along with others, is available at a modest price from Dependable Lists Inc., 257 Park Avenue South, New York, N.Y. 10010.

Planning, organizing, and directing your firm's direct mail efforts will consume a great deal of your time and energies, not to mention the considerable depletion of your financial reserves. A tight and secure system for handling internal operations is mandatory if you are to be successful in your mail order enterprise. At the outset, you will most likely be doing all of the related work by yourself, or with the help of your spouse and/or children. After your company has been firmly established and is in a growth track, you may wish to delegate this work to an employee to free your time for other, more important tasks. But by this time, your system should be firmly in place—and your "mail room" well managed under a trained executive (see the checklist in Figure 11-6). (There is additional material on mail rooms in the Appendix.)

Of course, keeping expenses down in your direct mail operation involves more than running your mail room properly. In an informative article in *Direct Marketing,* direct mail executive Luke Kaiser, chairman of the board of the Premier Company, discussed 17 categories of approaches to cutting the rising costs of direct mail production:

1. Establish your objectives and budget.
2. Bring in your supplier as soon as possible.
3. Be sure the artwork is right.
4. Use standard sizes.
5. Make an accurate dummy.
6. Check the envelope design.
7. Check the permit numbers on the envelopes.
8. Count the names on your mailing list.
9. Use machines for inserting.
10. Gang run wherever possible.
11. Get more colors for less cost.
12. Use bleed within reason.
13. Watch that overtime.
14. Consider self-mailers.
15. Use a computer for list maintenance and label preparation.
16. Consider polyethylene envelopes.
17. Take advantage of your supplier's equipment.[2]

**FIGURE 11-6. Managing your mail room.**

Many mailing problems start in company mail rooms. This checklist will help avoid them.

1. Check postal scales—five quarters weight a little less than one ounce.
2. Scales that are not level do not weigh accurately.
3. Complete, unused meter stamps are redeemable at your local post office.

[2]L. U. Kaiser, "Saving Money in Direct Mail by Using Built-in Safeguards," *Direct Marketing* 38 (December 1975), pp. 43–45ff.

4. Stock different size envelopes—the right size for everything.
5. Use green diamond border on all large first-class mail flats.
6. Keep all personal mail out of company mail rooms.
7. Mail early and mail often for the best possible service.
8. Maintain a library of Postal Service publications for your mail room.
9. Explore the reliable, fast, guaranteed delivery of Express Mail.
10. Learn how to save money by presorting your First-Class letter mail.
11. Investigate the benefits of having a Postal Service clerk set the postage meter in your mail room.
12. Exchange your old ZIP Code Directory for a new one at the post office at no cost to you.
13. Learn the cut-off and dispatch times at your local postal facility.
14. Learn how the Postal Service tray program can help in the mail room.
15. Join and participate in your local Postal Customers Council program.
16. Watch mailing machine maintenance—illegible meter imprints may delay mail.
17. Don't waste time opening mail by hand.
18. Remember invoices may be enclosed with Third- and Fourth-class packages.
19. Establish a departmental mail pick up and delivery schedule; publish it and stick to it.
20. Establish a smooth flow for both incoming and outgoing mail.
21. Investigate nylon pouches for postal savings to your branch locations.
22. Try mail room memos to your management staff for more postal awareness.
23. Include advertising stuffers for maximum return on postage costs.
24. Investigate polyester film tape for maximum label protection.
25. Always bundle metered mail (it is required) and it moves faster.
26. Use a reinforced filament tape for maximum parcel protection.
27. Always use precision scales for international mail.
28. Explore all types of insulated, bubble and reinforced envelopes.
29. Purge mailing lists annually. Use "Address Correction Requested" on a planned basis.
30. Package properly.

**Source:** Lee Epstein, "Retailers and the U. S. Postal Services Working Together and Saving Together," in *Direct Mail Advertising & Selling for Retailers* (New York: National Retail Merchants Association, 1978), pp. 243–44. Reprinted with permission.

**SUGGESTED READING**

Books

COOKLIN, LAWRENCE, *Profitable Mail Order Marketing*. Philadelphia: International Ideas, 1976.

HODGSON, RICHARD S., *Direct Mail and Mail Order Handbook*, 3rd ed. Chicago: Dartnell Corp., 1980.

HOGE, CECIL C., SR., *Mail Order Moonlighting*. Berkeley, Calif.: Ten Speed Press, 1976.

JOFFE, GERARDO, *How You Too Can Make at Least $1 Million (But Probably Much More) in the Mail-Order Business*. San Francisco: Advance Books, 1978.

National Retail Merchants Association, *Direct Mail Advertising & Selling for Retailers*. New York: NRMA, 1978.

SIMON, JULIAN L., and JULIAN SIMON ASSOCIATES, *How to Start and Operate a Mail-Order Business,* 2nd ed. New York: McGraw-Hill, 1976.

STONE, BOB, *Successful Direct Marketing Methods,* 2nd ed. Chicago: Crain Books, 1979.

# 12

# PRINT MEDIA:
# THE NEWSPAPER

By now you know that success in your own mail order enterprise depends on a blend of the right ingredients, including:

- The merchandise (or service) you sell
- Your offer—and how you present it
- Your direct mail "package"
- The quality of your mailing list
- Accurate knowledge of your target prospects

All five factors are, of course, interdependent.

Additional sales will come from increasing the size of your mailing list through, for example, your personal efforts at compiling names and addresses, or by buying lists from other organizations. The print media—newspapers and magazines—represent a valuable additional source, as do the air media, television and radio. In fact, many small mail order companies start up in business by placing advertisements in the print media, rather than by attempting a mailing.

This is a healthy approach, whether you are trying to sell items directly from your advertisement or are simply looking to "pull" inquiries. Some advertisements pay for themselves at the outset; orders with cash or checks enclosed are sufficient to defray the entire cost of the space. Other advertisements can be made to pay off by following up inquiries right away with persuasive direct mail.

Case in point: The owners of Country Curtains, a successful retail and mail order operation in Stockbridge, Massachusetts, got their start some twenty-odd years ago with a single advertisement (the money had been borrowed) in the magazine section of the *Boston Herald*. Item featured: ruffled curtains made from unbleached muslin. Enough replies came in to encourage placing a second advertisement.[1]

The print media are where people go to read about what's happening now—and about the past and future as well. In this chapter we will discuss the American newspaper; Chapter 13 is devoted to the magazine, followed by coverage of the broadcast media in Chapter 14.

**NEWSPAPERS AND THE MAIL ORDER ADVERTISER**

As you know, a newspaper carries current news stories, special features, editorials, and other items of interest, including advertising. Of all the mass media, the newspaper attracts the greatest share of the nation's total expenditure for media, somewhere around 29 percent. Television has grown rapidly in recent years to where it now occupies a strong second-place position.

Traditionally, most of the advertising in newspapers has been retail—the department stores and the chains, the supermarkets and the discount houses, theaters and movie houses, and many other types of local retailers.

Surprisingly, there are comparatively few mail order (or direct marketing) advertisements in most newspapers. Some, like the *New York Times*—in the Sunday magazine section's "Shopping Guide"—do encourage this kind of business. *Grit* (Williamsport, Pennsylvania) and *Capper's Weekly* (Topeka, Kansas) are two weeklies famous for their mail order columns. The lack of mail order advertising should not rule out your use of this medium. It does have value as a "proving ground" for quickly assessing consumer response to new merchandise and new offers. Variations in art, alternate headlines, and copy changes can be tested. You can see your newly created advertisement published within a short time and be able to estimate its effectiveness by the time another week has passed. Magazines (see Chapter 13), on the other hand, are different. Each month's issue may be "closed" to the advertiser as early as six to ten weeks before the date of issue. Responses will start to come in over the next several weeks, but will continue to arrive, perhaps for many months. Thus, it is difficult to project what your total returns are going to be in a time frame much shorter than six or eight weeks after the magazine has been put on sale (or mailed to subscribers).

Newspaper space will cost you less, on the average, than magazine space or television or radio time. And it is certainly cheaper than mounting any direct mail campaign, unless perhaps, you make a limited mailing, using a simple, self-mailing circular.

Moreover, some offers can be quickly tested and evaluated at a modest cost, through the newspaper's classified columns. (Try this whenever you can.)

[1] "Country Curtains by Mail Finds Red Lion Inn Perfect Home," *Direct Marketing*, December 1975, pp. 35–39.

According to the '80 *Ayer Directory of Publications*, more than 9,600 different newspapers were distributed that year in the United States. Of these, nearly three out of four were weekly publications; most of the balance, or 1,744 were dailies. Evening dailies outnumbered morning by almost four to one.[2]

TYPES OF NEWSPAPERS

Many daily newspapers also put out Sunday editions, or, perhaps, a weekend edition; the *New York Post,* for example. Nearly all dailies are "local" in nature, being published in a particular city or town and distributed there, in surrounding suburbs, and often to neighboring villages and towns. A few papers, such as the *Christian Science Monitor* and the *Wall Street Journal,* are national in scope.

Daily Newspapers

The best-known newspapers in the country are those of the major metropolitan areas, such as the *New York Times, Chicago Tribune, Los Angeles Times, Philadelphia Inquirer,* and *Washington Post.* These metropolitan dailies boast of circulations in the many hundreds of thousands of readers. (The *New York Daily News* reaches a million and one half people each weekday.)

Toward the other end of the measuring stick are the mid-sized city dailies, with circulations that hover around the 50,000 mark, such newspapers as the *Modesto Bee* and the *Stockton Record* (California), the *Royal Oak Tribune* (Michigan), the *Sioux Falls Argus Leader* (South Dakota), and the *Ogden Standard Examiner* (Utah). There are, of course, many more daily newspapers with fewer readers.

Sunday editions are usually more widely circulated. The Sunday edition of the *Chicago Tribune,* for example, reaches nearly 45 percent more people than its average daily paper. (See Table 12-1 for Sunday circulations for some of the big metropolitan newspapers.) For this reason—and because they are read far more leisurely and usually by several members of the family, Sunday paper advertising is preferred by direct marketing firms. For somewhat similar reasons, the evening paper seems preferable to the morning paper for mail order purposes.

Although, as the name indicates, these papers are generally published once a week regularly throughout the year, some are issued twice weekly or on some other basis. Because they are for the most part more "local" than the dailies, the tendency today is to label all of these newspapers (weekly or otherwise) "community newspapers." Many are distributed in the suburbs of large metropolitan centers and throughout the cities themselves. However, a larger number reach the rural areas, hitting villages and hamlets where a daily newspaper is only occasionally to be found. Localities look forward to each new issue, avidly digesting the news, features, and other items of community interest just as soon as the paper appears.

Weekly Newspapers

Standard Rate and Data Service puts out a publication, on a semiannual basis, that lists the names and addresses of all community newspapers, by state and alphabetically, along with other

[2]*'80 Directory of Publications* (Bala Cynwyd, Pa.: Ayer Press, 1980), p. *viii.*

details of interest to advertisers. This book, *Community Publication Rates and Data,* is broken down basically into three important sections: (1) Metro Area Urban/Suburban Weekly Newspapers, (2) Nonmetro Area Weekly Newspapers, and (3) Shopping Guides. Among their listings, for instance, you will find pertinent data about such publications as the *Herald* (Hardin, Montana, circulation 3,110), the *Lahontan Valley News* (Fallon, Nevada, circulation 3,950), the *Chronotype* (Rice Lake, Wisconsin, circulation 8,623), and the *Rappahannock News* (Washington, Virginia, circulation 2,616).[3]

The agate line rate for these publications and others with similar small circulations will run between 18 and 30 cents. Small enough to test out a few ads, perhaps? Yes, provided, of course, residents of these small rural communities are representative of the kinds of people you have targeted as prime prospects for your merchandise or service. But remember, your "cost per thousand" might turn out to be quite a good deal higher this way than you would pay if you placed an ad in a large city daily or Sunday paper.

**TABLE 12-1.**
Some major metropolitan Sunday newspapers.

| City | 1980 Population* (1,000s) | Newspaper | Circulation** |
|------|---------------------------|-----------|---------------|
| New York | 7,482 | New York Times | 1,430 |
| | | New York Daily News | 2,125 |
| Chicago | 3,099 | Chicago Tribune | 1,144 |
| | | Chicago Sun-Times | 681 |
| Los Angeles | 2,727 | Los Angeles Times | 1,234 |
| | | Los Angeles Herald-Examiner | 306 |
| Philadelphia | 1,816 | Philadelphia Inquirer | 824 |
| Houston | 1,357 | Houston Chronicle | 444 |
| | | Houston Post | 399 |
| Detroit | 1,335 | Detroit News | 721 |
| | | Detroit Free Press | 829 |

*Estimated population as per Bureau of the Census, U. S. Department of Commerce, *Statistical Abstract of the United States (1980),* (Washington, D.C.: Department of Commerce, 1979).

**Based on information supplied in *Newspaper Rates and Data,* Vol. 63, No. 3, March 12, 1981 (Skokie, Ill.: Standard Rate and Data Service).

**Special Readership and Other Types of Papers**

"Special readership," a rather broad classification, encompasses, among others, many hundreds of newspapers for black readers, papers printed in dozens of foreign languages, college newspapers, and publications aimed at a variety of religious denominations. Their audiences are logical targets, not only for all types of consumer goods and services, but also for offerings of special interest to these various consumer segments.

Other types of papers include large numbers of shopping papers, both local and regional in scope, distributed throughout the United States. They are referred to as "shoppers," "shopping guides," "pennysavers," or "trading papers." Most are weeklies. Although they

[3]Based on information supplied in *Community Publication Rates & Data,* November 1, 1980, Vol. 63, No. 2. (Skokie, Ill.: Standard Rate and Data Service).

can be and are occasionally used for mail order selling, most of the advertisements they carry are placed by area residents and small retailers or service firms.

Many newspapers supply magazine supplements and comics pages in their Sunday editions. Both types of supplements are used by mail order advertisers. Unfortunately, for the smaller firm space costs may be out of reach where the circulation is substantial. *Parade,* for example, enjoys a circulation in excess of 20 million readers. *Puck—The Comic Weekly* reaches a similarly huge audience. However, it is distributed through a number of newspaper groups (the American Network and the Pacific Group are two examples) and you may purchase space by the group instead of buying the entire circulation. Nevrtheless, except for an occasional—and small—ad in a less widely circulated Sunday supplement, you probably should shy away from these media.

Somewhat similar to the Sunday supplements as media vehicles for mail order companies are the familiar, high-circulation weeklies known as the "supermarket newspapers," the *National Enquirer* and the *Star,* among others. These papers are purchased each week by millions of shoppers. They carry a good deal of direct marketing advertising. Because of their national distribution and general makeup, think of these publications more as magazines than as newspapers and consider their possibilities vis-a-vis other magazines.

All media, of course, have their good and bad points. To be able to make sensible choices among them, you should familiarize yourself with both the benefits and the drawbacks of every medium you think of using.

## NEWSPAPER MAIL ORDER: THE PROS AND CONS

### Advantages of Newspapers

### Fast Results
Replies and/or orders begin to arrive a day or two after your advertisement appears. You can expect to recieve up to 70 or 75 percent of all repsonses within the following seven days.

### Rapid ad placement
A valuable feature of this medium is the short lead time between ad construction and publication. Closing time for ordering space may run from a few hours to one or two days prior to publication. The newspaper is, therefore, an excellent vehicle for testing purposes. You can modify your advertising from one day to the next: new headlines, changes in copy, alternative illustrations, and so on.

### Flexibility
The short lead time gives you the ability to make quick changes you can profit by. For example, if a prolonged heat wave is expected to roll in within the next thirty-six hours, you might decide to insert an ad for a hand-held, battery-operated fan you carry in stock, instead of featuring some other item you had planned to run.

### Excellent penetration

Collectively, our daily newspapers reach some seven out of 10 adults every day. This means a rather intensive "reach" or coverage of the community wherever you choose to advertise. Even though, in some locales, the area residents may read a weekly paper because no daily is available, you can still be sure that the majority of homes will be reached.

### Geographic selectivity

You can target in on just about every corner of the land to reach prospective customers. You can select the largest metropolitan centers, small and medium-sized towns, and the remotest of villages. You can reach readers living in lakeside communities, mountain or seashore resorts, or cattle country, anywhere, in fact, where the local newspaper audience is composed of the kinds of people who you believe will be interested in what you have to sell.

Listings of all newspapers—including names and addresses, circulations, rates, and other data—are made available by the Standard Rate and Data Service of Skokie, Illinois. Their publications may be found in the reference rooms of college and university libraries, and in many public libraries.

### Unhurried reading

People generally read newspapers at a leisurely pace. Morning papers may be read on commuter trains, but certainly, most evening papers are read at home. This means, of course, that advertisements that are interesting are considered carefully by the reader. Often, ads are torn out and held for future action; this gives the newspaper a significant advantage over radio or television commercials, which are over—and lost—immediately after having been broadcast.

### Additional readers

There is an excellent chance that two or more individuals will read the same paper. This is especially true of the Sunday editions. For example, the magazine section of the Sunday *New York Times* may well stay around the house for an entire week, along with a number of other sections of the paper.

### Availability of special position

Newspapers are organized into different departments and sections. You can gain more attention for your display ad by requesting its placement in the section your prospects will be most likely to read with care: the sport pages, the business section, the entertainment or the food pages, and so on. This will, of course, depend on just what you are selling. Naturally, if the newspaper regularly carries a special mail order section (as is the case, for instance, with the Sunday *New York Times*), you will most likely want your ad to appear with the other mail order ads.

Space advertising is usually purchased on an R.O.P. ("run-of-publication") basis. This means that the paper, or magazine, decides where to position your ad. Often, by paying an additional charge, you can have your ad placed in a "preferred position"—for example, on page two or page three, on a right-hand page instead of the left-hand side, in the top corner of a page, and the like.

### Relatively low production costs

The typical newspaper mail order advertisement can be prepared quite inexpensively, involving a layout, some artwork, and copy that has been set into position. If you use an advertising agency, their preparation costs are, for the most part, quite low. If you have not yet expanded to the point where you do employ an agency, note that most newspapers will set your ads free of charge, except, perhaps, for the preparation of a "cut" of your art at a modest fee. (Stock cuts are made available by many papers.) The resulting advertisement may not, of course, look quite as "professional" as if it had been created by an agency.

Small space ads destined for the classified section of the newspaper pose no difficulties. Not only does the paper set your copy in print, but they are also ready to advise on improvements in the copy you have written.

Although the newspaper has its place in the media plans of many mail order companies (usually well behind direct mail and magazines in terms of planned expenditures), the sophisticated marketer is well aware of its deficiencies. The major disadvantages of the newspaper are indicated below.

**Drawbacks of the Medium**

### Waste circulation

The typical paper is filled with ads placed by local retailers. Supermarkets, discount houses, and other mass retailers advertise often in their area papers, and to good avail. Most of the paper's readers reside in these retailers' trading areas; most are logical prospects for the merchandise they sell. In your particular case, however, you distribute selected or specialty items (or a special service) by mail. Consequently, the majority of the newspaper's readers may not be potential users of your offerings, and many of those people may not be accustomed to buying regularly through the mails.

### Short ad life

The newspaper is bought, in the main, for the news and features it contains. Although some of the many advertisements do manage to catch the typical reader's attention and may be studied for a few moments, the bulk of such messages are glanced at and dismissed almost simultaneously. Another factor that hurts is that the entire newspaper may be discarded within 30 or 40 minutes—and that ends that!

### Clutter

To compound the problem, you ad will be surrounded by other ads. Often, advertisements make up the bulk of the newspaper. Your small ad may be so overpowered by other, much larger ads on the same page that most readers might not even notice yours. And a big ad, say a half-page advertisement (or even a quarter of a page) may be well out of reach of your modest ad budget. Luckily , there are some "tricks of the trade" you might resort to in order to make your "littler" advertisement more noticeable, like using bold and heavy margins, a catchy photograph, lettering in reverse (white print against a black background), and so on (see Chapter 9 for other ideas).

### Involves only one sense

The printed advertisement's capacity for doing the selling job is decidedly limited. It appeals to only one sense of the reader, the sense of sight. Through visual impact alone, it must attract readers to it, stimulate their interest, convince them of the offer's value, and persuade them to act. Contrast the effectiveness of any print advertisement with that of a typical television commercial, for instance. The latter works on two of the viewer's senses—sight and hearing—and is, therefore, far more powerful.

**BUYING NEWSPAPER SPACE**

Given the availability of several different media, which should you use? Choices among those media competing for your advertising dollars will involve consideration of the following factors:

- Audience you are trying to reach.
- Effectiveness of the medium for *your* purposes.
- Reach or coverage.
- Costs involved.

The term *reach* is used to measure that portion of the community reached, or "covered," by the particular medium; when we talk about the print media, we mean the circulation of the newspaper or magazine.

Of course, newspaper advertisers think also in terms of *frequency* of impressions, that is, how many times the same story is told to the same readers. Repeating the same advertisement two, three, or four times reinforces its effects on readers.

Circulation

Newspaper advertising rates reflect their circulations. As a rule, the greater the circulation, the more you will be asked to pay for space. The large metropolitan daily newspapers and many of the smaller papers have their circulations audited on a regular basis by the Audit Bureau of Circulations (Schaumburg, Illinois). Those that are not audited often present sworn statements of their circulation figures to would-be advertisers. (Only copies that are sold are counted, not those distributed free of charge.) Sales include both subscription copies and papers sold at newsstands, stores, and other outlets.

It is generally wise to contact whichever newspapers you are thinking of using. Write or call them and request copies of their latest rate cards. Tell them you want to know their *mail order* rates (see Figure 12-1).

At least two different rates are quoted advertisers by the newspaper. National advertisers pay the "national rate," which is the highest rate. Lower rates are available for department stores, supermarkets and other retailers, for bars and restaurants, places of amusement, and so on. Mail order firms are included in these low rates; they can run from 20 to 35 percent or more less than the national rate.

Newspaper rates are typically quoted by the agate line, or by the column inch. There are 14 agate lines to the inch. The width of the line or the inch depends, of course, on the width of the newspaper column, which can differ from one paper to the next. Basically, there are two different newspaper formats, the regular or standard size and the tabloid. Standard papers typically run about 14 to 14½ inches across, are about 23 inches high, and carry six or seven columns to the page. Tabloid dimensions approximate 10 x 14 (plus or minus fractions of inches); these papers average some five columns to the page.

---

**FIGURE 12-1.  Sample newspaper rate card.**

**7 EDITIONS DAILY**

25 CENTS  **AMERICA'S FASTEST GROWING NEWSPAPER**  DAILY SALES EXCEED  **700,000**

210 South Street
New York, New York 10002
(212) 349-5000

**Effective January 1, 1981**
**Subject to all conditions and regulations**
**of New York Post Generic Card G-81**

---

### MAIL ORDER
### ADVERTISING RATES
Display—ROP

|  | Gross Per Agate Line |
|---|---|
| **OPEN** | $3.15 |

**Bulk Space Within One Year**

| | |
|---|---|
| 1,200 lines | 2.85 |
| 2,500 lines | 2.80 |
| 5,000 lines | 2.65 |
| 10,000 lines | 2.60 |
| 25,000 lines | 2.50 |
| 50,000 lines | 2.35 |

Minimum size: 14 lines (one inch) deep.

### SPLIT RUNS
Minimum size: 600 lines
Flat Charge: $185.00 NET
Two (2) Separate Mechanicals are Necessary.

MEMBER AUDIT BUREAU OF CIRCULATION

---

**Source**: Mail Order Rate Card, *New York Post*, 210 South Street, New York, NY, 10002. Reprinted with permission.

## Space Contracts

Let's say you decide to place a small display advertisement in your local newspaper. The ad measures two columns wide and runs five inches deep. This makes for 10 inches in all (2 columns x 5 inches). The newspaper will charge you their "open rate"—the basic per-line (or per-inch) charge for a one-time insertion in the paper. (Remember that 10 inches will equal 140 agate lines.) You will probably pay more per agate line if you want exposure in the Sunday edition, simply because most Sunday papers enjoy more circulation than weekday editions.

You can enter into a bulk space contract with the newspaper and thereby benefit from a lower rate than their open rate. Newspapers, in effect, offer a discount schedule; the more space you buy, the less it costs you. (Refer to the rate cards in Figure 12-1.) Translated into operational terms for your mail order business, this will result in a lower cost "per inquiry" or "per sale."

Even though you may have contracted for 1,000 lines for the year in order to earn the discount rate, you are not compelled to use that amount of space. If, for example, you have used 750 lines by the time your contract expires, you will be "short rated." Your actual line usage will be recomputed by the newspaper at the next higher rate. And since you have probably already paid your bills to this point at the rate shown on the contract, you will be invoiced for the short-rate differential.

## Combo rates and other details

Where newspapers distribute both morning and evening editions (usually under separate names), your advertisement can appear in both, and you will earn a lower, combination rate for the two. Or, perhaps, you can be offered a combination rate for running your ad on three successive weekdays, several weekdays and the Sunday edition, and so on.

Most advertisements are submitted with the understanding that the newspaper will place them where it sees fit (R.O.P.). Usually, the paper will see that your ad appears in the section where it belongs, for example, in the business section if you are selling an item that is of interest to business and industry, or, depending on your merchandise, in the sports section, the amusement pages, and so on. Newspapers are usually only too happy to do this when they can, if you request it. Naturally, if the newspaper normally carries a "shop by mail" section, you will want your ad to be where the action is.

Many advertisers believe they obtain better results if their advertisements are displayed in the first few pages of the newspaper, rather than toward the back, or if the advertisement appears on a right-hand page (instead of the left-hand side), or at the top of a page, or in an "island" position surrounded by news or editorial matter. Newspapers will try to accommodate these and other special positions requested where they are able to, but they do charge additional for this service. In many cases, however, the premium you pay will be modest.

Other possibilities in many newspapers include the use of a second color in the ad, or the insertion of sheets, folders, or other enclosures that have been "preprinted" by the advertiser. Unfortunately, this latter approach is often well beyond the reach, financially, of the small mail order operator.

Comparing
Media Costs

Mail order firms constantly face the problem of where best to advertise their products or services. Decisions of media selection boil down to: (1) selecting the generic medium type to use in any particular case—newspaper, magazine, radio, television, or direct mail, and (2) intertype choice, which newspaper (or magazine, or other) to advertise in. Assuming the similarity of audiences, intertype decisions depend for the most part on circulations and costs.

The tool most commonly used by advertisers to compare the costs of advertising in different newspapers is the *milline rate*. This measure is defined as:

$$\text{Milline Rate} = \frac{\text{Line Rate X } 1{,}000{,}000}{\text{Total Circulation}}$$

As an illustration, you are considering three different newspapers for your next advertisement. You check their circulations and the latest rates and come up with the following information:

| Newspaper | Circulation | Line Rate |
|---|---|---|
| A | 210,000 | $ .95 |
| B | 265,000 | 1.05 |
| C | 330,000 | 1.70 |

You figure out the milline rate for paper A by multiplying the line rate of 95¢ by 1,000,000, then dividing the result ($950,000) by the circulation, 210,000. This comes to a milline rate of $4.52.

You calculate the milline rates of the other two newspapers to be $3.96 for B and $5.15 for C. Comparing the three, paper B would be the right choice.

NEWSPAPER
CLASSIFIED

Most newspapers carry classified advertising pages. The advertisements in these sections are all similar in appearance, set in the same small type by the newspaper itself. Of course, many carry headlines in somewhat larger type; some advertisements are longer than others (in numbers of lines used); some employ more white space than others. These all-copy advertisements are collectively referred to as "general classified" advertising. Many publications also offer "display classified" opportunities for firms wishing to use small units of space. Line cuts and other illustrations may be used in such advertisements. This type of space is generally sold by column inches.

The typical daily newspaper rarely carries mail order offers in its classified pages. Nevertheless, you might consider trying out an occasional new item, or new proposition, in a small classified ad, especially in some weekly and rural papers. These little ads can often generate inquiries at a very low cost. It really does not take too much of a response to pay for the space.

More commonly, mail order firms resort to magazine classified sections (discussed at greater length in the next chapter).

**SUGGESTED READING**

**Books**

HAIGHT, WILLIAM, *Retail Advertising: Management and Techniques*. Glenview, Ill.: Scott, Foresman, 1976.

HODGSON, RICHARD S., *Direct Mail and Mail Order Handbook,* 3rd ed. Chicago: Dartnell Corporation, 1980.

JOHNSON, J. DOUGLAS, *Advertising Today*. Chicago: Science Research Associates, 1978.

KLEPPNER, OTTO, and NORMAN A. P. GOVONI, collaborator. *Advertising Procedure,* 7th ed. Englewood Cliffs, N.J.: Prentice-Hall, Inc., 1979.

NYLEN, DAVID W., *Advertising: Planning, Implementation, & Control,* 2nd ed. Cincinnati: South-Western Publishing, 1980.

STONE, BOB, *Successful Direct Marketing Methods,* 2nd ed. Chicago: Crain Books, 1979.

SURMANEK, JIM, *Media Planning: Quick and Easy Guide*. Chicago: Crain Books, 1980.

WATKINS, DON, *Newspaper Advertising Handbook*. Columbia, S.C.: Newspaper Book Service, 1980.

YOUNT, JOHN T., *Mail Order Advertising Handbook*. San Angelo, Tex.: Educator Books, 1978.

**13**

## MAGAZINES: MEDIUM FOR THE LONG PULL

Most mail order concerns get their start either through mailing sales literature directly to a list of names or by placing advertisements in selected magazines. Both approaches are often used by the company, for the two really work in tandem. Names obtained through responses to magazine advertisements are added to the firm's mailing list. Follow-up sales efforts, especially when mailed according to a well-planned schedule, result in additional orders. These may also be used to generate additional customers.

An example is Mary Maxim, well-known retailer and catalog house that specializes in needlecraft and hooked rug kits (located in Port Huron, Michigan).[1] The firm's major strength lies in its unique, exclusive designs. The mail order business was launched in 1964, through advertisements in several women's magazines, among them *McCalls, Workbasket,* and *Needlecraft*. Today, the house continues to rely on the print media primarily, often using full-color advertisements to sell its merchandise.

Not long ago, one of my graduate students came across an item he felt might be successfully sold in the sunbelt states. It was a device that could be placed against the windshields of automobiles that would protect the interiors from getting too hot. At a rather modest cost, he placed advertisements in several regional editions of *TV Guide,* and got a fast reading on consumer reaction. Since then, he has expanded to other merchandise and has continued in direct

[1] "Doing-It-Yourself Interest Becomes Boon for Mary Maxim," *Direct Marketing* (October 1977), pp. 56ff.

**163**

marketing (both to consumers and to industry) through combined print advertising and direct mail.

**TYPES OF MAGAZINES**

Over 10,000 different magazines are regularly published in the United States. Nearly four out of every 10 are monthlies; most of the rest are published either weekly, bimonthly, or on a quarterly basis.[2] Collectively, they constitute a tremendous and potentially profitable medium for the mail order concern. Market segmentation possibilities are enormous; you can reach almost any type of audience: old, young, rich, poor, professional and business people, numismatists or stamp collectors, hunters or amateur cooks.

A convenient way of classifying these publications is by dividing them into general consumer magazines, special interest publications, business, trade, and professional magazines, and farm publications. (For another classification approach, see Figure 13-1.)

**FIGURE 13-1. Classifying magazines by audience specialization.**

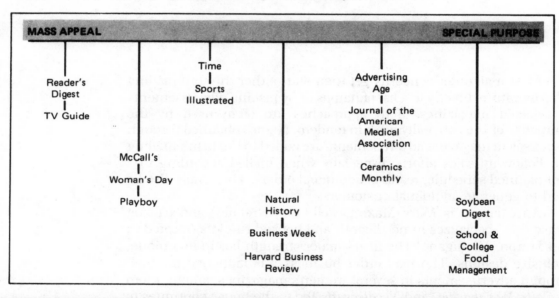

Source: David W. Nylen, *Advertising: Planning, Implementation, & Control*, 2nd ed. (Cincinnati: South-Western Publishing Co., 1980), p. 287.

**Special Interest Magazines**

These periodicals far outnumber those aimed at the general public. When categorized by reader interests, tastes, preferences, or lifestyles, the variety is astounding. In most cases, the titles of these magazines are a strong indication of the types of readers they seek to attract. Here is an abbreviated list:

American Hunter          Camping Journal
Baby Talk                Cats

[2]*'80 Ayer Directory of Publications* (Bala Cynwyd, Pa.: Ayer Press, 1980), p. *viii.*

| | |
|---|---|
| Ceramic Arts and Crafts | Motor Boating and Sailing |
| Country Song Roundup | National Racquetball |
| Crafts Magazine | Outdoor Life |
| Cruising World | Popular Ceramics |
| Cycle | Popular Mechanics |
| Dirt Bike | Popular Science |
| Electronics Hobbyist | Railroad Model Craftsman |
| Family Handyman | Rider |
| Family Health | Rolling Stone |
| Flower and Garden | Sail |
| Golf Digest | Shooting Times |
| Guns and Ammo | Skiing |
| High Fidelity | Trailer Life |
| Horticulture | Travelin' Vans |
| Hot Rod | Venture |
| Model Railroader | Your Astrology |

Some publications are of special attraction to the residents of many cities, such as *Cleveland, Houston City Magazine, Los Angeles Magazine,* and so on. Still other "special interest" periodicals focus on the members of fraternal orders and other organizations, theatergoers and hotel guests, and religious groups.

Included in this category are a fair number of general business magazines (*Business Week* and *Fortune,* as examples) and a far greater number of specialized periodicals of interest to different industries, trades, professional groups, and technical personnel. As with the special interest magazines, you can readily determine audience composition from the titles. (For a more detailed description of business publications, see Figure 13-2.) Examples include:

**Business, Trade, and Professional Publications**

| | |
|---|---|
| Antiques Dealer | Landscape Industry |
| Beer Wholesaler | Lodging |
| Beverage World | Luggage and Travelware |
| Builder and Contractor | Packaging Digest |
| Candy and Snack Industry | Plastics Engineering |
| Ceramic Industry | Purchasing Administration |
| Chain Store Age Executive | Radio World |
| Chemical Engineering | Restaurant Business |
| Computer Decisions | Sales and Marketing |
| Cosmetics and Toiletries | Management |
| Flooring | Sporting Goods Business |
| Insurance Sales | Textile World |
| | Theatre Journal |

Some authorities include these magazines with the "business, trade, and professional" category on the strength of an obvious fact: farming is a vocation. It is, however, also a way of living—a life-style for vast numbers of American farmers, ranchers, cattlemen, and the like. So, these magazines do merit a separate classification.

**Farm Publications**

Many farm publications are circulated only within a given state (rural areas, of course); others may be regional or even national in distribution. A few of the titles follow.

| | |
|---|---|
| American Fruit Grower | National Hog Farmer |
| Beef | Ohio Farmer |
| Big Farmer | Oklahoma Rural News |
| Colorado Rancher and Farmer | Progressive Farmer |
| Dakota Farmer | Rural Louisiana |
| Farm Journal | Rural Missouri |
| Farmer-Stockman | Successful Farming |
| Hoard's Dairyman | Sunbelt Dairyman |
| Hoosier Farmer | Texas Agriculture |
| Missouri Ruralist | Wisconsin Agriculturist |

**ADVANTAGES AND DISADVANTAGES**

Every advertising medium has advantages and drawbacks. Magazines are no exception. Yet, they can be a valuable component of the mail order company's media plan.

---

**FIGURE 13-2. Business publications.**

Business publications are of three types: (1) General business publications (usually called *business magazines);* (2) specialized business publications (called *business papers);* and (3) farm publications (called *farm papers).*

• *Business magazines* are edited primarily for top management. Most of them are national in scope, though some are limited to state or local coverage. In some, the editorial content is entirely business oriented. Others are basically news or general-interest magazines but carry business news or articles of special interest to businessmen.

Business magazines carry a good deal of business advertising. Because their readership covers all industries and businesses and the cost of space is relatively high, they are best suited for the advertising of big businesses.

• *Business papers* are periodicals issued either for a single industry, in which case they are called *vertical* business papers, or for men with similar duties but in different industries—chemists, for example, or purchasing agents. Periodicals of the latter type are called *horizontal* business papers.

Business papers may also be classified as industrial papers (for manufacturing, construction, and similar fields); trade papers (for retailers, wholesalers, and others concerned with merchandising); and professional papers (for professional people, who usually buy little themselves but often exert a strong influence on what others buy). More than half of all business papers in the country are industrial papers.

Most business papers are actually magazines in format, but the word *papers* is used to distinguish them from business *magazines* of the type described above. You will find at least one business paper—usually several—for every kind of business and job.

Business papers are used by large advertisers, but small advertisers predominate both in number of advertisers and in the total amount spent for advertising in these publications.

- *Farm papers* are a distinct group because of their combined business-consumer content. Because farming has traditionally been a family operation, the editorial content of farm papers and also their advertising concern both the occupation of farming and the farm home. No other medium is so specialized for advertising products for farms and rural living.

**Source:** Harvey C. Cook, "Selecting Advertising Media: A Guide for Small Business," *Small Business Management Series No. 34* (Washington, D.C.: Small Business Administration, 1969), pp. 27–28.

Mail order marketers allocate a far greater share of their promotion dollars to magazines than to newspapers. They prefer the magazine for some rather compelling reasons.

**Magazines: A Fine Mail Order Medium**

### Long publication life

Typically, we toss the daily paper into the trash container shortly after finishing it. On the other hand, each new issue of a magazine may be kept around the home, shop, or office for weeks on end. We may pick up the issue time and time again. We read it in spurts and in parts. So, experienced advertisers claim that, although up to one-half of the total number of replies to a magazine ad may arrive within the five weeks following the date of issue, responses will continue to trickle in for months. Sometimes, you will get replies as much as a year later, and even longer than that. A magazine is more "permanent" than a newspaper. In fact, some readers save the several issues of some publications and build home libraries.

### Secondary readership

The primary readers of a magazine include both the subscribers and those who purchase copies at newsstands or stationery stores. Yet, many magazines are also read and enjoyed by other members of the families of the primary readers, and by neighbors, friends, people in waiting rooms, visitors to public library branches, and the like. For some publications, the total number of persons who actually read a single issue may exceed their regular, "audited" average circulation by 300 percent or more.

### Reader specificity

In one way, advertising your mail order wares in this medium has a lot in common with your approaches to direct mail selling. Success in your direct mail efforts requires keeping in mind a firm image of your likely prospects, then searching for and finding lists of persons (or companies) whose characteristics most closely resemble that image.

You use much the same strategy when advertising in magazines. Knowing your customer, you canvas the field and select only those publications whose readers are most likely to buy from you. If, for example, you plan to distribute an innovative light filter or an improved attachment for cameras, you would check into magazines such as *Modern Photography* and *Popular Photography*. Or, if you want to offer a new fishing lure, you might consider publications like *Field and Stream* and *Fishing World*.

There are literally thousands of magazines, yet most appear to cater to a rather special, even unique, group of readers. Many publications research their audiences and have a pretty good idea of what these people are like. They are usually quite ready to furnish you with their "readership profile." (See Figure 13-3 for an example of one magazine's profile of its readers.)

Depending on just what you have to sell, you can choose publications targeted at farmers or businesspeople, young brides or young mothers, chemical engineers or insurance salespersons, lovers of country music or racing cars, skiers or joggers, racquetball or soccer fans, home owners or apartment dwellers, small businesspeople or corporation executives, and so on.

**FIGURE 13-3. Sample reader profile.**

*The HORTICULTURE Reader*

| | |
|---|---|
| Median Income | $ 27,400 |
| Average Income | $ 33,300 |
| Average Household Net Worth | $143,300 |

*Home Ownership*

| | |
|---|---|
| Own Principal Residence | 88.4% |
| Own Vacation or Second Home | 23.3% |

*Size of Property*

| | |
|---|---|
| ½ Acre or less | 37.9% |
| ½ to 1 Acre | 20.2% |
| 1 to 2 Acres | 14.0% |
| 2 to 10 Acres | 17.3% |
| Over 10 Acres | 10.6% |

*Location of Residence*

| | |
|---|---|
| City of 500,000+ Population | 8.7% |
| Suburb of City of 500,000+ | 15.4% |
| City under 500,000 | 15.6% |
| Urban Town | 23.0% |
| Rural Town or Area | 37.2% |

*Education and Occupation*

| | |
|---|---|
| Percent College Graduate | 49.8% |
| Percent Post Graduate | 29.2% |
| Professional/Executive | 39.3% |
| Manager/Proprietor | 18.0% |
| Teacher | 15.5% |
| Technician/Engineer | 11.1% |

*Average Amount Spent on Home Furnishings, Last Year*

| | |
|---|---|
| Antiques | $1137 |
| Floor Coverings | 882 |
| Furniture | 869 |
| Silver, China, Crystal | 318 |
| Total | $3206 |

**FIGURE 13-3.   Sample reader profile. (continued)**

*Credit Cards Held*
| | |
|---|---|
| Air Travel | 10.3% |
| American Express | 25.8% |
| Car Rental | 18.8% |
| Carte Blanche | 2.1% |
| Department Store | 26.9% |
| Diners Club | 3.7% |
| Gasoline Company | 58.9% |
| Master Charge | 49.2% |
| Visa | 54.2% |

*Activities, Past Year*
| | |
|---|---|
| Sewing | 61.0% |
| Limited Edition Collecting | 56.7% |
| Art Show Attendance | 53.5% |
| Photography | 52.5% |
| Carpentry | 52.1% |
| Boating/Fishing | 46.5% |
| Gourmet Cooking | 44.0% |
| Antique Collecting | 38.2% |
| Golf or Tennis | 32.8% |

*Club/Organization Officerships Held*
| | |
|---|---|
| Religious/Church Affiliated | 29.1% |
| Civic/City/Affairs | 22.0% |
| Scientific/Professional | 21.3% |
| Garden Club | 17.7% |
| Service Organization | 15.6% |
| Fraternal | 11.3% |
| Conservation | 5.7% |
| Political | 5.0% |

**Source:** From advertising material submitted March 1981 by *Horticulture,* 300 Massachusetts Avenue, Boston, Mass. 02115. Reprinted with permission.

### Reader loyalty

Most magazine audiences are intensely loyal to their publications. They consume issue after issue, reading from front to back cover. This can be a plus-factor for the mail order advertiser who seeks to enhance results through ad frequency—advertising regularly, month after month.

### Prestige of the medium

Somewhat tied into loyalty is a psychological factor: the very appearance of your advertisement in the readers' "beloved" publication endows your company—and its products—with an element of prestige and believability. This is probably due to the old adage that suggests one is known by the company he or she keeps.

### Special sections for mail order firms

Many publications devote special sections to merchandise and services that readers may purchase by mail. Some have classified pages where mail order firms that cannot afford to place display ads can advertise at a relatively low cost. In either case, you can be sure that regular readers of those pages are likely prospects for you (provided, of course, you have selected the right medium in the first place).

Often, these mail order sections or departments carry special names. Here are a few:

| | |
|---|---|
| *Elks Magazine* | —"Elks Family Shopper" |
| *Field and Stream* | —"Sportsman's Shopper" |
| *Good Housekeeping* | —"Shop By Mail" |
| *House Beautiful* | —"Window Shopping" |
| *Mechanix Illustrated* | —"Buyers Corner" |
| *Popular Science* | —"Shopper's Showcase" |
| *Redbook* | —"Tops in the Shops" |
| *World Tennis* | —"Tennis Mart" |

### Excellent reproduction

Photographs and drawings used to illustrate magazine advertisements reproduce amazingly well because fine screens (110 lines per inch, or more) are employed in preparing the halftones. (Illustrations in newspaper ads often leave much to be desired simply because coarser screens must be used.) This technical consideration is of even more importance in cases where full-color advertisements are used to enhance a product's appeal. An example is an ad that displays a gift package of assorted imported cheeses. (For more on the four-color process, see Chapter 10.)

## Drawbacks

As with the newspaper, the magazine appeals only to the reader's sense of sight. Your ad will need to be compelling enough to attract, interest, convince, and move the reader to act—all through the printed word, along with illustrations, symbols, spacing, and other techniques.

Again, there is the strong possibility of a lot of waste circulation. Many readers of any magazine you might advertise in are not regular "by mail" shoppers. Nor are they necessarily candidates for those special products you are attempting to sell.

A more serious disadvantage is the extraordinary amount of lead time required by this medium. You will need to reserve space in most publications long in advance of the scheduled date of issue; and deliver all the requisite components—the ad mechanical, plates, halftones, color separations (if using color), and so on—depending on whether the magazine is produced by letterpress or offset. Closing dates are typically listed on the publication's rate card; this may read "the first of the second month preceding the date of issue" (a common closing date). Or closing may fall on "the 25th of the third month preceding the date of issue."

The problem is further compounded by the fact that actual "issue dates" generally precede the dates shown on the covers of these periodicals by anywhere from several days to as much as two weeks, and sometimes more.

Magazines—like newspapers—usually offer different rate schedules to different classes of advertisers. The highest rate is the national rate; lower rates are offered to camps, schools, book and record clubs, mail order houses, and other types of organizations. The typical advertisement placed by a mail order operator will cost anywhere from 15 to 25 percent less than would a national advertisement, on the average. This is true whether it is to be printed in black and white, in two colors, or in full color. As an example, where a one-page advertisement scheduled for a single insertion would cost the national advertiser $7,200, a mail order company might be charged only $5,800.

**Fractional Pages and Color**

Space in magazines is sold on a fractional or full-page basis, and by the column inch. Where the publication offers a "shop by mail" section, there may be a minimum "unit" you will be required to buy; if the magazine carries classified advertising, you will be charged by the word or agate line, or by the inch if the section admits classified display advertisements.

When analyzed by the total amount of space for your investment, the full-page advertisement is your best buy. When you require less space for your message, you will actually be paying proportionately more for every line or every inch you use. This "premium" can run from only a tiny percentage to as much as 25 percent or higher on a half-page advertisement, for example. This can be readily seen in Table 13-1.

Check the entries in Table 13-1 for Magazine A. The space for a single insertion of your one-page mail order advertisement would cost you $4,550. You might then assume, quite logically, that half a page should cost you no more than $2,275 (or half of $4,550). Yet, the magazine will charge $2,500 for the space; $225 more than you calculated. You will be asked to pay a premium of nearly 10 percent above what the price theoretically ought to be.

**Table 13-1.**
Magazine mail order rates: fractional versus full-page costs.*

| Magazine | Cost of One Page | One-half Page | | | One-third Page | | |
| | | Cost at Page Rate | Actual Cost | Premium Percentage | Cost at Page Rate | Actual Cost | Premium Percentage |
|---|---|---|---|---|---|---|---|
| A | $4,550 | $2,275 | $2,500 | + 9.9% | $1,516.67 | $1,705 | +12.4% |
| B | 5,205 | 2,602.50 | 3,190 | +22.6 | 1,735 | 1,970 | +13.5 |
| C | 6,750 | 3,375 | 3,980 | +17.9 | 2,250 | 2,820 | +25.3 |
| D | 7,852 | 3,926 | 3,962 | ** | 2,617.33 | 2,642 | ** |
| E | 9,175 | 4,587.50 | 4,605 | ** | 3,058.33 | 3,070 | ** |
| F | 11,080 | 5,540 | 5,805 | + 4.8 | 3,693.33 | 4,040 | + 9.4 |
| G | 16,430 | 8,215 | 9,900 | +20.5 | 5,476.67 | 6,170 | +12.7 |

*All costs based on publication rate cards received January to March 1981.
**Insignificant differential; less than 1 percent.

What about the possibility of adding color to your advertisement? Depending on the publication, you will be charged as little as 8 to 10 percent, or up to 35 to 40 percent and more, over the normal black-and-white cost, should you want to add just a single color (to confirm this, see Table 13-2), provided you use one full page. Less space than that will cost you proportionately more. In fact, when it comes to full four-color advertising, this differential runs way, way up—to 50 percent and more over the one-page, black-and-white rate. On a smaller sized advertisement of, say, one-third of a page, the premium can rise to over 100 percent.

**Table 13-2.**
Magazine mail order rates: color versus black and white.*

| | Single Insertion Costs per Full Page | | | | |
|---|---|---|---|---|---|
| Magazine | Black and White | Two Color | Premium Percentage | Four Color | Premium Percentage |
| A | $ 4,550 | $ 5,155 | +13.3% | $ 6,340 | +39.3% |
| B | 5,205 | 6,555 | +25.9 | 6,975 | +34.0 |
| C | 6,750 | 7,325 | + 8.5 | 9,330 | +38.2 |
| D | 7,852 | 9,493 | +20.9 | 11,103 | +41.4 |
| E | 9,175 | 12,670 | +38.1 | 14.015 | +52.8 |
| F | 11,080 | 12,188 | +10.0 | 16,620 | +50.0 |
| G | 16,430 | 18,670 | +13.6 | 22,705 | +38.2 |

*All costs based on publication rate cards received January to March 1981.

It should be noted that the majority of publications that accept four-color advertising will not print anything less than one-third of a page. Some require a minimum space of one-half page or a full page.

**Space Contracts**

Again, just as is the case with the newspaper, magazines offer special frequency rates as well as discounted rates on the total amount of space used within the contract period. A good example of this approach can be seen in Figure 13-4, which shows a current rate card for advertising in the special mail order section of a major consumer magazine. In the first section, note a 5 percent savings for the advertiser if the advertisement appears in three issues of the publication, and even more of a discount when six or twelve issues are used.

The short-rate procedure is explained in Chapter 12; should you not use all of the space contracted for, your billings will be recomputed and you will be expected to pay the differential.

**Some Current Rates**

A regular, large-space R.O.P. display advertisement in the major consumer magazines is often well beyond the capabilities of the small mail order firm, yet such operators do "take a flyer" from time to time. With circulations in the hundreds of thousands—and some of them up in the millions, such publications may charge anywhere from several thousand dollars to as much as $30,000 and more for a one-page, black-and-white advertisement, even at the lower mail order rate. However, a goodly number of magazines contain special sections, or at least pages, devoted to merchandise sold by mail. Advertisements in these sections are typically smaller than their R.O.P. counterparts. And space in them can be purchased more readily by the small operator since the magazine accepts minimum-sized advertisements, sometimes as small as a column inch. Some publications run "editorial style" mail order advertisements; in these instances, there may be a minimum size requirement, such as 28–, 33–, 42–, or 60-lines or more.

Table 13-3 shows a sample listing of publications with each magazine's total circulation, the cost per page for B/W (black-and-white) mail order advertising, and the computed "cost per thousand." This last figure is arrived at by dividing the cost of a full-page B/W advertisement, after multiplying this cost by 1,000, by the total circulation. This approach gives you a basis for comparing media buys. The formula looks like this:

$$\text{Cost per M} = \frac{\text{Page Rate (B/W) X 1,000}}{\text{Total Circulation}}$$

Added to the above information, Table 13-3 also gives perhaps more useful data for the smaller company—the size of the minimum space unit normally accepted by the magazine, and the cost of that unit.

**Table 13-3.**
Mail Order Rates: Magazine Advertising.[a]

| | Publication Circulation[b] | B/W Page Rate (Mail Order) | Cost per Thousand[c] | Minimum Mail Order Unit | Unit Cost |
|---|---|---|---|---|---|
| American Legion Magazine | 2,500,000 | $9,110 | $3.64 | 28 lines | $715.12 |
| Better Homes and Gardens | 8,000,000 | 47,160 | 5.89 | 21 lines | 2,373.84 |
| Car and Driver | 725,000 | 6,265 | 8.64 | 1 inch | 430.00 |
| Cosmopolitan | 2,250,000 | 15,230 | 6.77 | 35 lines | 1,255.00 |
| Elks Magazine | 1,450,000 | 5,600 | 3.86 | 28 lines | 408.80 |
| Esquire | 650,000 | 7,245 | 11.15 | ⅙ page | 1,505.00[d] |
| Family Circle | 7,400,000 | 35,000 | 4.73 | 1 inch | 1,257.00 |
| Field and Stream | 2,000,000 | 16,320 | 8.16 | 1 inch | 627.20 |
| Glamour | 1,700,000 | 12,840 | 7.55 | 1/12 page | 1,070.00 |
| Good Housekeeping | 5,000,000 | 28,658 | 5.73 | 14 lines | 1,155.00 |
| Horticulture | 122,800 | 1,050 | 8.55 | 1 inch | 85.00 |
| Hot Rod | 850,000 | 7,460 | 8.78 | 1 inch | 410.00 |
| House and Garden | 1,000,000 | 11,825 | 11.82 | 1/12 page | 985.00 |
| House Beautiful | 929,500 | 9,175 | 9.87 | 1/12 page | 795.00 |
| Ladies Home Journal | 5,500,000 | 31,300 | 5.69 | 1 inch | 1,170.00 |
| McCall's | 6,200,000 | 45,860 | 7.40 | agate line | 143.95 |
| Mademoiselle | 900,000 | 6,480 | 7.20 | 1/12 page | 540.00 |
| Mechanix Illustrated | 1,600,000 | 10,590 | 6.62 | 1 inch | 495.00 |
| Metropolitan Home | 700,000 | 7,852 | 11.22 | 1/12 page | 669.00 |
| Ms. Magazine | 500,000 | 5,205 | 10.41 | ⅙ page | 1,075.00 |
| Parents | 1,550,000 | 13,135 | 8.47 | 1/36 page (11 lines) | 435.00 |
| Playboy | 5,000,000 | 40,515 | 8.10 | ⅙ page | 6,835.00 |
| Popular Electronics | 395,000 | 6,750 | 17.09 | ⅙ page | 1,710.00 |
| Popular Mechanics | 1,600,000 | 9,435 | 5.90 | 1 inch | 425.00 |
| Popular Science | 1,800,000 | 11,080 | 6.16 | 1 inch | 510.00 |
| Redbook | 4,300,000 | 23,693 | 5.51 | 14 lines | 811.00 |
| Road and Track | 630,000 | 6,140 | 9.75 | 1 inch | 375.00 |
| Runner's World | 475,000 | 5,950 | 12.53 | 1 inch | 150.00 |
| Saturday Evening Post | 625,000 | 4,586.40 | 7.34 | 14 lines | 171.21 |
| Seventeen | 1,500,000 | 8,650 | 5.77 | 14 lines | 284.00 |
| Sports Afield | 500,000 | 5,250 | 10.50 | 1 inch | 255.00 |
| Star Magazine | 3,350,000 | 12,250 | 3.66 | 1 inch | 189.00 |

**Table 13-3.**
Mail Order Rates: Magazine Advertising.[a] (continued)

| | Publication Circulation[b] | B/W Page Rate (Mail Order) | Cost per Thousand[c] | Minimum Mail Order Unit | Unit Cost |
|---|---|---|---|---|---|
| Woman's Day | 7,400,000 | 38,555 | 5.21 | 14 lines | 1,410.00 |
| Working Woman | 440,000 | 4,575 | 10.40 | 1/12 page | 468.75 |
| World Tennis | 400,000 | 5,180 | 12.95 | 1/12 page | 620.00 |

[a]Rates in effect as of early 1981.
[b]Circulation rate base in most instances (as per magazine rate cards).
[c]Obtained by dividing the cost of a full-page black-and-white advertisement by the circulation figure.
[d]At the discretion of the publisher.

---

**FIGURE 13-4.  Excerpt from magazine rate card.**

## MAIL ORDER RATES

| BLACK & WHITE | 1 Issue | 3 Issues | 6 Issues | 12 Issues |
|---|---|---|---|---|
| 1 page | $8,900 | $8,455 | $8,010 | $7,565 |
| 2 columns | 5,930 | 5,634 | 5,337 | 5,041 |
| 1 column | 2,960 | 2,812 | 2,664 | 2,516 |
| 3/4 column | 2,220 | 2,109 | 1,998 | 1,887 |
| 1/2 column | 1,490 | 1,416 | 1,341 | 1,267 |
| 1/4 column | 750 | 713 | 675 | 638 |

| 4 COLOR | | | | |
|---|---|---|---|---|
| 1 page | 12,740 | 12,103 | 11,466 | 10,829 |
| 2 columns | 9,780 | 9,291 | 8,802 | 8,313 |
| 1/2 page | 9,160 | 8,702 | 8,244 | 7,786 |

These rates are based upon the use of any combination of standard units of space in different issues within any twelve-month period. Time rates are allowed in advance only on contract giving specific units of space and issues to be used; otherwise, discounts allowed are earned. If an advertiser cancels any portion of his contract, he will automatically be short-rated at the rate earned. Time-rate funds will be credited (or paid in cash, if requested) as earned during each advertiser's contract year.

**COPY REQUIREMENTS**

**A.** Mail Order Department will accept advertising only from firms or from companies selling merchandise by mail.
**B.** There can be no mention of product distribution. Ads which include the name of a designer, trade mark, or registered trade name are eligible only when such mention is in body copy without undue emphasis.
**C.** No Mail Order advertising may be used in any way (trade paper advertising, display cards, dealer newspaper advertising, direct mail, etc.) as a means of promoting business with, or securing business from, dealers.
**D.** A mailing address to which mail orders and inquiries can be sent must be included in the copy.
**E.** Unless selling a service, all advertisers selling by mail must state exact price of merchandise and postage instructions relating to delivery.
**F.** All advertisers, except those selling personalized services, must agree to refund full price of any advertised item to unsatisfied readers who return the merchandise promptly and in an unused condition.

Specifications, mechanical requirements, copy and contract regulations as set forth in previous pages of this Rate Card apply to all Mail Order advertisers. Particularly note disclaimer paragraph F under Copy & Contract Regulations.

**Source:** Mail Order Rate Card, issued September 1981, *Mademoiselle® Magazine* ©1981 the Conde Nast Publications Inc., 350 Madison Avenue, New York, New York 10017. Reprinted with permission.

**Other Pointers**

Some of the more widely circulated magazines put out regional editions. Advertisements placed in these editions will, of course, cost far less than if you were to use the entire distribution. However, you will pay proportionately more for the space on a per M basis.

"Split-run" possibilities are also available from some publications. This means that the magazine can split its total circulation into two, three, or more segments; this enables the advertiser to try out alternate advertisements—all of the same size—simultaneously. A good example of an extremely flexible medium is *Popular Mechanics*. It offers advertisers "as many as 2,500 different combinations of states and copy splits. Through this program, advertisers may tailor-make their own regionals and/or copy splits according to individual marketing needs rather than be bound by predetermined state groupings"[3] (see Figure 13-5).

[3]From "Popular Mechanics Regional & Split-Run Availabilities," advertising brochure, 1979. Reprinted with permission.

**FIGURE 13-5. State circulations available (Popular Mechanics).**

| State | Circulation |
|---|---|
| Alabama | 18,625 |
| Alaska | 4,757 |
| Arizona | 18,110 |
| Arkansas | 10,535 |
| California | 142,210 |
| Colorado | 21,951 |
| Connecticut | 25,696 |
| Delaware | 4,999 |
| Dist. of Columbia | 4,263 |
| Florida | 54,883 |
| Georgia | 25,632 |
| Hawaii | 6,133 |
| Idaho | 8,008 |
| Illinois | 88,702 |
| Indiana | 46,527 |
| Iowa | 30,154 |
| Kansas | 25,504 |
| Kentucky | 16,324 |
| Louisiana | 18,361 |
| Maine | 9,344 |
| Maryland | 24,950 |
| Massachusetts | 39,861 |
| Michigan | 75,910 |
| Minnesota | 47,172 |
| Mississippi | 8,537 |
| Missouri | 31,510 |
| Montana | 9,917 |
| Nebraska | 16,070 |
| Nevada | 5,771 |
| New Hampshire | 8,388 |
| New Jersey | 49,179 |
| New Mexico | 7,042 |
| New York | 116,225 |
| North Carolina | 28,451 |
| North Dakota | 8,253 |
| Ohio | 88,923 |
| Oklahoma | 19,523 |
| Oregon | 22,470 |
| Pennsylvania | 102,901 |
| Rhode Island | 6,435 |
| South Carolina | 13,935 |
| South Dakota | 7,863 |
| Tennessee | 20,917 |
| Texas | 71,668 |
| Utah | 7,907 |
| Vermont | 4,542 |
| Virginia | 32,523 |
| Washington | 38,649 |
| West Virginia | 11,309 |
| Wisconsin | 48,385 |
| Wyoming | 3,946 |
| Canada | 52,862 |
| TOTAL CIRCULATION | _____ |

PLEASE NOTE: Minimum Circulation: 250,000 Must Follow State Lines
States Must Be Contiguous

Advertiser _____  Product _____

Agency _____  Contact Name _____

Popular Mechanics Salesman _____  Date _____

| Rates Requested: | Black & White | 2 Color | 4 Color |
|---|---|---|---|
| Per Page | ☐ $ | ☐ $ | ☐ $ |
| Other Units | ☐ $ | ☐ $ | ☐ $ |

**Source:** *"Popular Mechanics Regional and Split-Run Availabilities,"* advertising brochure, 1979. Reprinted with permission.

For either regional editions or split runs, most publications will insist that you use a minimum space of at least one-third or one-half of a page.

Special positions for your display advertisement, outside of the regular mail order section, are usually difficult to get. If the magazine decides to honor your request, you pay an extra charge. As to your chances of being able to purchase an inside or back cover position, these are next to nil. Some publications will not take a mail order advertisement in these positions; many will consider only a full-color page. And the cost can be twice, three times, or far more than that of a single B/W full-page advertisement.

On occasion, advertisers will use inserts in connection with their offers. A business reply card is an example. These inserts must be printed and paid for by the advertising firm and delivered to the publication for insertion. Their use often dramatically increases the total number of responses. In most cases, you will be required to pay for this service at the rate usually charged for a full-page B/W advertisement.

Some magazines use their own business reply cards to encourage readers to send for information regarding advertisements carried in the publication. Responses thus obtained are forwarded to the individual advertisers. This is commonly called a magazine "bingo card" (see Figure 13-6).

## CLASSIFIED ADVERTISING

Many magazines have classified sections, just as the newspapers do. These can be very profitable columns for the smaller mail order house. Some advertisers appear in the same publication month after month, for years. Costs are comparatively low when contrasted with the cost of a display advertisement or even with the cost of a minimum-space mail order unit. After all, what most small firms are looking for is either a low cost-per-inquiry or a low cost-per-sale; the trick is to have the advertisement pay for itself if at all possible.

An interesting alternative, especially where publications offer no regular classified pages, is the "Market Place," handled by Classified, Inc., of 676 St. Clair, Chicago, Ill. 60611. This is a classified column that the company introduces into a variety of publications. The column is sectioned off from the surrounding text and topped by the "Market Place" masthead. The firm usually sells space in the column for a group of magazines. For example, there is a group of women's magazines that includes, among others, *True Story, Movie Life, Real Confessions*, and *Modern Screen*. With one men's group, you can reach the readers of *Saga, Inside Detective, Male*, and *Ring Magazine*, along with those of other publications as well. Another combination is the organization group; your advertising there will appear in both *Moose Magazine* and *VFW Magazine*. The column may also be found in such mass-audience magazines as *Family Circle* and *Redbook*.

As noted in Chapter 12, mail order companies and other direct-response organizations use very little newspaper classified advertis-

FIGURE 13-6. Sample magazine "bingo" card.

## SHOP BY THE NUMBERS

To receive more information on the products or services advertised in this issue, circle the Reader Service numbers from the advertisements. If your interest demands immediate attention, write those numbers in the space provided under Item 7. Their salesman will call on you.

Be sure to answer all of the questions completely. This information is designed to help the manufacturers reply more specifically to your request.

## TO RECEIVE MORE INFORMATION.

Name _____ Title _____

Company _____

Address _____

City _____ State _____ Zip _____

Telephone _____

**PLEASE CHECK THE APPROPRIATE INFORMATION:**

**1) Type of Firm**
☐ 1. Manufacturing
☐ 2. Retail/Wholesale
☐ 3. Financial Service
☐ 4. Business Service
☐ 5. Other _____

**2) Title**
☐ A. Owner
☐ B. President
☐ C. Vice-President
☐ D. General Manager
☐ E. Treasurer
☐ F. Other _____

**3) Purchasing Authority**
☐ A. Recommend
☐ B. Specify
☐ C. Approve

**4) Number of Employees**
☐ 1. 1-19
☐ 2. 20-49
☐ 3. 50-99
☐ 4. 100-499
☐ 5. 500-999
☐ 6. 1000-2499
☐ 7. 2500 or more

**5) Annual Dollar Volume**
☐ A. Under $1.0 million
☐ B. $1 to $4.9 million
☐ C. $5 to $9.9 million
☐ D. $10 to $14.9 million
☐ E. $15 to $24.9 million
☐ F. Over $25 million

**6) Reason for Inquiry**
☐ 1. Future Project
☐ 2. Immediate Purchase

**7) I have a special interest in the following items. Please have a salesman contact me:**

☐ **PLEASE SEND ME 12 MONTHLY ISSUES OF INC. AND BILL ME $18.00.**

| 1 | 31 | 61 | 91 | 121 | 151 | 181 | 211 | 241 | 271 | 301 | 331 | 361 |
| 2 | 32 | 62 | 92 | 122 | 152 | 182 | 212 | 242 | 272 | 302 | 332 | 362 |
| 3 | 33 | 63 | 93 | 123 | 153 | 183 | 213 | 243 | 273 | 303 | 333 | 363 |
| 4 | 34 | 64 | 94 | 124 | 154 | 184 | 214 | 244 | 274 | 304 | 334 | 364 |
| 5 | 35 | 65 | 95 | 125 | 155 | 185 | 215 | 245 | 275 | 305 | 335 | 365 |
| 6 | 36 | 66 | 96 | 126 | 156 | 186 | 216 | 246 | 276 | 306 | 336 | 366 |
| 7 | 37 | 67 | 97 | 127 | 157 | 187 | 217 | 247 | 277 | 307 | 337 | 367 |
| 8 | 38 | 68 | 98 | 128 | 158 | 188 | 218 | 248 | 278 | 308 | 338 | 368 |
| 9 | 39 | 69 | 99 | 129 | 159 | 189 | 219 | 249 | 279 | 309 | 339 | 369 |
| 10 | 40 | 70 | 100 | 130 | 160 | 190 | 220 | 250 | 280 | 310 | 340 | 370 |
| 11 | 41 | 71 | 101 | 131 | 161 | 191 | 221 | 251 | 281 | 311 | 341 | 371 |
| 12 | 42 | 72 | 102 | 132 | 162 | 192 | 222 | 252 | 282 | 312 | 342 | 372 |
| 13 | 43 | 73 | 103 | 133 | 163 | 193 | 223 | 253 | 283 | 313 | 343 | 373 |
| 14 | 44 | 74 | 104 | 134 | 164 | 194 | 224 | 254 | 284 | 314 | 344 | 374 |
| 15 | 45 | 75 | 105 | 135 | 165 | 195 | 225 | 255 | 285 | 315 | 345 | 375 |
| 16 | 46 | 76 | 106 | 136 | 166 | 196 | 226 | 256 | 286 | 316 | 346 | 376 |
| 17 | 47 | 77 | 107 | 137 | 167 | 197 | 227 | 257 | 287 | 317 | 347 | 377 |
| 18 | 48 | 78 | 108 | 138 | 168 | 198 | 228 | 258 | 288 | 318 | 348 | 378 |
| 19 | 49 | 79 | 109 | 139 | 169 | 199 | 229 | 259 | 289 | 319 | 349 | 379 |
| 20 | 50 | 80 | 110 | 140 | 170 | 200 | 230 | 260 | 290 | 320 | 350 | 380 |
| 21 | 51 | 81 | 111 | 141 | 171 | 201 | 231 | 261 | 291 | 321 | 351 | 381 |
| 22 | 52 | 82 | 112 | 142 | 172 | 202 | 232 | 262 | 292 | 322 | 352 | 382 |
| 23 | 53 | 83 | 113 | 143 | 173 | 203 | 233 | 263 | 293 | 323 | 353 | 383 |
| 24 | 54 | 84 | 114 | 144 | 174 | 204 | 234 | 264 | 294 | 324 | 354 | 384 |
| 25 | 55 | 85 | 115 | 145 | 175 | 205 | 235 | 265 | 295 | 325 | 355 | 385 |
| 26 | 56 | 86 | 116 | 146 | 176 | 206 | 236 | 266 | 296 | 326 | 356 | 386 |
| 27 | 57 | 87 | 117 | 147 | 177 | 207 | 237 | 267 | 297 | 327 | 357 | 387 |
| 28 | 58 | 88 | 118 | 148 | 178 | 208 | 238 | 268 | 298 | 328 | 358 | 388 |
| 29 | 59 | 89 | 119 | 149 | 179 | 209 | 239 | 269 | 299 | 329 | 359 | 389 |
| 30 | 60 | 90 | 120 | 150 | 180 | 210 | 240 | 270 | 300 | 330 | 360 | 390 |

sxlrxtv                      This card expires April 1, 1981.

**Source:** January 1981 issue of *INC.* (INC. Publishing Company, 38 Commercial Wharf, Boston, Mass. 02110). Reprinted with permission.

FIGURE 13-7. List of classified advertising categories.

## SELECT THE HEADING FOR YOUR AD from this list. Then please WRITE IN the number of the heading you choose on the other side of order form →

| Category | No. |
|---|---|
| Agents & Salespersons Wanted* | 56 |
| Airedales & Terriers | 35 |
| All Terrain Vehicles | 21A |
| Animal Wildlife Carvings | 55B |
| Antique Firearms | 2A |
| Antiques & Relics | 66 |
| Archery Equipment | 27 |
| Arms Equipment | 1 |
| Art Instruction & Cartooning | 55 |
| Athletic Equipment | 29 |
| Author's Service | 77 |
| Autos, Supplies & Equipment | 79 |
| Aviation | 80 |
| Beagles & Bassets | 36 |
| Binoculars & Telescopes | 7 |
| Birds, Pets & Animals | 15 |
| Boats, Motors & Marine Supplies | 31 |
| Body Building, Self-Defense Courses | 30A |
| Books & Magazines | 78 |
| Bowhunting | 28 |
| Box Traps | 12 |
| Business Opportunities* | 57 |
| Buy It Wholesale | 58 |
| Cameras & Photo Supplies | 81 |
| Campers & Trailers | 21 |
| Campgrounds | 22 |
| Camping Equipment | 23 |
| CB Radio | 87A |
| Christmas Gifts | A-1 |
| Coins & Currency | 75 |
| Collies | 37 |
| Decoys, Calls & Blinds | 10 |
| Detectives | 84 |
| Dog Accessories & Kennel Equipment | 34 |
| Dogs — Miscellaneous | 45 |
| Do-It Yourself | 85 |
| Education & Instruction | 54 |
| Electronics, Radio-TV | 87 |
| Emblems & Brassards | 9 |
| Employment Information* | 59 |
| Fancy Poultry | 68 |
| Fishing, Misc. | 46 |
| Flies & Fly Tying | 48 |
| For the Home & Garden | 69 |
| For Sale, Miscellaneous | 63 |
| Frogs & Fish | 51 |
| Fur Bearing Animals | 18 |
| Game Birds | 16 |
| German Shepherds | 38 |
| Gifts | 71 |
| Good Eating | 70 |
| Government Surplus | 62 |
| Gun Books | 4 |
| Gun Cabinets | 5 |
| Gunsmithing | 6 |
| Hamsters, Guinea Pigs & Mice | 19 |
| Hawks, Falcons & Owls | 17 |
| Hearing Aids | 95A |
| Hobbies & Crafts | 32 |
| Home Craftsman | 85A |
| Home Movies, Color Slides | 83 |
| Horse Training | 20 |
| Hounds | 39 |
| Hunting Equipment & Information | 8 |
| Ice Fishing | 47 |
| Import-Export | 72 |
| Knives & Stones | 4A |
| Live Bait | 50 |
| Loans by Mail | 96A |
| Log Cabin & Home Building | 53 |
| Magic Tricks | 32A |
| Minerals & Precious Stones | 26 |
| Miscellaneous | 93 |
| Money Making Opportunities* | 60 |
| Motorcycles, Scooters & Bicycles | 91 |
| Musical Instruments | 88 |
| Nursery Stock | 73 |
| Of Interest to All | 67 |
| Old Gold, Jewelry & Watches | 65 |
| Patents & Inventions* | 74 |
| Personal | 96 |
| Photo Finishing | 82 |
| Pointers & Setters | 40 |
| Printing, Office Supplies, etc. | 92 |
| Profitable Occupations* | 61 |
| Prospecting | 25 |
| Real Estate | 52 |
| Records & Tapes | 89 |
| Reloading Supplies | 2 |
| Remailing Services | 95 |
| Retrievers | 41 |
| St. Bernards | 42 |
| Sights, Scopes & Mounts | 3 |
| Snowmobiles | 31A |
| Songwriters | 90 |
| Spaniels | 43 |
| Special Services | 94 |
| Sporting Equipment | 30 |
| Stamp Collecting | 76 |
| Survival Equipment | 23A |
| Tackle & Lures | 49 |
| Tanning | 13 |
| Taxidermy | 14 |
| Tents | 24 |
| Tobacco, Pipes & Cigars | 97 |
| Toys, Games & Novelties | 33 |
| Trapping | 11 |
| Trophies | 9A |
| Wanted To Buy | 64 |
| Wearing Apparel | 98 |
| Weimaraners | 44 |
| Where-To-Go, Travel, Resorts | 99 |
| Wildlife Art | 55A |

Source: *Outdoor Life*, Times Mirror Magazines, Inc., 380 Madison Avenue, New York, N.Y. 10017. Reprinted with permission.

ing. The opposite is true with magazine classified. These columns are filled with small advertisements from an amazing variety of firms that seek replies by mail. Some advertisements offer merchandise directly for sale; these are usually low cost items that sell for up to $2–$3. Mail order operators often prefer a two-step approach for merchandise that costs more than that. The classified advertisement will offer a booklet, free details, or other information—perhaps asking the respondent to send a stamped, self-addressed envelope (SASE) or a modest amount, perhaps a quarter, to rule out curiosity seekers. The follow-up material sent by the advertiser tries to sell the respondent. This kind of approach is practically a must for anything priced over $10.

Magazine readers often read the classified pages thoroughly. They have come to expect all sorts of offers that may interest them and answer their needs. Books like *Popular Mechanics* and *Popular Science* contain many pages of such advertisements; some of the advertisements have been running for many years (with changes of copy, of course).

To help the reader locate advertisements that may be of interest, the publication groups these ads under different headings. A listing from one publication is shown in Figure 13-7. In this case, the headings are listed on the back of the classified advertising department's order form, for the benefit of the mail order advertiser.

As is true in newspaper classified, magazine classified includes both "regular" (words only) and "display" classified. Table 13-4 contains a short list of magazines that offer classified space. In addition to providing names, addresses, and telephone numbers of these publications, current rates for regular classified advertising—and, where available, for display classified—are shown. Also indicated are the minimum sizes offered by the magazine.

**Table 13-4.**
ABBREVIATED LIST OF PUBLICATIONS WITH CLASSIFIED SECTIONS.

| COST INFORMATION FOR CLASSIFIED ADS* | | |
| --- | --- | --- |
| Name and Address of Publication | Regular Classified | Display Classified |
| *American Business* 1775 Broadway New York, N.Y. 10019 (212-581-2000) | $2 per word; minimum 10 words** | 1-inch minimum, $198 |
| *Atlantic Monthly* 8 Arlington Street Boston, Mass. 02116 (617-536-9500) | $1.50 per word | 1-inch minimum, $90 |
| *Backpacker* Ziff-Davis Publishing Co. 1 Park Avenue New York, N.Y. 10016 (212-725-3925) | $2.35 per word; minimum $35.25 | 1-inch minimum, $145 |
| *Baseball Digest* Century Publishing Co. 1020 Church Street Evanston, Ill. 60201 (312-491-6440) | 95¢ per word; minimum 10 words | |

**Table 13-4. (continued)**
ABBREVIATED LIST OF PUBLICATIONS WITH CLASSIFIED SECTIONS.

| Name and Address of Publication | COST INFORMATION FOR CLASSIFIED ADS* | |
|---|---|---|
| | Regular Classified | Display Classified |
| *Boating*<br>Ziff-Davis Publishing Co.<br>1 Park Avenue<br>New York, N.Y. 10016<br>(212-725-3925) | $1.60 per word; minimum $24 | 1-inch minimum, $130 |
| *Capper's Weekly*<br>616 Jefferson<br>Topeka, Kan. 66607<br>(913-295-1102) | 63¢ per word | $3.20 per line; minimum 5 lines |
| *Car and Driver*<br>Ziff-Davis Publishing Co.<br>1 Park Avenue<br>New York, N.Y. 10016<br>(212-725-3755) | $3.30 per word; minimum 15 words | 1-inch minimum, $260 |
| *Catholic Digest*<br>441 Lexington Avenue<br>New York, N.Y. 10017<br>(212-867-9766) | $2.25 per word; minimum 12 words | 1-inch minimum, $175 |
| *Fate*<br>500 Hyacinth Place<br>Highland Park, Ill. 60035<br>(312-433-4550) | 95¢ per word | |
| *Field and Stream*<br>1515 Broadway<br>New York, N.Y. 10036<br>(212-975-7548) | $71 for minimum 14 words; $5.10 for each additional word | 1-inch minimum, $350 |
| *Grit*<br>Grit Publishing Co.<br>Williamsport, Pa. 17701<br>(717-326-1771) | $1.20 per word; minimum 10 words | 1-inch minimum, $123 |
| *Horticulture*<br>300 Massachusetts Avenue<br>Boston, Mass. 02115<br>(617-536-9280) | 90¢ per word; minimum $18 | |
| *Let's Live*<br>444 No. Larchmont Blvd.<br>Los Angeles, Calif. 90004<br>(213-469-3901) | $48 minimum for 20 words or less; $2.50 for each additional word | 2-inches minimum, $77 |
| *Mechanix Illustrated*<br>1515 Broadway<br>New York, N.Y. 10036<br>(212-975-7549) | $4.75 per word; minimum 10 words | |
| *Money*<br>P.O. Box 1510<br>Clearwater, Fla. 33517<br>(813-443-7666) | $3.95 per word; minimum 10 words | 1-inch minimum, $340 |
| *National Enquirer*<br>Lantana, Fla. 33464<br>(305-586-1111) | $4.60 per word | |

**Table 13-4.**
ABBREVIATED LIST OF PUBLICATIONS WITH CLASSIFIED SECTIONS.

COST INFORMATION FOR CLASSIFIED ADS*

| Name and Address of Publication | Regular Classified | Display Classified |
|---|---|---|
| *National Review*<br>150 East 35th Street<br>New York, N.Y. 10016<br>(212-679-3330) | 90¢ per word; minimum 10 words | |
| *New York Magazine*<br>755 Second Avenue<br>New York, N.Y. 10017<br>(212-880-0732) | $4.50 per word; minimum 10 words | 1-inch minimum, $268 |
| *Outdoor Life*<br>380 Madison Avenue<br>New York, N.Y. 10017<br>(212-687-3000) | $4.35 per word; minimum 14 words | 1-inch minimum, $290 |
| *Popular Electronics*<br>Ziff-Davis Publishing Co.<br>1 Park Avenue<br>New York, N.Y. 10016<br>(212-725-3568) | $3 per word; minimum $45 | 1-inch minimum, $370 |
| *Popular Mechanics*<br>224 West 57th Street<br>New York, N.Y. 10019<br>(212-262-4284) | $4.30 per word; minimum 10 words | |
| *Popular Photography*<br>Ziff-Davis Publishing Co.<br>1 Park Avenue<br>New York, N.Y. 10016<br>(212-725-3779) | $5.25 per word; minimum $78.75 | 1-inch minimum, $455 |
| *Popular Science*<br>Times Mirror Magazines, Inc.<br>300 Madison Avenue<br>New York, N.Y. 10017<br>(212-687-3000) | $6 per word, minimum 10 words | 1-inch minimum, $330 |
| *Psychology Today*<br>Ziff-Davis Publishing Co.<br>1 Park Avenue<br>New York, N.Y. 10016<br>(212-725-3900) | $6.65 per word, minimum $99.75 | 1-inch minimum, $485 |
| *Runner*<br>Ziff-Davis Publishing Co.<br>1 Park Avenue<br>New York, N.Y. 10016<br>(212-725-3925) | $2.25 per word, minimum $33.75 | 1-inch minimum, $95 |
| *Runner's World*<br>1400 Stierlin Road<br>Mountain View, Calif. 94043<br>(415-965-8777) | $2.50 per word; minimum $50 | |
| *Saturday Evening Post*<br>1100 Waterway Boulevard<br>Indianapolis, Ind. 46202<br>(317-634-1100) | $2.60 per word; minimum 10 words | |

**Table 13-4. (continued)**
ABBREVIATED LIST OF PUBLICATIONS WITH CLASSIFIED SECTIONS.

COST INFORMATION FOR CLASSIFIED ADS*

| Name and Address of Publication | Regular Classified | Display Classified |
|---|---|---|
| *Skiing*<br>Ziff-Davis Publishing Co.<br>1 Park Avenue<br>New York, N.Y. 10016<br>(212-725-3925) | $2.65 per word; minimum $39.75 | 1-inch minimum, $340 |
| *Spinning Wheel*<br>Fame Avenue<br>Hanover, Pa. 17333<br>(717-632-3535) | 25¢ per word | |
| *Star Magazine*<br>News Group Publications, Inc.<br>730 Third Avenue<br>New York, N.Y. 10017<br>(212-557-9210) | $13.50 per line | |
| *Travel/Holiday*<br>Travel Building<br>Floral Park, N.Y. 11001<br>(516-352-9700) | $2.20 per word; minimum 20 words | |
| *True West*<br>700 East State Street<br>Iola, Wis. 54945<br>(715-445-2214) | $3.20 minimum for up to 10 words; $4.80 for 11–15 words; etc. | |
| *World Tennis*<br>CBS Publications<br>1515 Broadway<br>New York, N.Y. 10036<br>(212-975-7300) | $50 for minimum 20 words; $2 for each additional word | |

*All rates as of February–March, 1981.

**As a bonus, classified ad repeated free in *Better Living*.

**SUGGESTED READING**

Books

HAIGHT, WILLIAM, *Retail Advertising: Management and Techniques*. Glenview, Ill.: Scott, Foresman, 1976.

HODGSON, RICHARD S., *Direct Mail and Mail Order Handbook*, 3rd ed. Chicago: Dartnell Corporation, 1980.

KLEPPNER, OTTO and NORMAN A. P. GOVONI, collaborator. *Advertising Procedure*, 7th ed. Englewood Cliffs, N.J.: Prentice-Hall, Inc., 1979.

MOORE, CHARLES, *Guidebook to Classified Advertising Costs*. Richboro, Pa.: Richoboro Press, 1980.

NYLEN, DAVID W., *Advertising: Planning, Implementation, & Control,* 2nd ed. Cincinnati: South-Western Publishing, 1980.

STONE, BOB, *Successful Direct Marketing Methods,* 2nd ed. Chicago: Crain Books, 1979.

YOUNT, JOHN T., *Mail Order Advertising Handbook*. San Angelo, Tex.: Educator Books, 1978.

# 14

## THE
## BROADCAST
## MEDIA

Even though the greater share of their promotion budgets typically goes into direct mail activity and advertising in the print media, many direct marketing companies rely on radio and/or television—the broadcast media—for some of their sales. Each day, somewhere, the air waves carry messages to consumers about long-playing records and eight-track tapes, hardware items and kitchen utensils, encyclopedias and magazine subscriptions, garden supplies and burglar alarms, and a host of other products and services.

Of course, both radio and television, especially the local variety, are far more widely used by both retail and manufacturing businesses than by mail order houses. Yet, they can play an important role in mail order selling. Radio can be an asset both as an alternative to and in addition to your print advertisements and your mailings. Television can be valuable as a medium where the product you want to advertise will enjoy greater sales *if* it can be demonstrated, or shown in full color.

Media people in advertising agencies like to refer to the broadcast media as "universal" media, in the sense that through either radio or television you can reach most every household in the nation. Radios, often as many as four or more, are found in most homes, and also in millions of automobiles, trucks, and other vehicles. Most households are equipped with at least one television set, but many have two or more, and color sets are found today in a majority of TV households. There is also fast-growing cable television. By 1978, some 16 percent of all TV homes were receiving cable broadcasts.[1]

A few years ago, a study of television viewing habits reported that "heavy viewers" averaged more than 100 hours of prime time television during a month, and that even "light viewers" watched during prime time for some thrity-five hours over the month.[2]

A major attraction of these broadcast media for direct marketing firms is the almost instantaneous audience response to radio announcements or television commercials.

## RADIO

Well over 6,000 radio stations are distributed throughout the country. More than two-thirds of them are AM stations; the balance, FM stations.[3] (These statistics come from a government source for the year 1978. But the 1981 edition of *Radio Facts,* a publication of the Radio Advertising Bureau, indicates that a total of 7,871 commercial stations were broadcasting during 1980.[4])

Most radio stations are independents. Only a small fraction of the total number belongs to a giant national network, like the American Broadcasting Company (ABC), the National Broadcasting Company (NBC), the Columbia Broadcasting System (CBS), and the Public Broadcasting System (PBS). These networks are used only infrequently by direct marketing firms because of the cost. More often, such advertisers will use "local" radio; they advertise on individual stations in selected areas or, perhaps, schedule their announcements on a number of such stations during the same time period.

## Attractions of Radio

As a medium, radio attracts the retailer for several reasons, and for the same reasons it should interest the mail order firm as well.

### Quick consumer reaction

Consumers may respond almost instantaneously to offers broadcast over both radio and television. Most direct marketing companies using these media will provide the listener (or viewer) with telephone numbers to call to place orders directly or to give their name and addresses so that information, catalogs, and the like can be mailed to them. On radio, these numbers are usually repeated several times for the listening audience. Telephone operators or recording machines may stand by 24 hours a day, so that even an announcement aired at two or three o'clock in the morning can generate immediate results.

---

[1]Arnold M. Barban and Dean M. Krugman, "Cable Television and Advertising: An Assessment," *Journal of Advertising* 7 (Fall 1978), pp. 4–8.

[2]Kathryn E. A. Villani, "Personality/Lifestyle and Television Viewing Behavior," *Journal of Advertising Research* 15 (November 1975), pp. 432–39.

[3]U.S. Bureau of the Census, *Statistical Abstract of the United States: 1979,* 100th ed. (Washington, D.C.: 1979), p. 585.

[4]Radio Advertising Bureau, *Radio Facts* (New York: RAB, 1981).

### Short lead time and flexibility

Newspapers may require a lead time of one or two days for the advertiser. They have to set the ads up in print, select the pages on which they are to appear, and so on. Radio announcements, on the other hand, can be broadcast within hours after the copy has been written. This means exceptional flexibility in copy changes, a definite assist to the advertiser.

Larry Butner, who heads an agency that specializes in direct marketing, participated in a panel discussion at an ANA/RAB workshop in 1979, commenting on this aspect of flexibility.

Radio also offers us one of the fastest and most accurate barometers to success or failure. We know the next day if we're on the right track, we don't have to wait for ratings, we don't have to wait for in-store surveys, for results. We can turn on a dime. We can change our copy overnight if we have to, and be on the air in little less than 24 hours also if we have to. What other medium can do this for you?[5]

### Radio goes everywhere

It is true that newspapers reach a majority of the households in the nation, but radios can be found in just about every one. Most automobiles also are equipped with radios, and many with FM reception as well. If you advertise on radio, your messages may be heard by people driving to and from work, those on vacation at beaches or in the mountains, bicyclists, and teenagers out for a walk. You will reach places where newspapers are seldom found.

### Audience targeting

Over time, every successful radio station attracts a solid core of regular listeners. Station audiences are intensely loyal; people often listen to the same radio station hour after hour, day after day without turning the dial (unlike television viewers, who often switch channels). So the possibilities of targeting selected segments of consumers are practically unlimited. You can aim advertisements at listeners who appreciate classical or semiclassical music, at rock fans or country music lovers, at those who prefer talk shows, or at specific nationality groups or certain parts of the population. There are, for instance, hundreds of radio stations targeted at black Americans. You can also reach such large groups as young men and women under 21 years of age, many of whom appear not to be oriented toward newspaper readership.

### Help in preparing announcements

The radio advertiser can count on the station's staff for help in writing copy, selecting background music, and so on.

Although radio always has been and is being used successfully by direct marketing firms, this medium does have several significant drawbacks.

**Disadvantages of Radio**

[5]Report on ANA/RAB Workshop, 1979—Direct Marketing Panel, p. 19. Reprinted with permission of the Radio Advertising Bureau, Inc.

### Restricted presentation

If you advertise in the print media or on television, you can show your audiences the merchandise you are featuring. Moreover, on television you can also address the viewers with enthusiasm, reinforcing the visual message with the added power of direct, one-to-one selling. You cannot demonstrate your product over the radio. You must rely on sound alone to trigger the listener's imagination—to attract his or her attention, arouse interest, build desire, and secure action. Your only tools are words, music, and perhaps sound effects; with these you need to construct skillfully an impressive picture in the listener's imagination, one strong enough to motivate that person to respond.

### Distractions

Even though many people do listen attentively to their radios, in a large percentage of cases, the radio is heard with "half an ear." Often, radio music or talk is little more than background sound for the individual engaged in other activities demanding his or her attention: driving an automobile, cleaning the house, cooking, speaking to friends, and so on.

### Short-lived messages

Typically, the mail order radio announcement runs one minute in length. No sooner has it been broadcast then its message is gone—lost to the listener. There is no way an interested party can refer back to it, as one can with advertisements in magazines or newspapers; hence the need, in radio advertising, for scheduling repeated airings of your announcements.

### Fragmentation

In most areas of the country, anywhere from five or six to as many as two dozen or more radio stations, both AM and FM, may be transmitting at the same time. What this means to the advertiser is clear. Despite radio's practically universal reach (in that it enters 99 percent of the nation's homes), this massive audience is "spread" across a number of stations at any one time—day or night, and over the weekends as well. So, your chances of the listeners in a specific locale catching a single announcement of yours are not much better than poor to fair; all the more reason to think in terms of repetition, of frequency.

**Buying Radio Time**  Although national advertisers may sponsor parts of or entire programs on radio, the mail order operator thinks in terms of spot announcements, more precisely, *local* spot radio. These, for the most part, are full one-minute spots; shorter ones cannot really get the story across.

Rates on local radio vary according to the time of day or night the advertiser wants his or her announcements to be aired. The 24 hours of the day are broken down into time segments called "day parts." Although these may vary somewhat from station to station, the information in Table 14-1 is a fairly accurate representation of these segments. (See also Table 14-2 for spot rates on a major station in a metropolitan area.)

**Table 14-1.**
A TYPICAL TIME CLASSIFICATION FOR RADIO STATIONS.

| Time Class | Description | Hours |
|---|---|---|
| AA | Morning drive time | 6 A.M. to 10 A.M. |
| B | Housewife time | 10 A.M. to 4 P.M. |
| A | Evening drive time | 4 P.M. to 7 P.M. |
| C | Evening time | 7 P.M. to Midnight |
| D | Night time | Midnight to 6 A.M. |

**Source:** Harvey R. Cook, "Selecting Advertising Media: A Guide for Small Business," *Small Business Management Series No. 34* (Washington, D.C.: Small Business Administration, 1969), p. 67.

**Table 14-2.**
RADIO TIME CATEGORIES AND SPOT RATES—
METROPOLITAN STATION.*

| Time Category | Description | Flat Rate One-Minute Spot |
|---|---|---|
| A.M. Drive Time | Monday–Saturday, 5–10 A.M. | $600 |
| P.M. Drive Time | Monday–Friday, 3–8 P.M. | 400 |
| Daytime | Monday–Friday, 10 A.M.–3 P.M. | 300 |
| Weekend | Saturday, 10 A.M.–8 P.M. Sunday, 6 A.M.–8 P.M. | 300 |
| Night | Monday–Sunday, 8 P.M.–1 A.M. | 200 |
| Postmidnight | Monday–Sunday, 1–6 A.M. | 100 |

*Based on information in *Spot Radio Rates and Data,* Vol. 63, No. 3, March 1, 1981 (Skokie, Ill.: Standard Rate and Data Service).

The Standard Rate and Data Service regularly publishes information regarding rates. You can use their service if you will be doing a lot of radio advertising. You may also contact those stations you are interested in to request copies of their current rate cards. Ask if they offer special rates for mail order advertisers, and about their "package plans." (See Figure 14-1 for examples of radio station rate cards.)

When using this medium, think in terms of a series of announcements scheduled over a period of, perhaps, one to three weeks. Frequency of advertising is the key to success here; advertisers look for the cumulative effect of their radio commercials, and the cumulative reach attained. The same commercial can be broadcast repeatedly at different times of the day and night, and on different days of the week. Or, you can create two or three totally different commercials, all presenting the same proposition, and schedule them to be rotated by the station as the scheduled times come up. The more you repeat your message over the air, the greater the chance that listeners who have missed earlier broadcasts will be exposed to it. And along with repeated announcements, the chances for customer response increases. (Incidentally, results will be much better if you arrange to use a toll-free 800 number in connection with your advertising message.)

The mail order company generally avoids the more popular time slots, such as morning and evening drive time, because they command the highest prices of all categories. Moreover, it is far easier to obtain off-hours time because Class AA and Class A time is snapped up rapidly by the bigger advertisers. In fact, many mail order people prefer to have their commercials broadcast late at night and on

**FIGURE 14-1.  Sample radio station rate cards.**

## RATE CARD #35

Effective April 15, 1981

### SECTION

| | | |
|---|---|---|
| I | Monday THRU Saturday<br>Saturday | 5:00A-10:00A<br>10:00A-9:00P |
| II | Monday THRU Friday<br>Sunday | 3:00P-9:00P<br>8:00A-9:00P |
| III | Monday THRU Friday | 10:00A-3:00P |
| IV | Monday THRU Sunday | 9:00P-1:00A |
| V | Monday THRU Sunday | 1:00A-5:00A |

### 30″ ANNOUNCEMENTS

EIGHTY PERCENT (80%)

### 10″ ANNOUNCEMENTS

FIFTY PERCENT (50%)

### SPONSORSHIPS

NEWS/SPORTS/SPECIAL PROGRAMMING
FIXED POSITION RATES AVAILABLE
UPON REQUEST

### 60″ ANNOUNCEMENTS

| | Section<br>I | Section<br>II | Section<br>III | Section<br>IV | Section<br>V |
|---|---|---|---|---|---|
| Grid 1 | $600 | $250 | $200 | $175 | $100 |
| Grid 2 | $500 | $225 | $180 | $160 | $ 75 |
| Grid 3 | $450 | $200 | $160 | $145 | $ 50 |
| Grid 4 | $425 | $175 | $140 | $130 | |
| Grid 5 | $400 | | | | |

30 Rockefeller Plaza, New York, N.Y. 10020 ■ (212) 664-4444

**Source**: Rate Card /35. WNBC, New York, NY 10020.

Sundays and Saturdays because most people are at home then. The thinking is that listening is so much more relaxed at home—and that the audience will have paper and pencil nearby to jot down box numbers, addresses, or telephone numbers as soon as they are broadcast.

Kenneth J. Costa, Vice President of Marketing Information for the Radio Advertising Bureau (RAB), confirms this thinking with the following comment:

The obvious attribute in radio for direct response is the in-home audience ... because one needs to write down a phone number or mailing address if the

FIGURE 14-1. (continued)

## WOR✧RADIO
### 710
THE HEART OF NEW YORK

RATE CARD #45
EFFECTIVE 7/1/81

| GRIDS | AAA<br>5-10 AM M-SAT | | AA<br>3-8PM M-F | | A<br>10 AM-3PM M-F | | B<br>2-8 PM SAT<br>2-6 PM SUN<br>8-12 PM M-SAT | |
|---|---|---|---|---|---|---|---|---|
| | 60 sec | 30 sec | 60 sec | 30 sec | 60 sec | 30 sec | 60 sec | 30 sec |
| I | 450 | 360 | 215 | 175 | 170 | 135 | 160 | 130 |
| II | 375 | 300 | 175 | 140 | 140 | 110 | 130 | 105 |
| III | 350 | 280 | 160 | 130 | 130 | 105 | 120 | 95 |
| IV | 325 | 260 | 145 | 115 | 120 | 95 | 110 | 90 |
| V | 300 | 240 | 130 | 105 | 110 | 90 | 100 | 80 |

**WOR✧RADIO**
Regular Personalities

- John A. Gambling
- Patricia McCann
- Bernard Meltzer
- Jack O'Brian
- Ralph Snodsmith
- Sherrye Henry
- Arlene Francis
- Carlton Fredericks

- The Fitzgeralds
- Joe Franklin
- John R. Gambling
- Joan Hamburg
- Kathy Novak
- George Meade
- Don Criqui
- Bill Korbel

1. Specially Priced Features– rates provided upon request.
- News
- Weather
- Sports
- Traffic Reports
- Business Reports
- Daily News Tonite Edition
- Ralph Snodsmith
- Bernard Meltzer
- Carlton Fredericks
- Larry King

2. Grids, I, II, III, IV, and V are based on availability at time of sale.
3. Call WOR or your RKO Radio Representative for prevailing grid.

**Source**: Rate Card /45. WOR Radio, New York, NY 10018.

ad is to be fully effective. In-home listening represents 60.7% of the total over the full week ... but it's higher in the evening hours and on weekends.[6]

Radio announcements are usually quite inexpensive to write and prepare. Most direct-response (mail order) commercials are of the "straight-offer" type, where a station announcer delivers the message in a professional manner. The one-minute spot announcement usually contains somewhere between 110 and 145 or so words. If you have not employed the services of an advertising agency, the radio station will often help prepare your radio copy for better results. Sound effects and music (to introduce, end, or accompany a message as background) can also be used, often to good avail.

**Radio Commercials**

Advertisers, of course, use other formats for radio announcements. Otto Kleppner, author of an excellent textbook on advertising, mentions techniques such as the customer interview, the slice-of-life, and the two-announcer approach, along with the straight announcement and other types.[7] In Sol Robinson's informative book on radio advertising, he describes nine different formats (see Figure 14-2).

[6]Letter from Kenneth Costa to author, dated 12 February 1981.
[7]Otto Kleppner, and Norman A. P. Govoni, *Advertising Procedure,* 7th ed. (Englewood Cliffs, N.J.: Prentice-Hall, Inc., 1979), pp. 433–34.

**FIGURE 14-2. Basic types of radio commercials.**

COMMERCIAL TYPES

The nine basic types of commercials now generally used by the radio industry are:

1. **The straight announcement:** A straightforward sales talk or advertising message delivered without the use of gimmicks, sound effects, or musical backgrounds.

2. **The dramatized announcement:** A commercial employing two or more voices presented in the form of a skit or play.

3. **The dialog announcement:** A discussion between two or more persons concerning the product or service that is not delivered in play form.

4. **The comedy announcement:** A commercial in which the sales message is written and presented in a humorous atmosphere.

5. **The "punch" announcement:** Also referred to as the hard-sell. The commercial is emphatic and urgent in its approach. This type of message requires a well-controlled delivery on the part of the announcer.

6. **The soft-sell announcement:** A commercial that is easy going, one that creates an atmosphere of a face-to-face, relaxed conversation.

7. **The singing jingle announcement:** A commercial in which the message is presented entirely in music as part of a song.

8. **The musical announcement:** A spoken commercial which has some music with which to introduce or finish the message, or music playing softly in the background as the message is delivered orally.

9. **Special effects announcement:** Commonly referred to as attention grabbers and used to capture the listener's attention. Often, the echo chamber technique is used during the message, or at the opening or close of the message.

**Source:** Reprinted from *Radio Advertising—How to Sell It & Write It* (#565),, copyright 1974 by TAB BOOKS Inc., Blue Ridge Summit, PA 17214. $12.95 hardbound edition.

## Writing Radio Copy

Most of the copywriting guidelines for the print media covered in Chapter 9 apply as well to the creation of radio copy. After all, good writing is good writing! But this medium of radio differs radically from newspaper and magazine advertising, and from television as well, in two important aspects. First, your listener cannot see the item you are trying to sell. Second, you must rely on spoken words, possibly along with music and/or sound effects, to create in your listener's mind an image of the product, and *then* do an effective selling job thereafter—and all in a whole minute's time (or, perhaps in 90 or 120 seconds)!

That is quite a handicap you will be working under. Yet, what a challenge to your creativity and talent! Still, if you are lucky enough to afford an ad agency, you can turn over the challenge to them.

To help sharpen your skills at writing radio advertising, read the ten suggestions below, and refer to the many "copy hints" in Chapter 9 before you start practicing.

1. Clarify your mental image of your listener before you write a single word.

2. As you start to write—and all along, while working—maintain an open, friendly attitude toward this prospect you are trying to persuade to buy.

3. Do some role-playing; pretend you are talking with someone you know personally. (Keep that image firmly in mind!)

4. Talk to the air around you. You are trying to convince the individual listener, on a one-to-one basis, not an entire audience.

5. Write as you speak, and as you normally do speak. Use a conversational style, and the kinds of simple words and short sentences you use among friends.

6. Realize that your presentation is limited to a matter of seconds; select every single word—and sound—with extreme caution.

7. Important selling points need to be repeated. This is essential for reinforcement in the listener's mind.

8. Clearly state both the selling price of the merchandise and the directions for ordering. Repeat those directions.

9. After finishing your commercial, reread it. Examine every word; ask what contribution it makes to the whole. Then, cut, pare, and polish for more effectiveness with the same total number of words.

10. Make sure you read the commercial aloud, preferably to others. Test it for organization, clarity, possible difficulties in pronunciation, and to see if it can be delivered unhurriedly and smoothly within the allotted time frame.

## TELEVISION

A TV commercial is radio and print advertising—and personal selling as well—all wrapped together in one neat, astounding package. It enters the intimacy of most all American homes through "the tube."

There is no more effective medium for persuading the public to buy.

### Advantages of Television

Although chances are you will not be using television to promote your merchandise for some time, it is never too early to begin learning about what this medium can do for you. Below are some of the reasons why many advertisers prefer television.

#### Strongest appeal to the senses

Because television reaches not one but two of the human senses, sight and sound, its impact is far stronger than those of the other mass media. Then, too, the prevalence of color television in homes today further enhances the impact of a presentation. Television is tops for any product that needs to be demonstrated. We have all seen the closeups on camera, in full color, of a pair of hands demonstrating a special tool for quickly slicing vegetables into different and appetizing shapes; pots and pans with special "nonstick" surfaces arrayed attractively over a tablecloth; a running list of song titles accompanied by music and a series of colorful rustic scenes flashed on the screen to advertise a new long-playing record or tape; and so on.

### Quick response

As with radio, responses to offers made over TV—whether inquiries or actual orders—are immediate. I have been present in a "telephone room" for a direct marketing company where a dozen or more salespeople manned the phones. No sooner is the "number to call" announced and flashed on the screen, then incoming calls begin to light up the switchboard and the room's atmosphere turns from one of quiet anticipation to frenzied excitement.

### Tremendous reach

There are far fewer television than radio stations. Many parts of the country are penetrated by only one or two TV stations, so audiences are sizeable and rather loyal. In the more populated areas viewers can easily number in the hundreds of thousands, and even millions.

## The Negatives

Television is such an attractive medium that you would think the mail order company would jump into it frantically. After all, TV audiences are sizeable and public reaction is quick. But there is one problem sure to make you think, not twice, but three and four times before approaching a single television station—the cost of TV time itself. It is *high!* A single one-minute spot can run from several hundred to a few thousand dollars. Then, there is the cost of producing a television commercial. It is practically inane to consider producing one yourself; generally, you need the help of experts, which could mean more thousands.

You can, of course, do what many direct marketers do—look for "nonprime time" buys at every station you are interested in. Even postmidnight spots can generate business.

Television also has some of the disadvantages found in radio. Like the radio announcement, the TV commercial must be short, and, as soon as it has been broadcast, there is no way the viewer can study the offer. Moreover, some of the audience dislikes commercials. They use the time to run to the kitchen for a snack, or perhaps to flick the dial to see what other channels are showing. Others turn most commercials off mentally.

Another drawback is the fact that most television audiences are broadly heterogeneous. You can't benefit from the selectivity factor, as you can with radio and magazine advertising. As a result, thousands of viewers are not going to be proper targets for your messages.

## Television Time and Commercials

Because it is so infrequently used by the small mail order firm, only a few comments on television marketing are included here.[8] (The interested reader is directed to several of the books in the Suggested Reading section at the end of this chapter.)

Just as in radio, television time is offered to advertisers according to day parts. Top rates are asked for those hours where viewing is

---

[8]Information on television can also be obtained by contacting organizations such as the Television Bureau of Advertising, 485 Lexington Avenue, New York 10017, and the Television Information Office, 745 Fifth Avenue, New York 10022.

traditionally heaviest. These differ, however, from the scheduling of radio stations; class AA time on TV is not "drive time," rather, it is the evening hours. These would usually be the hours between 7:30 and 11:00 P.M.

Again, as in radio, direct marketing people tend to buy spots on local television at times that carry the lowest costs. The commercials are generally 60 seconds in length, although purchasing 90 or 120 seconds is fairly common. Commercials must be professionally done; the use of technical production companies is common.

Copy for the audio, or sound, portion of the commercial script is similar in intent, style, and delivery to radio announcements. There is an additional refinement: it must, of course, tie in completely with what the audience will be viewing on their TV sets.

Action for the viewing, or video, component is also planned in advance by developing "storyboards." These are rough sketches of the various scenes and events, done in sequence, as they will be presented on the screen. Instructions for the camera are also worked out. The final script is divided into two halves, with video instructions on the one side and audio copy on the other.

Television commercials themselves may be created according to different formats, such as is the case in radio. According to the authors of a textbook on advertising, here are nine of the most common formats:[9]

Vignettes
Standup
Song-and-Dance Routine
Mini-Drama/Slice of Life
Testimonial
Dramatization
Demonstration
Documentary
Animation

**SUGGESTED READING**

**Books**

BELLAIRE, ARTHUR, *Controlling Your TV Commercial Costs*. Chicago: Crain Books, 1979.

BOOK, ALBERT C., and NORMAN D. CARY, *Radio and Television Commercial*. Chicago: Crain Books, 1978.

CAPLES, JOHN, *Tested Advertising Methods,* 4th ed. Englewood Cliffs, N.J.: Prentice-Hall, Inc., 1974.

GILSON, CHRISTOPHER, and HAROLD W. BERKMAN, *Advertising: Concepts and Strategies*. New York: Random House, 1980.

HAIGHT, WILLIAM, *Retail Advertising: Management and Technique*. Glenview, Ill.: Scott, Foresman, 1976.

KLEPPNER, OTTO, and NORMAN A. P. GOVONI, collaborator. *Advertising Procedure,* 7th ed. Englewood Cliffs, N.J.: Prentice-Hall, Inc., 1979.

[9]Christopher Gilson and Harold W. Berkman, *Advertising: Concepts and Strategies* (New York: Random House, 1980), p. 436.

Murphy, Jonne, *Handbook of Radio Advertising.* Radnor, Pa.: Chilton, 1980.

National Retail Merchants Association, *How to Profit from Radio Advertising.* New York: NRMA, 1975.

Stone, Bob, *Successful Direct Marketing Methods,* 2nd ed. Chicago: Crain Books, 1979.

Terrell, Neil, *Power Technique of Radio-TV Copywriting.* Blue Ridge Summit, Pa.: Tab Books, 1971.

Wainwright, Charles A., *Television Commercials: How to Create Successful TV Advertising,* rev. ed. New York: Hastings House, 1970.

Wright, John S., and Daniel S. Warner, *Advertising,* 4th ed. New York: McGraw-Hill, 1977.

# 15

## GROWTH
## AND EXPANSION

Congratulations on your success! Through effort and persistence, you have managed to establish and build a strong, exciting new business. It may have taken you only a year, or more likely, three to five years to arrive at this stage. Each day brings bundles of mail, many pieces with checks or money orders. Activity at your place is constant: opening the mail, sorting orders from inquiries and other correspondence, typing shipping labels, pulling merchandise from the shelves to be wrapped for mailing, carting packages to the post office, and so on.

Along the way, you have developed a handsome catalog business, set up toll-free telephone numbers for your customers to call in their orders, instituted a good customer credit program to encourage more buying, experimented with telephone selling to increase catalog distribution, and perhaps even gone into drop-shipping some of your merchandise items for other mail order houses.

By now, you may be so intoxicated with your success that you are thinking "Where do I go from here?"

This is the exact point when you need to ponder alternatives. Would it be best to continue concentration on mail order selling, perhaps moving to larger quarters and automating your handling and processing methods? Should you consider the benefits and drawbacks in seeking more precipitous growth through acquisition of one or more mail order firms? Would a merger make more sense?

You might think of integrating backward a single step, forming your own wholesale establishment so that you can buy your merchandise at lower cost. This move might also enable you to sell your products to other mail order houses or to retail stores. Or you could take two steps backward and set up your own manufacturing facility.

Another choice, and one to consider seriously, is to open a retail store in conjunction with your mail order business. (This is discussed at greater length in Chapter 16.)

But before you decide on any major change of direction, make sure that your current business is in excellent shape, and that you have done everything you can to tone it up so that it runs smoothly without your close personal supervision. Moreover, you need to free yourself from needless interruptions and unimportant daily chores (in this connection, see Figures 15-1 and 15-2).

---

**FIGURE 15-1.  Tips on time management.**

1. Consolidate similar tasks.
2. Tackle tough jobs first.
3. Delegate and develop others.
4. Learn to use idle time.
5. Get control of the paper flow.
6. Avoid the cluttered-desk syndrome.
7. Get started immediately on important tasks.
8. Reduce meeting time.
9. Take time to plan.
10. Learn to say "no."

---

**Source:** H. Kent Baker, "Techniques of Time Management," *Management Aids 239* (Washington, D.C.: Small Business Administration, January 1979), pp. 5–6.

---

**FIGURE 15-2.  Twenty major time wasters.**

*External Time Wasters*

| | |
|---|---|
| Telephone interruptions | Excessive paperwork |
| Meetings | Communication breakdown |
| Visitors | Lack of policies and procedure |
| Socializing | Lack of competent personnel |
| Lack of information | Red tape |

*Internal Time Wasters*

| | |
|---|---|
| Procrastination | Failure to plan |
| Failure to delegate | Poor scheduling |
| Unclear objectives | Lack of self-discipline |
| Failure to set priorities | Attempting to do too much at once |
| Crisis management | Lack of relevant skills |

---

**Source:** H. Kent Baker, "Techniques of Time Management," *Management Aids 239* (Washington, D.C.: Small Business Administration, January 1979), p. 3.

Whether you plan to expand your present business, seek to acquire other mail order operations, or set out in an entirely new direction, one ingredient above all else is essential: *money.* Growth capital is not easy to come by.

You may, of course, be determined to plough back repeatedly every cent of your earned profits to enlarge your firm's treasury over a period of time. This can be done, but it usually takes at least a few years before you can accumulate enough funds to make the attempt.

A sizeable bank loan is a distinct possibility. It wouldn't be, if you had not already been running a business successfully for some time. Banks are wary of the entrepreneur without a track record. If you present the bank official with a well-structured growth plan—one that details your realistic appraisal of the opportunities and includes both past and projected income statements and balance sheets, you may well expect your loan application to be approved. The problem here, however, is the high interest rate you have to pay for your indebtedness, and the strain on your business assets caused by having to return the principal in installments.

You might consider instead searching for investment capital. There are people and firms willing to invest in companies that show promise, in return for some ownership percentage. These "venture capitalists" include private individuals, partnerships, investment banking firms, small business investment companies (licensed by the SBA), and professionally managed firms that work with institutional monies. (See Figure 15-3 for a listing of the contents of the usual venture proposal to be submitted to such people.)

---

**FIGURE 15-3. Elements of a venture proposal.**

ELEMENTS OF A VENTURE PROPOSAL

**Purpose and Objectives**—a summary of the what and why of the project;

**Proposed Financing**—the amount of money you'll need from the beginning to the maturity of the project proposed, how the proceeds will be used, how you plan to structure the financing, and why the amount designated is required;

**Marketing**—a description of the market segment you've got now or plan to get, the competition, the characteristics of the market, and your plans (with costs) for getting or holding the market segment you're aiming at;

**History of the Firm**—a summary of significant financial and organizational milestones, description of employees and employee relations, explanations of banking relationships, recounting of major services or products your firm has offered during its existence, and the like;

**Description of the Product or Service**—a full description of the product (process) or service offered by the firm and the costs associated with it in detail;

**Financial Statements**—both for the past few years and pro forma projections (balance sheets, income statements, and cash flows) for the next 3–5 years,

Growth and Expansion **197**

showing the effect anticipated if the project is undertaken and if the financing is secured (This should include an analysis of key variables affecting financial performance, showing what could happen if the projected level of revenue is not attained.);

**Capitalization**—a list of shareholders, how much is invested to date, and in what form (equity/debt);

**Biographical Sketches**—the work histories and qualifications of key owners/employees.

**Principal Suppliers and Customers**

**Problems Anticipated and Other Pertinent Information**—a candid discussion of any contingent liabilities, pending litigation, tax or patent difficulties, and any other contingencies that might affect the project you're proposing;

**Advantages**—a discussion of what's special about your product, service, marketing plans or channels that gives your project unique leverage.

---

**Source:** LaRue Tone Hosmer, "A Venture Capital Primer for Small Business," *Management Aids No. 235* (Washington, D.C.: Small Business Administration, 1978), p. 3.

## EXPLORING OPPORTUNITIES IN WHOLESALING

Only a modest percentage of manufacturing companies sell their products directly to the consumer. Most prefer to concentrate their energies and assets on the production of goods and leave the problems associated with distribution to intermediaries. These latter firms are specialists who act as "go-betweens" between manufacturer and consumer: brokers, wholesalers, and retailers. Each type performs (and is compensated for) its particular function along the "marketing channel"—that theoretical passageway through which the goods will travel to their end users.

Also known as "distributors" and "jobbers," wholesalers buy products in large quantities at a sizable trade discount from manufacturers, either directly or sometimes through the services of a broker. They take possession of the goods, storing them in warehouses to be held against future orders. Typically, the wholesale establishment needs enough warehouse space to store merchandise for literally hundreds of accounts. And the stock may represent hundreds, and perhaps thousands, of different items, depending on the nature of the lines carried. They sell, of course, to retail stores—and to door-to-door sales organizations, fund-raising outfits, and mail order firms. Some also supply commercial and industrial companies, government agencies and departments, utilities, and other types of institutions.

All of which means—for you—a heavy capital investment: for the warehouse (and its equipment and complement of personnel) and for the inventory you will need to maintain. And that's without mentioning the need for sales representation to take orders! Moreover, the wholesaler typically must extend credit to its retail customers, so you will need sufficient financial strength to be able to maintain hundreds of unpaid balances at all times in your receivables ledger—for periods of up to 90 days, and occasionally longer, without fear of jeopardizing your operation.

Additional requirements for success in the wholesale trades include an efficient order handling and billing system, tight inventory control (usually with the aid of data processing equipment or the services of a computer bureau), and effective warehouse supervision.

A few types of "limited service" wholesalers normally do not maintain warehouses of their own, nor do they call for too heavy an initial investment. Among others, these include the truck jobber and the rack jobber. The first type is generally found in the food industry, visiting supermarkets and groceries regularly to deliver dairy products, fresh fruits and vegetables, and other perishable goods. The rack jobber places display stands or racks in various kinds of stores, fills the racks with merchandise, then periodically services the displays for the retailer. With both types of distributors, credit is seldom extended; the customers pay them on delivery (hence the term "limited service" rather than "full service"). Both the truck and the rack jobber load their trucks or vans each day with goods, at the manufacturer's or distributor's warehouse, then go on their rounds making deliveries.

For further information regarding particular wholesale trades, find out the name and address of the trade association and contact the organization's secretary. (See Figure 15-4 for a partial listing of some wholesale trade associations.)

---

**FIGURE 15-4. Some trade associations for wholesalers.**

American Surgical Trade Association
11 East Adams Street
Chicago Ill. 60603

American Traffic Services Association
525 School Street, S.W.
Washington, D. C. 20024

Appliance Parts Distributors Association, Inc.
228 East Baltimore
Detroit, Mich. 48202

Associated Equipment Distributors
615 West 22nd Street
Oak Brook, Ill. 60521

Association of Footwear Distributors
c/o McBreen/Bonn Shoe Company
310 Peoria Street South
Chicago, Ill. 60607

Association of Institutional Distributors
1750 Old Meadow Road
McLean, Va. 22101

Association of Steel Distributors
2680 N. Moreland Boulevard
Cleveland, Ohio 44120

Automotive Service Industry Association
230 North Michigan Avenue
Chicago, Ill. 60601

Bearing Specialists Association
221 North LaSalle
Chicago, Ill. 60601

Beauty and Barber Supply Institute, Inc.
551 Fifth Avenue, Suite 517
New York, N. Y. 10017

Bicycle Wholesale Distributors Association, Inc.
c/o Hans Johnsen Company
8901 Chancellor Row
Dallas, Tex. 75247

Biscuit and Cracker Distributors Association
111 East Wacker Drive
Chicago, Ill. 60601

Ceramics Distributors of America
410 North Michigan Avenue, Suite 982
Chicago, Ill. 60601

Copper and Brass Warehouse Association, Inc.
1900 Arch Street
Philadelphia, Pa. 19103

Council for Periodical Distributors Association
488 Madison Avenue
New York, N. Y. 10022

Farm Equipment Wholesalers Association
1100 Upper Midwest Building
Minneapolis, Minn. 55401

Federal Wholesale Druggists' Association
393 Seventh Avenue, Room 2018
New York, N. Y. 10001

Flat Glass Marketing Association
1325 Topeka Avenue
Topeka, Kan. 66612

Food Industries Suppliers' Association
P. O. Box 1213
Sedona, Ariz. 86338

Food Service Equipment Distributors
Association
332 South Michigan Avenue
Chicago, Ill. 60604

General Merchandise Distributors Council
2530 Crawford Avenue
Evanston, Ill. 60201

Hobby Industry Association of America, Inc.
200 Fifth Avenue
New York, N. Y. 10010

International Sanitary Supply Association
5330 North Elston Avenue
Chicago, Ill. 60630

Laundry and Cleaners Allied Trades
Association
543 Valley Road
Upper Montclair, N. J. 07043

Lawn and Garden Distributors Association
1900 Arch Street
Philadelphia, Pa. 19103

Material Handling Equipment Distributors
Association
102 Wilmot Road, Suite 210
Deerfield, Ill. 60015

National-American Wholesale Grocers'
Association
51 Madison Avenue
New York, N. Y. 10010

National Association of Aluminum
Distributors
1900 Arch Street
Philadelphia, Pa. 19103

National Association of Brick Distributors
1750 Old Meadow Road
McLean, Va. 22101

National Association of Chemical
Distributors
1406 Third National Building
Dayton, Ohio 45402

National Association of Container
Distributors
c/o M. Jacob and Sons
10101 Lyndon
Detroit, Mich. 48238

National Association of Electrical
Distributors
600 Madison Avenue
New York, N. Y. 10022

Napional Association of Fire Equipment
Distributors
111 East Wacker Drive
Chicago, Ill. 60601

National Association of Floor Covering
Distributors
221 North LaSalle Street
Chicago, Ill. 60601

**Source:** Darlene J. Forte, "Wholesaling," *Small Business Bibliography No. 55* (Washington, D.C.: Small Business Administration, rev. September 1973), p. 5.

**BECOMING A MANUFACTURER**

Although they fulfill somewhat different needs in the distribution sector, both wholesalers and retailers buy finished products, store them for a time, and then resell them. Their major contribution to the economy is that they help propel manufactured goods along the marketing channels toward the end user.

The manufacturing company represents a different type of business. A manufacturer is a producer; that is to say, a firm that makes, forms, constructs, fabricates, or even assembles the finished products that distributors and retail outlets make available to all of us. In effect, they are the sources of supply that provide the momentum to keep our economy humming along.

A typical producer purchases raw materials, semiprocessed or semifinished goods, and/or components. Within the company plant, certain operations are performed with or on these ingredients; examples include extruding, stamping, welding, pressing, shaping, turning, mixing, cutting, and so on. Most often, these processes involve machinery, although frequently operations are performed by hand. The outcome of this activity is finished goods. Subsequently, the products may be packaged, placed into cartons, transferred to the plant's finished goods stock, and eventually sent to the shipping department from which they depart for their destinations.

Why should the mail order company consider this avenue? Occasionally, the firm will come across a product—or a line of products—that enjoys an immediate and resounding sales success. Its potential seems exciting. It may be that by investing in a piece of equipment the item can be produced internally at a much lower cost per unit than the firm has been paying the supplier. Moreover, the same machine might be able to produce other salable products. A big benefit here is that the firm now controls the supply of this merchandise; you need not worry about being out of stock or obtaining the kind of markup on your goods that you need. Then, too, if you can manufacture greater quantities than you can use, there is the opportunity of selling the excess to other mail order dealers or to retail stores.

Indeed, you may already be in some phase of manufacturing. If you have been selling handicrafts, bagging or packing merchandise, making rubber stamps, mixing chemicals, cutting patterns, or stringing beads for bracelets and necklaces, you already are a producer. Bringing in machinery or equipment may eventually cut your costs and sharply increase your output.

Setting yourself up properly in manufacturing calls for a considerable investment in a suitable plant, for machinery, equipment, and supplies, in the materials you will need for producing your line of merchandise, and perhaps for skilled or semiskilled workers to operate the machines. You must think about plant layout, production scheduling and control (include setting production standards), and efficient stockkeeping procedures.

The following short list of manufacturing possibilities may give you some worthwhile ideas.

| | |
|---|---|
| advertising specialties | embroidery |
| apparel | foods |
| athletic equipment | furniture |
| athletic goods | garden supplies |
| automotive care products | giftware |
| baked goods | glassware |
| bathroom accessories | greeting cards |
| beaded novelties | handicrafts |
| beauty aids and supplies | health foods |
| books | health-related equipment |
| business cards | hobby kits |
| canned preserves | hobby supplies |
| ceramic items | household furnishings |
| chemicals | jewelry |
| cleaning compounds | kitchen utensils |
| cosmetics | knitting supplies |
| curtains and draperies | lighting fixtures |
| decorative accessories | lubricants |
| dolls | machinery and equipment |
| electrical supplies | marine supplies |
| electronic games | maternity clothes |

| | |
|---|---|
| metal products | plastic products |
| models and kits | pool chemicals |
| molded novelties | printed specialties |
| monogrammed items | printing |
| neckties | religious articles |
| needlework kits | signs and posters |
| paints | slippers |
| paper goods | sporting goods |
| party supplies | sports equipment |
| pet supplies | toiletries |
| photography | tools |
| | toys |

## BUILDING YOUR ORGANIZATION

Whatever the direction you choose, you need to start thinking about putting together an organization that can deal effectively with an expanding list of duties and responsibilities. It must be strong enough to ensure the continued and successful growth of your company.

But right from the beginning, be cautious! Hire only when you must; you will be amazed at how much you need to do in additional sales to cover even the seemingly minor expense of a single part-time worker. For the sake of illustration, assume that your end-of-year gross margin percentage is 40 percent of sales. (Recall that gross margin, or gross profit, is what you have earned after subtracting cost of goods sold from sales figures.) In concrete terms, this means that only forty cents of every dollar you take in can be used to cover your overhead expenses and produce a few cents of profit. The other 60 cents must go to pay for the merchandise you have sold. Now, you consider hiring a full-time, entry level employee at a modest salary of, say, $175 a week. When you add to this expense the worker's fringe benefits and your contribution to the federal government of a matching percentage of his or her social security tax, your total outlay may exceed $11,000 annually. Putting those two data together, forty cents out of every sales dollar and $11,000 a year, you will need to do some $27,500 more in sales over the year just to break even on this cost of adding one employee!

## What Types of Job Openings

If you elect the wholesale route, an immediate need will be for one or more clerical employees to handle orders, type invoices, answer correspondence and the telephone, file, and so on. On the outside, you will need some sort of sales representation even if you plan on doing much of the selling yourself. You will need someone to oversee your outgoing shipments and arrange for their transportation, and another person to supervise incoming deliveries of merchandise to your warehouse. In these two positions, you have the beginnings of the shipping and receiving departments. You will need warehouse workers to load and unload stock and to pick orders; drivers if you plan to use your own delivery trucks instead of public carriers; and operators if you use fork-lifts or other types of heavy equipment within the warehouse. Eventually, you may require a warehouse manager, one or more bookkeepers to handle your accounts and payroll, and a credit manager to watch your receivables.

If you chose instead to go into manufacturing, you need to fill many of the same kinds of positions. In addition, you have to consider adding production staff, like expeditors and machine operators, maintenance employees, an experienced purchasing agent, and perhaps a quality control supervisor.

On the other hand, launching a retail store calls for little more than one or a few salesclerks and a stock clerk (at least, until your business has grown substantially and you begin to need more specialized personnel).

These are the major policy areas in which you must make decisions regarding your personnel:

**Personnel Management**

- Recruitment and selection
- Pay plan
- Training
- Supervision
- Management development
- Compliance with labor legislation

For more detailed study of these areas, review the SBA publications on personnel aspects in the bibliography at the end of this chapter. You can also read several books on personnel management available in many public libraries.

### Recruitment and selection

Analyze the job requirements for each position you anticipate in your company, then set up job specifications for them. In this way, you will have a clear idea of the kind of individual you should be searching for to fill an opening. Sources of prospective employees include newspaper advertisements (classified for many jobs, display ads for higher level positions), neighborhood schools and colleges, both public and private employment agencies, recommendations from other employees, customers, and friends, posted signs, and "walk-ins" or "write-ins."

To help you select new employees from among the applicants, introduce some professionalism into your selection procedure. Use those familiar tools: the employment application, the personal interview, reference checking, and, possibly for some positions, standardized performance tests. You can purchase employment application forms at your local business stationery store. Depending on the nature and level of the job opening, one or more personal interviews may be indicated. These are not only useful for broadening your perceptions of the information shown on the application, but also for gaining valuable insights into the applicant's personality, depth of knowledge and/or training, command of the English language, self-control, and other aspects. The interview is also an excellent vehicle for telling the job hunter about your company, as well as what his or her prospects with you may be.

*Pay plan*

You must devise the kind of pay scale that will appropriately reward your employees for their work. For most workers, this means a daily wage rate or a weekly salary that compares favorably with those earned by those in equivalent positions with competitive firms. You strive to keep them satisfied so that they remain in your employ, rather than seek greener pastures elsewhere. (An excellent SBA booklet is available that will help you work up a wages and salary administration package for your company—Gene F. Scollard's "Setting Up a Pay System," *Management Aid No. 241,* published March 1979.)

Along with the basic plan, you must decide on the kinds of fringe benefits to offer that will round out the total employee compensation program.

---

**FIGURE 15-5. Required payroll information.**

Federal regulations do not prescribe the form in which your payroll records must be kept, but the records should include the following information and documents:

1. The names, address, and Social Security number of each employee.

2. The amount and date of each wage payment and the period covered by the payment.

3. The amount of wages subject to withholding included in each payment.

4. The amount of withholding tax collected and the date it was collected.

5. If applicable, the reason that the payable amount is less than the total payment.

6. Your employer identification number.

7. Duplicate copies of returns filed.

8. Dates and amounts of deposits made with government depositories.

9. The periods for which your employees are paid by you while they are absent because of sickness or personal injury, and the amount and weekly rates of the payments.

10. Your employees' withholding exemption certificates.

11. Any agreement between you and an employee for withholding of additional amount of tax.

You will also have to keep these documents and records.

1. Copies of statements furnished by employees relating to nonresident alien status, residence in Puerto Rico or Virgin Islands, or residence or physical presence in a foreign country.

2. The value and date of any noncash compensation paid to a retail salesperson from which no tax was withheld.

3. The dates in each calendar quarter on which an employee performed services not in the course of your trade or business, and the amount you paid for these services.

4. Copies of employees' statements of tips they received in the course of their employment, unless this information is reported on another item in this list.

5. Employees' requests to have their withholding tax computed on the basis of their cumulative wages.

Regarding Social Security (FICA) taxes, you must maintain these additional records.

1. The amount of wages that are subject to FICA tax.

2. The amount and date of FICA employee tax collected for each payment and the date collected.

3. If applicable, the reason that the total wage payment and the taxable amount are not equal.

Under the Federal Unemployment Tax Act, you must maintain these records.

1. The total amount you paid your employees during the calendar year.

2. The amount of the wages subject to the unemployment tax, and, if applicable, why this amount differs from the total compensation.

3. The amount you paid into the state unemployment fund, showing the payments deducted or to be deducted, and the payments not deducted or to be deducted from your employees' wages.

**Source:** Robert C. Ragan, "Financial Recordkeeping for Small Stores," *Small Business Management Series No. 32* (Washington, D.C.: Small Business Administration, 1976), pp. 121–23.

*Training, supervision, management development*

New employees require indoctrination into the ways of your organization. They need to know your firm's history, the kinds and quality of your products, your pricing and promotion approaches, what their responsibilites will be and who they will report to, existing personnel policies and procedures, opportunities for personal growth and promotion, and the like. All this should be taken care of immediately after they have been hired. Preferably, you should conduct this initial training personally, at least until the size of your organization is such that a specialist must be hired to take over this function to enable you to devote your time to other aspects of your business.

Consider assigning each new worker to a more experienced person holding the same position; in this way, the job of breaking in the newcomer becomes easier. Another valuable assist could come from developing and distributing a good employee handbook.[1]

To ensure organizational flexibility, along with a healthy level of productivity, prepare intermediate and advanced training programs for the future. Use them to broaden the existing skills of your employees, to prepare people for promotion to the supervisory ranks

[1]Obtain a copy of Management Aids No. 197, "Pointers on Preparing an Employee Handbook," from the Small Business Administration.

or for transfer to other departments, and to train others to fill your top management slots. Familiarize yourself with management training methods, perhaps by taking one or two relevant courses at a nearby college of business administration or by attending one of the intensive, five-day programs for top managers offered by the American Management Associations.

Work on your own self-development, too. Read all the books you can find on personnel administration and on the principles of management. Strive also to improve your own human relations skills; in the final analysis, running a company successfully means working effectively with people to get the required work done (see Figure 15-6).

### Labor legislation

Seek your lawyer's counsel regarding the many labor laws and regulations with which you need to comply. If you employ people, you are bound by both federal and state legislation, and regulated by local ordinances as well. You must become familiar with the major provisions, and their implications for your company, of such laws as:

- Fair Labor Standards Act
- Equal Pay Act
- Civil Rights Act
- Age Discrimination in Employment Act
- Equal Employment Opportunity Act
- Pension Reform Act
- Occupational Safety and Health Act
- National Labor Relations Act

---

**FIGURE 15-6. Some suggestions for improving your human relations.**

1. Improve your own general understanding of human behavior.
2. Accept the fact that others do not always see things as you do.
3. In any differences of opinion, consider the possibility that you may not have the right answer.
4. Show your employees that you are interested in them and that you want their ideas on how conditions can be improved.
5. Treat your employees as individuals; never deal with them impersonally.
6. Respect differences of opinion.
7. Insofar as possible, give explanations for management actions.
8. Provide information and guidance on matters affecting employees' security.
9. Make reasonable efforts to keep jobs interesting.
10. Encourage promotion from within.
11. Express appreciation publicly for jobs well done.
12. Offer criticism privately, in the form of constructive suggestions for improvement.
13. Train supervisors to be concerned about the people they supervise, the same as they would be about merchandise or materials or equipment.
14. Keep your staff up-to-date on matters that affect them.

15. Quell false rumors, and provide correct information.
16. Be fair!

---

**Source:** Martin M. Bruce, "Human Relations in Small Business," *Small Business Management Series No. 3,* 3rd ed. (Washington, D.C.: Small Business Administration, 1969), pp. 14–15.

BALLOU, RONALD H., *Basic Business Logistics: Transportation, Materials Management, Physical Distribution.* Englewood Cliffs, N.J.: Prentice-Hall, Inc., 1978.

BRANNEN, WILLIAM H., *Successful Marketing for Your Small Business.* Englewood Cliffs, N.J.: Prentice-Hall, Inc., 1978.

BUFFA, ELWOOD S., *Basic Production Management,* 2nd ed. New York: Wiley, 1975.

BURSTINER, IRVING, *The Small Business Handbook: A Comprehensive Guide to Starting and Running Your Own Business.* Englewood Cliffs, N.J.: Prentice-Hall, Inc., 1979.

DANENBURG, WILLIAM P., RUSSELL L. MONCRIEF, and WILLIAM E. TAYLOR, *Introduction to Wholesale Distribution.* Englewood Cliffs, N.J.: Prentice-Hall, Inc., 1978.

HEDRICK, FLOYD D., *Purchasing Management in the Smaller Company.* New York: American Management Associations, 1971.

KIRKPATRICK, C. A., and FREDERICK A. RUSS, *Salesmanship,* 6th ed. Cincinnati: South-Western, 1976.

LEE, LAMAR, JR., and DONALD W. DOBLER, *Purchasing and Materials Management,* 3rd ed. New York: McGraw-Hill, 1977.

LINNEMAN, ROBERT E., *Shirt-Sleeve Approach to Long-Range Planning for the Smaller Growing Corporation.* Englewood Cliffs, N.J.: Prentice-Hall, Inc., 1980.

LOCK, DENNIS, *Factory Administration Handbook.* New York: Beekman, 1976.

MOORE, FRANKLIN G., and THOMAS HENDRICK, *Production/Operations Management,* 7th ed. Homewood, Ill.: Irwin, 1977.

PEDERSON, CARLTON A., and MILBURN D. WRIGHT, *Selling: Principles and Methods,* 6th ed. Homewood, Ill.: Irwin, 1978.

ROBBINS, STEPHEN P., *Personnel: The Management of Human Resources.* Englewood Cliffs, N.J.: Prentice-Hall, Inc., 1978.

RUSSELL, FREDERIC A., FRANK H. BEACH, and RICHARD D. BUSKIRK, *Textbook of Salesmanship,* 10th ed. New York: McGraw-Hill, 1978.

SIPPL, CHARLES, and FRED DAHL, *Computer Power for the Small Business.* Englewood Cliffs, N.J.: Prentice-Hall, Inc., 1979.

STANLEY, RICHARD E., *Promotion: Advertising, Publicity, Personal Selling, Sales Promotion.* Englewood Cliffs, N.J.: Prentice-Hall, Inc., 1977.

*Management aids*

#41 ODELL, CHARLES E., "How the Public Employment Service Helps Small Business," reprinted January 1974.

#171 MATTS, REX, "How to Write a Job Description," revised September 1976.

#179 GOLDE, ROGER A., "Breaking the Barriers to Small Business Planning," reprinted May 1977.

#186 SMITH, LEONARD J., "Checklist for Developing a Training Program," reprinted January 1977.

#190 LOEN, RAYMOND O., "Measuring the Performance of Salesmen," reprinted January 1977.

#193 LENNON, VICTOR A., "What Is the Best Selling Price?" reprinted June 1974.

#196 GRUBB, KENNETH, "Tips on Selecting Salesmen," reprinted May 1974.

#200 BOBROW, EDWIN E., "Is the Independent Sales Agent for You?" reprinted January 1977.

#201 WEBER, JR., FRED I., "Locating or Relocating Your Business," reprinted January 1974.

#206 FELLER, JR., JACK H., "Keep Pointed Toward Profit," reprinted April 1974.

#207 KLINE, JOHN B., "Pointers on Scheduling Production," reprinted January 1977.

#212 MAYER, RAYMOND R., "The Equipment Replacement Decision," reprinted February 1974.

#218 Office of Management Assistance, "Business Plan for Small Manufacturers," July 1973.

#220 WOELFEL, CHARLES J., "Basic Budgets for Profit Planning," 1979.

#222 Institute of Life Insurance, "Business Life Insurance," March 1975.

#234 GOULET, PETER G., "Attacking Business Decision Problems with Breakeven Analysis," March 1978.

#235 Hosmer, LaRue Tone, "A Venture Capital Primer for Small Business," August 1978.

#236 SMITH, IVAN C., "Tips on Getting More for Your Marketing Dollar," December 1978.

#238 MARIS, TERRY L., and ROBERT L. MATHIS, "Organizing and Staffing a Small Business," January 1979.

#239 BAKER, H. KENT, "Techniques of Time Management," January 1979.

#240 Staff Members, "Introduction to Patents," revised January 1979.

#241 SCOLLARD, GENE F., "Setting Up a Pay System," March 1979.

#243 Office of Management Information and Training, "Setting Up a Quality Control System," April 1979.

#244 LEACH, GORDON L., "Product Safety Checklist," April 1979.

#245 KONIKOW, ROBERT B., "Exhibiting at Trade Shows," January 1979.

#246 GOULD, DOUGLAS P., "Developing New Accounts," May 1979.

#250 KRAMER, EDWARD C., "Can You Use a Minicomputer?" October 1979.

## Small business bibliographies

#9 DEBOER, LLOYD M., "Marketing Research Procedures," revised December 1974.

#12 Office of Management Information and Training, "Statistics and Maps for National Market Analysis," revised August 1974.

#55 FORTE, DARLENE J., "Wholesaling," revised September 1973.

#58 CARBERRY, FRANK J., "Automation for Small Offices," reprinted July 1973.

#82 LOEN, RAYMOND O., "Personnel Management," reprinted January 1974.

#89 COX, KEITH K., JAMES E. STAFFORD, AND ART PALMER, "Marketing for Small Business," revised November 1978.

## Small marketers aids

#101 SERIF, MED, "Pointers for Developing Your Top Assistant," reprinted April 1974.

#122 VANDEMARK, ROBERT L., "Controlling Inventory in Small Wholesale Firms," September 1966.

#131 COSTELLO, JR., FRANK J., "Retirement Plans for Self-Employed Owner Managers," reprinted April 1974.

#132 MURPHY, BETTY S., "The Federal Wage-Hour Law in Small Firms," revised December 1974.

#135 STONE, MORRIS, "Arbitration: Peace-Maker in Small Business," June 1968.

#147 MURPHY, JOHN F., "Sound Cash Management and Borrowing," reprinted July 1977.

#148 GREENE, MARK R., "Insurance Checklist for Small Business," July 1971.

#149 CALEY, JOHN D., "Computers for Small Business: Service Bureau or Time-Sharing," reprinted August 1973.

#153 Office of Management Assistance, "Business Plan for Small Service Firms," October 1973.

#163 GARVEY, L. KIM, "Public Relations for Small Business," December 1977.

#167 LAUMER, JR., J. FORD, JAMES R. HARRIS, and HUGH J. GUFFEY, JR., "Learning About Your Market," April 1979.

## Small business management series

To Order from the
Superintendent of
Documents

#15 ZWICK, JACK, "A Handbook of Small Business Finance," *Small Business Management Series No. 15*, 8th ed. Washington, D.C.: Small Business Administration, 1975. (Stock #045-000-00139-3.)

#22 SEMON, THOMAS T., "Practical Business Use of Government Statistics," *Small Business Management Series No. 22*. Washington, D.C.: Small Business Administration, 1975. (Stock #045-000-00131-8.)

#26 LOEN, ERNEST L., "Personnel Management Guides for Small Business," *Small Business Management Series No. 26*. Washington, D.C.: Small Business Administration, 1974. (Stock #045-000-00126-1.)

#27 MILLER, ROBERT W., "Profitable Community Relations for Small Business," *Small Business Management Series No. 27*. Washington, D.C.: Small Business Administration, 1961. (Stock #045-000-00033-8.)

**16**

## GETTING INTO STORE RETAILING

A common route for the successful mail order company, especially one that deals in consumer goods, is to establish a retail outlet. This is a natural direction for growth because in selling merchandise by mail you are already involved in running a retail operation. You sell individual items to individual consumers—a "store by mail."

This type of expansion has its advantages. You continue your mail order activity at the store address, given a large room or, even better, several rooms in back of your store, or in the basement. This means your two businesses will then share one rent along with other overhead costs. But your store will complement your mail order operation in other ways, and vice versa. You will be able to use some merchandise in both, turn slow-sellers into fast-movers by running special promotions, add the names and addresses of store customers to your mailing list to make additional sales, order stock in larger quantities to obtain larger discounts, and so on.

You should, however, try to keep separate records. By regarding each business as a distinct "profit center," you can keep on top of what's happening and make the kinds of decisions that will ensure end-of-year profits in both.

You know little about running a store, you say? Nonsense! You haven't owned one before? So what?

**INDEPENDENT RETAILING**

How many different stores have you visited or shopped in during your lifetime? So many that you must be aware by now of what customers expect to see and find in a store, and the kinds of attention and service they want from the merchant. Compare your present thoughts with those of some 195 small store merchants who offered their opinions as to why customers liked to shop at their outlets (see Table 16-1).

Census data indicate that there are close to two million retail establishments in the United States. Retail stores account for about one-half of these, once we cull out of the government's statistics the figures for restaurants and bars (368,000), gas stations (176,000), motor vehicle dealers (68,000), and a few other types—along with the so-called nonstore retailers (mail order houses, direct selling companies, and vending machine operators).[1]

**Table 16-1.**
REASONS WHY PEOPLE SHOP AT SMALL STORES.

| Reasons | Stores Reporting | % of Total |
|---|---|---|
| Good treatment, personal attention | 93 | 47.7% |
| Convenient location | 89 | 45.6 |
| Reasonable prices | 59 | 30.3 |
| Quality merchandise | 57 | 29.2 |
| Breadth, depth of product mix | 46 | 23.6 |
| Prompt service | 39 | 20.0 |
| Reliable reputation | 27 | 13.9 |
| Miscellaneous service* | 24 | 12.3 |
| Attractiveness of store, displays | 15 | 7.7 |
| Cleanliness of store | 11 | 5.6 |
| Extension of credit | 10 | 5.1 |

*Includes prompt deliveries, good refund and exchange policy, alterations, guarantees, etc.
**Source:** Irving Burstiner, "The Small Retailer and His Problems," *Journal of Business Education*, (March 1975), p. 244.

Although they account for a sizable share of total annual retail sales in the country, department stores, supermarkets, discount houses, and chain stores are numerically in the minority. The vast majority of American stores are small, single-unit establishments run by independent merchants. These people are a hardy, courageous lot. They work long hours, diligently applying their energies and talents to the daily decisions that must be made. Some prosper indeed; most earn a good livelihood, managing to keep their business in the black year after year despite the inroads of inflation, economic downturns, and the pressures of ever-present competition.

These are the people you will be joining.

Is there room for another store? Certainly! There are so many varieties of stores that you may be surprised to learn how few exist of a particular type. For example, the 1977 census of business indicated fewer than 7,000 stationery stores in operation during the entire year across the country. Luggage and leather goods stores numbered only 2,600; bookstores, some 12,800; and hardware stores, admittedly a prevalent type, only 26,500.

[1]U.S. Bureau of the Census, *Statistical Abstract of the United States: 1979,* 100th ed. (Washington, D.C.: Department of Commerce, 1979).

Naturally, you would seek a location for your new store where you can attract enough of the kinds of customers who will buy your merchandise—and where the competition is light or nonexistent.

It is often best to carry over into your new retail operation the kinds of merchandise you have had success with in mail order. If, for instance, you have been selling books by mail (a popular line for direct marketers), opening a traditional bookstore or a used book exchange would seem a logical choice. Following along the same line of reasoning, mail order experience with giftwares or household items ought to lead to the launching of a souvenir and gift shop, a variety store, or even a hardware store. Compatible or complementary lines may, of course, be added to your basic merchandise lines.

Only a cursory treatment of the salient aspects of retailing can be accorded in this chapter. Check into the references listed in the Suggested Reading section at the end. Most of the government publications shown deal with the retailing environment; this is so because the majority of the 350,000 or so new businesses that are started up every year are retail establishments.

## YOUR RETAIL BUSINESS PLAN

In Chapter 6, we discussed an outline designed to help you work up a business plan for your new mail order enterprise. Granted, it was hard work preparing all the details, but it allowed you to chart the course that established you in mail order marketing.

Now you are faced with the problem of generating a second plan. Starting a retail store is another, and quite different, business. Nevertheless, if you want to improve your chances for succeeding in this new venture, plug away at it. And do it well!

First, look over the chart in Figure 16-1, an overview of what retail store management is all about. It contains all the areas you need to be concerned with. Then check the more detailed outline in Figure 16-2. This information, as presented, suggests that you prepare five subplans, all part of your overall retail plan. Get a notebook, preferably a looseleaf type, and divide it into five sections. Use a separate page for each of the entries shown in Figure 16-2 under the major headings. Of course, you may need to add more pages to some of them, which is why a looseleaf book is best. And along with your planning, continually ask yourself the "Five W's" to help shape your decisions.

## YOUR STORE LOCATION

Like many other aspiring mail order entrepreneurs, you most likely initiated your business from your home and in your spare time. Then, when business activity outgrew the limited confines of your attic, basement, or spare room (if you were lucky enough to have one), you rented an office nearby. Location was not too important at the time, so long as it was convenient for you to get to and the landlord proposed a rental figure that you could tolerate.

Finding a store location is another matter entirely. The majority of store types depend heavily on the traffic that passes by. Mostly, this is pedestrian traffic, although vehicular traffic can also be important in many situations. You need to go where the traffic is, for location is often the single most important factor in a store's success or failure.

**FIGURE 16-1.  Retail store management.**

| | | |
|---|---|---|
| RETAIL STORE MANAGEMENT<br><br>Planning,<br><br>Organizing,<br><br>Directing,<br><br>and<br><br>Controlling | THE STORE | Store front<br>Decor<br>Layout<br>Fixturization<br>Maintenance and so on |
| | STORE PERSONNEL | Recruitment<br>Selection<br>Induction<br>Training<br>Supervision and so on |
| | BUYING | Determining needs<br>Locating sources<br>Negotiating prices<br>Scheduling deliveries |
| | MERCHANDISING | Unit control<br>Dollar control<br>Taking inventory<br>Pricing<br>Markdowns and so on |
| | CUSTOMER SERVICES | Store hours<br>Delivery<br>Wrapping<br>Returns<br>Credit and so on |
| | PROMOTION | Advertising<br>Window displays<br>Interior displays<br>Salespersonship<br>Publicity and so on |
| | SYSTEMS | Accounting methods<br>Sales systems<br>Expense control<br>and so on |

**Source:** From the book, *The Small Business Handbook* by Irving Burstiner. © 1979 by Prentice-Hall, Inc. Published by Prentice-Hall, Inc., Englewood Cliffs, New Jersey 07632.

**FIGURE 16-2.  Business plan for a retail store.**

A. My Store Plan
    1. Thorough description of my location.
    2. Analysis of my competition.
    3. What my customers are like.
    4. Terms of lease.
    5. Licenses, permits, local ordinances, and other legal requirements.

6. The store front.
7. Interior decor.
8. Store layout.
9. Store lighting.
10. Show windows.
11. Fixturization.
12. Equipment.
13. Supplies.

B. My Stock Plan
1. Merchandise line(s) to be carried.
2. Depth of merchandise offerings.
3. Merchandise resources: list of suppliers' names and addresses, terms, credit and delivery policies, and the like.
4. Price ranges; quality levels.
5. Opening stock.
6. Expected turnover rate (overall; by classification).
7. Markdown and discount policies.
8. Inventory and stock control method.
9. Customer services.
10. Customer credit extension program.

C. My Promotion Plan
1. One-year promotional calendar.
2. Display and advertising budgets.
3. Window display program.
4. Interior display program.
5. Selection of advertising media.
6. Cooperative advertising efforts.
7. Public relations program.
8. Sales training program.

D. My Personnel Plan
1. Employee needs assessment.
2. Job specifications for all positions.
3. Sources of prospective employees.
4. Compensation plans and pay guidelines.
5. Employee benefits to offer.
6. Promotional ladder.
7. Training program.

E. My Financial Plan
1. Pro forma accounting statements (P&Ls, balance sheets).
2. Bookkeeping method to be followed.
3. Cash flow projections.
4. Payroll and other record-keeping approaches.
5. Insurance program.
6. Internal risk-reduction approaches.
7. Tax liability and responsibilities.
8. Bank relations.

**Source**: From the book, *Run Your Own Store: From Raising the Money to Counting the Profits* by Irving Burstiner, Ph.D. © 1981 by Prentice-Hall, Inc. Published by Prentice-Hall, Inc., Englewood Cliffs, New Jersey 07632.

Choosing a location involves three sequential decisions:

1. Picking out the right town or city for your business and for *you*.

2. Determining the right retail area in that town or city.
3. Getting the right store site within that area.

A helpful guide for the new retailer who is searching for a store location is the material in Figure 16-3, reproduced from the SBA's "Business Plan for Retailers." You can also profit by looking over the checklist in Figure 16-4 from another SBA publication.

---

**FIGURE 16-3. Selecting a store location.**

### SECTION ONE—DETERMINING THE SALES POTENTIAL

In retail business, your sales potential depends on location. Like a tree, a store has to draw its nourishment from the area around it. The following questions should help you to work through the problem of selecting a profitable location.

In what part of the city or town will you locate?
In the downtown business section?
In the area right next to the downtown business area?
In a residential section of the town?
On the highway outside of town?
In the suburbs?
In a suburban shopping center?
List the reasons for your choice here:

I plan to locate in _____ because

_____

_____

_____

_____

_____

What is the competition in the area you have picked?
The number of stores there that handle my lines of merchandise is _____
How many of these stores look prosperous?_____
How many look as though they are barely getting by? _____
How many similar stores went out of business in this area last year? _____
How many new stores opened up in the last year? _____
What price line does competition carry? _____
Which store or stores in the area will be your biggest competition? _____

_____

List the reason for your opinion here: _____

_____

**FIGURE 16-3. (continued)**

Is the area in which you plan to locate supported by a strong economic base? For example, are nearby industries working fulltime? Only parttime? Did any industries go out of business in the past several months? Are new industries scheduled to open in the next several months?

Write your opinion of the area's economic base and your reason for that opinion here. _____

_____

_____

When you find a store building that seems to be what you need, answer the following questions:

Is the neighborhood starting to run down? _____

*Is the neighborhood new and on the way up? _____

Are any super highways or throughways planned for the neighborhood? _____

Is street traffic fairly heavy all day? _____

Do the pedestrians who pass the building look as though they would be prospects for your store? _____

How close is the building to the bus line or other public transportation? _____

Are there adequate parking facilities convenient to the building? _____

Are the sidewalks in good repair? _____

Is the street lighting good? _____

Is the parking lot well-lighted if you are open at night? _____

What is the occupancy history of this store building? Does the store have a reputation for failures? (that is, stores opening and closing after a short time? _____

If the store has housed several failures in recent years, can you find out why they failed? Was it the location, excessive rent, or some other factor? _____

What rent will you have to pay each month? _____

What is the physical condition of the store? _____

What services, if any, does the landlord provide? _____

_____

What are the terms of the lease? _____

_____

I expect to do $_____ in annual sales in this location.

*Finally,* when you think you have solved the site-location of your new business, ask your banker to recommend the three people who in his opinion know the most about locations in your line of business. Contact these people and listen to their advice, weigh what they say, then decide.

---

*The local Chamber of Commerce may have information on the population of the area or be able to refer you to other local sources. Census Tracts on Population, published by the Bureau of Census, may also be useful. Other sources of such marketing statistics are trade associations and directories, such as, THE EDITOR & PUBLISHER MARKET GUIDE. Published annually in September. $15. Editor & Publisher Co., 850 Third Avenue, New York, N. Y. 10022
SURVEY OF BUYING POWER. Published annually in June. $10. Sales Management Inc., 630 Third Avenue, New York, N. Y. 10017. (The latter breaks population down into eight age groups, to mention two examples, 18 to 24 years old and 25 to 34 years old.)

**Source:** Office of Management Assistance, Small Business Administration, "Business Plan for Retailers," *Small Marketers Aid No. 150* (Washington, D.C.: Small Business Administration, reprinted March 1973), pp. 4–5.

**FIGURE 16-4.   Store Location: some considerations.**

- How much retail, office, storage or workroom space do you need?
- Is parking space available and adequate?
- Do you require special lighting, heating or cooling, or other installations?
- Will your advertising expenses be much higher if you choose a relatively remote location?
- Is the area served by public transportation?
- Can the area serve as a source of supply of employees?
- Is there adequate fire and police protection?
- Will sanitation or utility supply be a problem?
- Is external lighting in the area adequate to attract evening shoppers and make them feel safe?
- Are customer restroom facilities available?
- Is the store easily accessible?
- Does the store have awnings or decks to provide shelter during bad weather?
- Will crime insurance be prohibitively expensive?
- Do you plan to provide pick up or delivery?
- Is the trade area heavily dependent on seasonal business?
- Is the location convenient to where you live?
- Do the people you want for customers live nearby?
- Is the population density of the area sufficient?

**Source:** Jeffrey P. Davidson, "Store Location: 'Little Things' Mean a Lot," *Small Marketers Aid No. 168* (Washington, D.C.: Small Business Administration, June 1979), pp. 5–6.

The Retail
Structure

Although you can readily find an occasional store sitting all by itself in any city of your choice, as is the case with some discount houses or furniture stores located along major highways, most experienced merchants prefer to go where the action is. They know that surrounding stores act as magnets, drawing shoppers to a particular area. The greater the number, and the better the "mix," of stores, the heavier the traffic will be. They benefit by this increase, for many of the shoppers may visit their stores, too.

A convenient way of categorizing the retail sections is to break them down, first of all, into two main classifications: the "old type" or "unplanned" groupings and the more modern "planned" retail centers. The former term embraces the downtown area's business section, secondary business districts, neighborhood shopping streets, and small "store clusters." These types grew over the decades without the benefit of any overall coordination, in the sense that many different landlords and builders may have been involved in their development.

In the downtown section, the central business district is where the department stores, banks, largest buildings, and main branches of chain stores are usually found. Both pedestrian and automobile traffic are heavy, and store rents are exceedingly high. (Of course, this may not be true where the area has been seriously depressed or has deteriorated badly.) Usually found along the main roads leading out of the downtown area toward the outskirts of the city, there may be several secondary business districts. Stores there are much like those of the central business district. They are, however, ordinarily smaller in size, have less window frontage, and carry a more limited selection of merchandise than their counterparts downtown. The streets are normally busy during the daytime, and the merchants fare nicely. Rents run rather high, but are considerably less than those of the central business district.

Neighborhood shopping streets are found throughout the city and its suburbs. They attract customers from surrounding apartment houses and homes up to a few city blocks away in all directions. Although there are some specialty and shopping goods stores in these areas, as in the business districts, a greater percentage of the shops sell convenience goods. Here are fruit and vegetable stands, bakeries, pizza parlors, meat stores, independent pharmacies, hardware stores, and so on; also a number of service-type stores, like launderettes, beauty parlors, barber shops, and the like.

A final type characterizing the older retail structure of the city is the store cluster. There may be many of these: groups of as few as three or four stores to as many as eight or 10. Usually, they are nestled among rows of private homes or in a block of large apartment buildings.

Shopping center locations, the "newer" types, comprise three basic kinds. Smallest of all is the neighborhood shopping center, where one typically finds a row of small stores with one larger, "traffic-builder" store at one end. Frequently, this is a supermarket, variety store, or drugstore. Neighborhood centers average 40,000 to 50,000 square feet in total area and have parking facilities for anywhere from several dozen to as many as 150 automobiles. A larger variety, the community shopping center, may run from 100,000 to 150,000 square feet. As contrasted with the neighborhood type of center, more of the stores carry specialty or shopping goods. There are also several larger stores; these may include one or more discount or variety stores (such as a Times Square Stores unit, a K-mart, or a Zayre's store), and, perhaps, a junior department or large specialty store. These centers have a more extended trading area; they will draw shoppers from as far away as 20 minutes by car.

The real giants are the so-called regional shopping centers. They are large complexes that contain, in addition to as many as 50 to 100 stores, one to four branches of department stores, banks, movie houses, fast food shops and regular restaurants, offices, and so on. Many of these centers are fully enclosed, climate-controlled shopping

**Shopping Centers**

malls that attract crowds the year round, from 9:30 in the morning to 9:30 at night. Their "draw" is tremendous; people drive to these centers from as far away as 45 minutes by car. Some of the regionals run as big as half a million to three quarters of a million square feet in total area.

## SETTING UP YOUR STORE

The sculptor readily perceives the extraordinary asthetic possibilities in an ordinary block of stone. The artist regards the blank canvas stretched across the easel as a challenge to create a masterpiece. And the poet is invited by a single sheet of paper to weave words together so intriguingly as to evoke the emotions.

That place you plan to lease for your new retail enterprise merits no less spirit—or soul, as the case may be—on your part. Often, you rent little more than four bare walls, a floor and ceiling, and an outside show window, with entrance alongside. From this raw material, you must shape a suitable and attractive environment that will invite shoppers to enter, make their purchases, and leave satisfied so that they will return again and again. You would be wise to seek professional assistance; hire a store designer to help you lay out and decorate your store.

Here are the major facets you need to be concerned with:

- The store front
- The spore interior (decor, layout, fixturization)
- Proper lighting, heating, and air conditioning
- Displays
- Your opening stock

Your store front is, of course, the first contact that passersby will have with your new outlet. Overhead sign, front decor, and entrance must all carry through the kind of image you want to project. Store window(s) should be kept attractively trimmed and spotlessly clean. Merchandise displayed should be representative of the kind and quality of goods carried in the store so that the public is attracted to the window(s) and then invited to come in. Merchandise and trim should be changed regularly; for most types of stores, changes every two or three weeks are recommended.

You may have been fortunate enough to have found a store that needs little redecorating, with suitably finished ceiling, flooring, and walls. Usually, however, that is not the case. If you are handy, you may be able to save a substantial amount of money by doing some of the decorating yourself, for example, laying an asphalt tile floor, putting up wallpaper, or painting. Many kinds of floor coverings are available; select one that not only is attractive and fits the overall decor, but is also durable and needs little maintenance. Ceilings may be dropped low to convey a sense of intimacy or else left high, perhaps covered with acoustical tile so that the store inside looks spacious.

To illuminate the interior, use fluorescent lighting. It does a better job of brightening up the place than incandescent lighting and is more efficient (your electric bills will be lower). You may want to place incandescent bulbs here and there to highlight one or more sections of the store and to show merchandise more effectively.

As with store decorating, laying out the interior should be done with professional guidance. Selling and work areas must be separated. Ample space must be left for unimpeded customer traffic. Aisles behind counters and showcases must be planned so that sale personnel may pass easily. Fixtures must be put into place; you can use simple drawings of the store interior to locate display cases, back bars, shelves, register, and so on. (For calculating your costs, see Figure 16-4).

**FIGURE 16-4. Worksheet No. 3.**

WORKSHEET NO. 3

LIST OF FURNITURE, FIXTURES, AND EQUIPMENT

| Leave out or add items to suit your business. Use separate sheets to list exactly what you need for each of the items below. | If you plan to pay cash in full, enter the full amount below and in the last column. | If you are going to pay by installments, fill out the columns below. Enter in the last column your downpayment plus at least one installment. | | | Estimate of the cash you need for furniture, fixtures, and equipment |
|---|---|---|---|---|---|
| | | Price | Downpayment | Amount of each installment | |
| Counters | $ | $ | $ | $ | $ |
| Storage shelves, cabinets | | | | | |
| Display stands, shelves, tables | | | | | |
| Cash register | | | | | |
| Safe | | | | | |
| Window display fixtures | | | | | |
| Special lighting | | | | | |
| Outside sign | | | | | |
| Delivery equipment if needed | | | | | |
| **TOTAL FURNITURE, FIXTURES, AND EQUIPMENT** (Enter this figure also in worksheet 2 under "Starting Costs You Only Have To Pay Once".) | | | | | $ |

**Source:** "Checklist for Going into Business," *Small Marketers Aids No. 71* (Washington, D.C.: Small Business Administration, 1977), p. 12.

Like the two sides of a single coin, buying and merchandising are complementary activities essential to successful store operation. Proper buying and merchandising will mean that you have the right merchandise on hand, at the right prices and in the right quantities, at the right time. Both elements involve considerable planning and continuous attention. Because your store inventory represents a major investment, as well as a means of earning profit, an overriding objective is to maintain as lean a stock at all times as is possible. It

**BUYING AND MERCHANDISING**

should be sufficient to satisfy customer needs without needlessly tying up your capital.

## Buying

You already had some experience buying merchandise for resale in your mail order business. Now you must seek out other sources, suppliers who can provide the kinds of goods that are ordinarily sold in your particular type of store. Your shop is certain to be visited by sales representatives from wholesalers and manufacturers; these salespeople will be quick to show you their lines, extend the usual trade credit, and vie generally for your business. You can gain information about other sources from the trade association in your field, whether you have a hardware store, gift shop, variety store, or sell men's apparel. (There seems to be such an association for nearly every retail line.) You should also check whether there is an independent buying office that services your type of store; these organizations, located in the major metropolitan areas, may be able to represent you for a relatively small annual fee. Their buyers will scout the market continually, looking for items you can sell in your store and even placing orders on your behalf. In this way, if your store is located far from "the market," you can be assured of the latest styles, prices, "deals," and the like without the need to make a business trip several times a year.

Here are the kinds of activities you will be involved in if your store is to be properly stocked:

- Determining the needs and wants of your shoppers
- Anticipating demand and deciding on quantities needed
- Locating suppliers who are reliable and with whom you can work
- Negotiating good prices and favorable terms
- Scheduling in deliveries
- Receiving and checking the merchandise
- Maintaining a careful inventory control

Both merchandising and buying are important to you. There is lots of money to be saved—and some headaches, too—each year by developing expertise in these fields. You can profit by a thorough study of several of the books listed at the end of this chapter, especially:

Diamond and Pintel's *Retail Buying*
Shipp's *Retail Merchandising: Principles and Applications*
Wingate and Friedlander's *The Management of Retail Buying*

## Controlling Your Store Merchandise

A store's inventory typically consists of one or more broad merchandise lines that represent the kinds of goods its customers would normally expect to find in a store of that type. As a familiar example, today's supermarket carries such lines as dairy products, meats, produce, groceries, drugs, household items, and several others. Each of these broad categories is, of course, broken down into literally hundreds of products. A children's wear store would carry both everyday and play clothes, sleepwear, outerwear, and so on.

Managing your store's stock encompasses, first of all, selecting the major lines you ought to carry, and then developing the desired breadth of assortment you need to stock within each of the lines. Personal visits to several representative stores should acquaint you with the kinds of items that are traditionally offered. Your trade association can probably provide you with a detailed list of products that should form the basic stock assortment for your kind of store; in some instances, you may even be able to learn the more popular styles, materials, colors, and sizes of these items.

Deciding how much stock to carry is a different problem. You must anticipate the amount of business you will be doing well in advance, then translate the expected dollar volume into your inventory requirements. Retailers quickly learn about "stockturn"—how fast or how slow their stock sells, or "turns over." It is expressed by the ratio of sales to average stock, as shown in the following formula:

$$\text{Stockturn} = \frac{\text{Sales}}{\text{Average Stock}}$$

Here is an example. Assume you plan on first-year sales of $80,000. From your trade association (or from another source, such as Dun and Bradstreet), you find that the typical stock turnover rate for your kind of merchandise is 2.5 times per year, at retail. Plug the knowns into the formula, and you come up with:

$$2.5 = \frac{\$80,000}{x}$$

The "x" represents the one unknown quantity—the average stock. To solve the equation, divide the $80,000 by 2.5, to find an average inventory figure of $32,000. This tells you that you must maintain, on the average, an inventory valued at $32,000 at retail prices. Of course, you must convert this valuation to cost figures in order to know how much you will have to spend for the stock. If you work on a "keystone" markup, that is, you double your cost of an item to arrive at its retail price, you must purchase an inventory of some $16,000 at cost.

But remember that this is an average figure. During certain months or seasons, you will stock less; other times, such as during December, you may need more than this average amount.

Inventory and record-keeping are required elements of your stock control. Keep a close watch on fast-moving products. Get rid of slow movers through special promotions and sales or by marking down their prices. Keep track of all items by units, rather than by their overall dollar volume. Take physical inventory of your stock at least quarterly, and preferably each month. Work up a simple inventory form: list all items you carry on ruled sheets of paper, arrange them by classifications of merchandise and by product variants within the categories, show each item's price, leave space to enter figures as the counting is being done, and provide space for extension of inventory values. As you gain experience in merchandise management, develop minimum and maximum inventory levels for every item in your store, taking into account the necessary lead time for ordering and delivery.

**RETAIL PROMOTION**

In retailing, it is said that nothing happens until the sale is made. You may have a beautiful store laden with all kinds of goodies for your customers, but until you can get them to come in, your cash register will be bare.

Your store is new. You must communicate with the public to get people to know you're there—and to sample your wares. Promotion is needed. And what is promotion? Communication, pure and not-so-simple.

Retailers communicate with their prospective customers through three complex sets of activities: advertising, personal selling, and sales promotion. Let us take a brief look at each of these categories.

Advertising

Most store owners allocate far fewer dollars from their promotion budget to media advertising than to either sales promotion or personal selling. They prefer to rely more on their window displays to attract shoppers into the store, and on their salespeople and interior displays to sell these shoppers. So, the typical independent merchant spends somewhere between one and two percent of annual sales for advertising.

Of course, it does depend on the type of store you own. Retailers who sell hard goods—refrigerators, washing machines, television sets, and the like—may spend as much as five to 10 percent of their sales volume in the media; especially if they are highly promotional stores.

If you are planning a first-year sales volume of $200,000 and you limit your advertising expense to the median store expenditure of, say, 1.5 percent, you will have only about $3,000 available for the entire year for advertising purposes. (You should realize, too, that your sales estimate is rather ambitious; it is well above the average for many store types!) Where will you spend this amount? If you try to spread the sum equally across all 12 months, you will have about $250 each month to plunge into advertising. With that kind of money, you certainly could not afford even the briefest television commercial! Seldom, however, is an annual advertising budget broken down into such even segments. Usually, the retailer tries to assign monthly percentages that roughly correspond with monthly sales. In this way, more money is available for advertising when customer interest is brisk, and less during the slow periods of the year.

A new store needs lots of publicity. There is a greater need to let the public know where the store is located, what it stands for, the kinds of merchandise it offers, and the types of customers it seeks to attract. You should spend no less than twice the average of an established retail business during your first year of operation. Even five or six percent of your anticipated sales might not do the job!

**224** Getting Into Store Retailing

Review again the suggestions in Chapters 9 through 14 for help in planning, creating, and placing your retail advertising.

## Personal Selling

You know that every salesperson working for you should always present a pleasant, helpful personality to your shoppers. However, this alone will not assure a profitable business. Your employees must be trained from the very first day you hire them. They need to know the store merchandise well and where every item is located. They need to be taught that customer servicing comes before all other activities within the store. They need to learn the prices of the merchandise as well as the selling points of every item. But, above all, they need to be trained in *how to sell*. The ability to sell is not born with us; it is developed through training and practice on the job.

With thought and effort, it should not be too difficult for you to work up a modest sales training program for your newly hired salesclerks. Review Chapter 8, and refer to several of the sources listed at the end of this chapter; three valuable references from that bibliography are:

- Buskirk's *Retail Selling: A Vital Approach*
- Hartzler's *The Retail Salesperson: A Programmed Text*
- Mills and Paul's *Successful Retail Sales*

Such a program ought to encompass, at the very minimum, these subjects:

- How to meet—and greet—the customer
- How to determine what the customer is looking for
- How to present the merchandise effectively (and involve the customer in the presentation)
- How to meet—and counter—objections
- How to close the sale
- How to increase sales through "suggestive selling"

## Sales Promotion

This term merits some elaboration, for it includes just about every kind of communication with the public that the store merchant can bring into play except for personal selling and advertising. Both window and interior display are included. Indeed, these two constitute the heart of sales promotion activity in the store. Added to these two basics is a wide range of other techniques: sampling, demonstrations, premiums, giveaways, special sales events, contests, publicity stunts, and so on.

The key element in your sales promotion efforts, however, is display. Your show window is a powerful promotional tool. It represents the shopper's first exposure to your store and to your store's merchandise and pricing. Frequent window changes have already been suggested. Plan your windows well in advance so that you can prepare and, if necessary, purchase beforehand any materials, signing, or decorations you may need. When ready to trim the window, make sure you have already laid out all props, window posters, merchandise, display stands, sign tickets, and the like. Select the merchandise items with care; goods shown should be both timely and in demand. Group your items attractively and allow plenty of "air space" between groups. Use combinations of different sizes of stands and pedestals, along with shelves (of glass or wood), to help group the merchandise and to raise your displays to various heights.

The window center is its most compelling space. Center features should be selected with care and presented effectively, even dramatically. Try to show merchandise in use whenever you can. Small signs and large posters may accent the window theme. For example, one or two posters depicting foreign countries may be borrowed from a neighboring travel agency to lend authenticity and weight to a "vacation time" theme. Indeed, every new window should have a theme, for this makes the display more powerful and integrated.

A helpful practice is to prepare, with the aid of a calendar, a six-month schedule and timetable for all window changes. You then choose appropriate themes around which the windows are to be constructed, selecting from the many "standard" ones—like Washington's Birthday, Halloween, back-to-school, winter holiday, and so on—and by using your own creativity to devise new and exciting themes. Finally, list all the supplies, merchandise, fixtures, and signs that will be needed to dress each window. Thus, you end up with a complete window-dressing plan for half a year.

Many small store owners hire the services of a part-time window trimmer for a more professional job than they could do themselves.

Displays inside the store need the same attention as your windows do, but their purpose is different. Where the store window is designed primarily to stop passersby and induce them to come in, interior displays help to add to the shoppers' interest and perhaps convince them to make purchases. They complement the efforts of the salesclerks. For additional information, see *Checklist for interior arrangement and display* in the Appendix.

## OTHER ASPECTS OF STORE MANAGEMENT

Other important facets of retail store operation must be explored by the neophyte merchant. They include such areas as sales and expense control, personnel management, store maintenance, and problems of security (shoplifting, money handling procedures, avoidance of theft, and so on). Table 16-2 will give you some idea of the kinds of problems the small storekeeper faces.

Such information, however, more properly belongs in an entire book devoted to independent retailing. Read several such books thoroughly before embarking on your retail venture. You will also find additional useful material in *Checklist for increasing transactions* in the Appendix.

## SUGGESTED READING

Books

BODLE, YVONNE GALLEGOS, and JOSEPH A. COREY, *Retail Selling*. New York: McGraw-Hill, 1972.

BOLEN, WILLIAM H., *Contemporary Retailing*. Englewood Cliffs, N.J.: Prentice-Hall, Inc., 1978.

**Table 16-2.**
PROBLEMS OF THE SMALL RETAILER.

| Problems | Number of Stores Reporting | Percent of Total |
|---|---|---|
| With shoppers | | |
|   Shoplifting | 48 | 25.0% |
| Difficulties with customers[a] | 46 | 24.0 |
|   Resistance to high prices | 28 | 14.6 |
| With Store Personnel | | |
|   Getting and keeping competent help | 68 | 35.4 |
|   Conflicts among employees | 8 | 4.2 |
| With Store and Neighborhood | | |
|   More storage space needed | 29 | 15.1 |
|   More display space needed | 20 | 10.4 |
|   Burglaries, robberies | 18 | 9.4 |
|   More selling space needed | 10 | 5.2 |
|   Vandalism | 9 | 4.7 |
| With Merchandise | | |
|   Deliver problems | 56 | 29.2 |
|   Maintaining proper inventory levels | 52 | 27.1 |
|   Spoilage, damange, breakage | 14 | 7.3 |
|   Keeping merchandise orderly and in place | 7 | 3.6 |
|   Changes in fashions | 6 | 3.1 |
| With Promotion and Sales | | |
|   Sales adversely affected by competition | 28 | 14.6 |
|   Declining sales (not due to competition) | 20 | 10.4 |
|   Adverse weather affecting sales | 7 | 3.6 |
|   Seasonal changes affecting sales | 6 | 3.1 |
| With Maintenance | | |
|   General store maintenance | 17 | 8.9 |
| With Financial Aspects | | |
|   Increasing costs of operation | 47 | 24.5 |
|   Credit problems with customers[b] | 13 | 6.8 |
|   High taxes | 10 | 5.2 |
|   Government regulations and reports | 8 | 4.2 |
|   High costs of utilities, insurance | 8 | 4.2 |
|   Lack of cash, capital for growth | 7 | 3.6 |
|   High rent | 7 | 3.6 |
|   Low markup, low profits | 6 | 3.1 |
| With Miscellaneous Aspects | | |
|   Long hours, six-day week | 20 | 10.4 |
|   Hard work | 5 | 2.6 |

[a]People who bargain, chronic complainers, language difficulties, confusion on guarantees, etc.
[b]Slow payments, uncollectibles, etc.
**Source:** Irving Burstiner, "The Small Retailer and His Problems," *Journal of Business Education*, (March 1975), p. 245.

BURSTINER, IRVING, *Run Your Own Store: From Raising the Money to Counting the Profits*. Englewood Cliffs, N.J.: Prentice-Hall, Inc., 1981.

————, *The Small Business Handbook: A Comprehensive Guide to Starting and Running Your Own Business*. Englewood, Cliffs, N.J.: Prentice-Hall, Inc., 1979.

BUSKIRK, RICHARD H., *Retail Selling: A Vital Approach*. San Francisco: Canfield Press, 1975.

CLARK, LETA W., *How to Open Your Own Shop or Gallery.* New York: St. Martin's Press, 1978.

DIAMOND, JAY, and GERALD PINTEL, *Retail Buying.* Englewood Cliffs, N.J.: Prentice-Hall, Inc., 1976.

EMORY, MICHAEL, *Windows.* Chicago: Contemporary Books, 1977.

GENTILE, RICHARD J. *Retail Advertising: A Management Approach.* New York: Lebhar-Friedman, 1976.

HAIGHT, WILLIAM, *Retail Advertising: Management and Technique.* Glenview, Ill.: Scott, Foresman, 1976.

HARTZLER, F. E., *The Retail Salesperson: A Programmed Text,* 2nd ed. New York: McGraw-Hill, 1979.

LANE, MARC J., *Legal Handbook for Small Business.* New York: American Management Associations, 1978.

MILLS, K., and K. PAUL, *Successful Retail Sales.* Englewood Cliffs, N.J.: Prentice-Hall, Inc., 1979.

MILLS, KENNETH H., and JUDITH EDISON PAUL, *Create Distinctive Displays.* Englewood Cliffs, N.J.: Prentice-Hall, Inc., 1974.

NOVAK, ADOLF, *Store Planning and Design.* New York: Lebhar-Friedman, 1977.

SHAFFER, HAROLD, and HERBERT GREENWALD, *Independent Retailing: A Money-Making Manual.* Englewood Cliffs, N.J.: Prentice-Hall, Inc., 1976.

SHIPP, RALPH D., JR., *Retail Merchandising: Principles and Applications.* Boston: Houghton Mifflin, 1976.

WINGATE, JOHN W., and JOSEPH S. FRIEDLANDER, *The Management of Retail Buying,* 2nd ed. Englewood Cliffs, N.J.: Prentice-Hall, Inc., 1978.

**Free Materials from the Small Business Administration**

*Small business bibliographies*

#10 PFEIFFER, PAUL L., "Retailing," revised July 1975.

#15 OLSHAN, NATHAN H., "Recordkeeping Systems—Small Store and Service Trade," revised May 1977.

#27 MYERS, DR. ROBERT H., "Suburban Shopping Centers," reprinted January 1974.

#31 BLAKE, WM. HENRY, "Retail Credit and Collections," revised April 1974.

#72 O. LOEN, RAYMOND, "Personnel Management," reprinted January 1974.

#79 BARTHOLOMEW, ROBERT P., "Small Store Planning and Design," December 1976.

*Small marketers aids*

#71 "Checklist for Going into Business," revised September 1977.

#95 GRUBB, KENNETH, "Are Your Salespeople Missing Opportunities?" September 1963.

#96 LIPSCOMB, CHARLES T., JR., "Checklist for Successful Retail Advertising," 1974.

#104 CURTIS, S. J. (BOB), "Preventing Accidents in Small Stores," reprinted April 1974.

#111 VALENTI, GABRIEL M., "Interior Display: A Way to Increase Sales," reprinted May 1974.

#113 MYERS, ROBERT H., "Quality and Taste As Sales Appeals," reprinted April 1974.

#114 LAWS, DWAYNE, "Pleasing Your Boss, the Customer," June 1965.

#116 MILLER, ERNEST A., "How to Select a Resident Buying Office," reprinted September 1976.

#118 LAUGHLIN, CHARLES W., "Legal Services for Small Retail and Service Firms," reprinted July 1977.

#120 COLLAZZO, CHARLES J., "Building Good Customer Relations," April 1966.

#121 SORBET, ELIZABETH M., "Measuring the Results of Advertising," 1966.

#123 HARLING, EDWIN L., "Stock Control for Small Stores," December 1966.

#124 BLACKWELL, ROGER D., "Knowing Your Image," reprinted May 1977.

#125 ELLIOTT, CHARLES B., "Pointers on Display Lighting," March 1967.

#129 VERRILL, ADDISON H., "Reducing Shoplifting Losses," September 1967.

#130 ABRAHAM, ALFRED B., "Analyze Your Records to Reduce Costs," reprinted July 1977.

#132 MURPHY, BETTY S., "The Federal Wage-Hour Law in Small Firms," revised December 1974.

#133 HALVERSON, GERALD B., "Can You Afford Delivery Service?" reprinted September 1976.

#134 CURTIS, S. J. (BOB), "Preventing Burglary and Robbery Loss," reprinted October 1973.

#139 KASS, BENNY L., "Understanding Truth in Lending," 1974.

#140 HILL, RICHARD M., "Profit by Your Wholesalers' Services," January 1970.

#143 McKEEVER, J. ROSS, "Factors in Considering a Shopping Center Location," May 1970.

#145 SCHWARTZ, IRVING, "Personal Qualities Needed to Manage a Store," reprinted April 1974.

#147 MURPHY, JOHN F., "Sound Cash Management and Borrowing," reprinted July 1977.

#148 GREENE, MARK R., "Insurance Checklist for Small Business," July 1971.

#149 CALEY, JOHN D., "Computers for Small Business: Service Bureau or Time-Sharing," reprinted August 1973.

#150 Office of Management Assistance, "Business Plan for Retailers," reprinted March 1973.

#152 LOWRY, JAMES R., "Using a Traffic Study to Select a Store Site," April 1974.

#154 VORZIMER, LOUIS H., "Using Census Data to Select A Retail Site," April 1974.

#156 KRESS, GEORGE, and R. TED WILL, "Marketing Checklist for Small Retailers," 1974.

#157 BERMAN, HERBERT, "Efficient Lighting in Small Stores," January 1976.

#159 ROSENBLOOM, BERT, "Improving Personal Selling in Small Retail Stores," reprinted April 1980.

#160 Riso, Ovid, "Advertising Guidelines for Small Retail Firms," 1977.

#161 Claus, Karen E., and R. J. Claus, "Signs and Your Business," April 1977.

#163 Garvey, L. Kim, "Public Relations for Small Business," December 1977.

#166 Hammel, Fred C., "Simple Breakeven Analysis for Small Stores," May 1978.

#168 Davidson, Jeffrey P., "Store Location: 'Little Things' Mean a Lot," June 1979.

**To Order from the Superintendent of Documents**

*Small business management series*

#3 Bruce, Martin M., "Human Relations in Small Business," *Small Business Management Series No. 3,* 3rd ed. Washington, D.C.: Small Business Administration, 1969. (Stock #045-000-00036-2.)

#15 Zwick, Jack, "A Handbook of Small Business Finance," *Small Business Management Series No. 15,* 8th ed. Washington, D.C.: Small Business Administration, 1975. (Stock #045-000-00139-3.)

#26 Loen, Ernest L., "Personnel Management Guides for Small Business," *Small Business Management Series No. 26.* Washington, D.C.: Small Business Administration, 1974. (Stock #045-000-00126-1.)

#27 Miller, Robert W., "Profitable Community Relations for Small Business," *Small Business Management Series No. 27.* Washington, D.C.: Small Business Administration, 1961. (Stock #045-000-00033-8.)

#32 Ragan, Robert C., "Financial Recordkeeping for Small Stores," *Small Business Management Series No. 32.* Washington, D.C.: Small Business Administration, 1976. (Stock #045-000-00142-3.)

#33 Wingate, John W., and Seymour Helfant, "Small Store Planning for Growth," *Small Business Management Series No. 33.* 2nd ed. Washington, D.C.: Small Business Administration, 1977. (Stock #045-000-00139-7.)

*Starting and managing series*

#1 Metcalf, Wendell O., "Starting and Managing a Small Business of Your Own," *Starting and Managing Series, No. 1.* 3rd ed. Washington, D.C.: Small Business Administration, 1973. (Stock #045-000-00123-7.)

# APPENDIX

---

**FIGURE A-1.  Checklist for going into business.**

Thinking of starting a business? Ask yourself these questions.

You want to own and manage your own business. It's a good idea provided you know what it takes and have what it takes.

Starting a business is risky at best. But your chances of making it go will be better if you understand the problems you'll meet and work out as many of them as you can before you start.

Here are some questions to help you think through what you need to know and do. Check each question if the answer is YES. Where the answer is NO, you have some work to do.

## BEFORE YOU START

### How about YOU?

Are you the kind of person who can get a business started and make it go? (Before you answer this question, use the worksheet on pages 4 and 5.)    *maybe*

Think about *why* you want to own your own business. Do you want to badly enough to keep you working long hours without knowing how much money you'll end up with?    ?  ____

Have you worked in a business like the one you want to start?    *no*

**231**

## WORKSHEET NO. 1

Under each question, check the answer that says what you feel or comes closest to it. Be honest with yourself.

*Are you a self-starter?*

☐ I do things on my own. Nobody has to tell me to get going.

☑ If someone gets me started, I keep going all right.

☐ Easy does it. I don't put myself out until I have to.

*How do you feel about other people?*

☑ I like people. I can get along with just about anybody.

☐ I have plenty of friends—I don't need anyone else.

☐ Most people irritate me.

*Can you lead others?*

☑ I can get most people to go along when I start something.

☐ I can give the orders if someone tells me what we should do.

☐ I let someone else get things moving. Then I go along if I feel like it.

*Can you take responsibility?*

☐ I like to take charge of things and see them through.

☑ I'll take over if I have to, but I'd rather let someone else be responsible.

☐ There's always some eager beaver around wanting to show how smart he is. I say let him.

*How good an organizer are you?*

☑ I like to have a plan before I start. I'm usually the one to get things lined up when the group wants to do something.

☐ I do all right unless things get too confused. Then I quit.

☐ You get all set and then something comes along and presents too many problems. So I just take things as they come.

*How good a worker are you?*

☐ I can keep going as long as I need to. I don't mind working hard for something I want.

☑ I'll work hard for a while, but when I've had enough, that's it.

☐ I can't see that hard work gets you anywhere.

*Can you make decisions?*

☐ I can make up my mind in a hurry if I have to. It usually turns out O.K., too.

☐ I can if I have plenty of time. If I have to make up my mind fast, I think later I should have decided the other way.

☐ I don't like to be the one who has to decide things.

*Can people trust what you say?*

☑ You bet they can. I don't say things I don't mean.

☐ I try to be on the level most of the time, but sometimes I just say what's easiest.

☐ Why bother if the other fellow doesn't know the difference?

*Can you stick with it?*

☐ If I make up my mind to do something, I don't let *anything* stop me.

☑ I usually finish what I start—if it goes well.

☐ If it doesn't go right away, I quit. Why beat your brains out?

*How good is your health?*

☐ I *never* run down!

☑ I have enough energy for most things I want to do.

☐ I run out of energy sooner than most of my friends seem to.

*Now count the checks you made.*

How many checks are there beside the *first* answer to each question? ___4___

How many checks are there beside the *second* answer to each question? ___6___

How many checks are there beside the *third* answer to each question? ___0___

If most of your checks are beside the first answers, you probably have what it takes to run a business. If not, you're likely to have more trouble than you can handle by yourself. Better find a partner who is strong on the points you're weak on. If many checks are beside the third answer, not even a good partner will be able to shore you up.

Have you worked for someone else as a foreman or manager? ___no___

Have you had any business training in school? ___no___

Have you saved any money? ___no___

## How about the money?

Do you know how much money you will need to get your business started?* ___no___

Have you counted up how much money of your own you can put into the business? ___no___

Do you know how much credit you can get from your suppliers—the people you will buy from? ___no___

Do you know where you can borrow the rest of the money you need to start your business? ___no___

*Use Worksheets 2 and 3

| ESTIMATED MONTHLY EXPENSES | | | |
|---|---|---|---|
| Item | Your estimate of monthly expenses based on sales of $ _____ per year | Your estimate of how much cash you need to start your business (See column 3.) | What to put in column 2 (These figures are typical for one kind of business. You will have to decide how many months to allow for in your business.) |
| | Column 1 | Column 2 | Column 3 |
| Salary of owner-manager | $ | $ | 2 times column 1 |
| All other salaries and wages | | | 3 times column 1 |
| Rent | | | 3 times column 1 |
| Advertising | | | 3 times column 1 |
| Delivery expense | | | 3 times column 1 |
| Supplies | | | 3 times column 1 |
| Telephone and telegraph | | | 3 times column 1 |
| Other utilities | | | 3 times column 1 |
| Insurance | | | Payment required by insurance company |
| Taxes, including Social Security | | | 4 times column 1 |
| Interest | | | 3 times column 1 |
| Maintenance | | | 3 times column 1 |
| Legal and other professional fees | | | 3 times column 1 |
| Miscellaneous | | | 3 times column 1 |
| STARTING COSTS YOU ONLY HAVE TO PAY ONCE | | | Leave column 2 blank |
| Fixtures and equipment | | | Fill in worksheet 3 and put the total here |
| Decorating and remodeling | | | Talk it over with a contractor |
| Installation of fixtures and equipment | | | Talk to suppliers from whom you buy these |
| Starting inventory | | | Suppliers will probably help you estimate this |
| Deposits with public utilities | | | Find out from utilities companies |
| Legal and other professional fees | | | Lawyer, accountant, and so on |
| Licenses and permits | | | Find out from city offices what you have to have |
| Advertising and promotion for opening | | | Estimate what you'll use |
| Accounts receiveble | | | What you need to buy more stock until credit customers pay |
| Cash | | | For unexpected expenses or losses, special purchases, etc. |
| Other | | | Make a separate list and enter total |
| TOTAL ESTIMATED CASH YOU NEED TO START WITH | $ | | Add up all the numbers in column 2 |

Have you figured out what net income per year you expect to get from the business? Count your salary and your profit on the money you put into the business. _____

Can you live on less than this so that you can use some of it to help your business grow? _____

## LIST OF FURNITURE, FIXTURES, AND EQUIPMENT

| Leave out or add items to suit your business. Use separate sheets to list exactly what you need for each of the items below. | If you plan to pay cash in full, enter the full amount below and in the last column. | If you are going to pay by installments, fill out the columns below. Enter in the last column your downpayment plus at least one installment. | | | Estimate of the cash you need for furniture, fixtures, and equipment |
|---|---|---|---|---|---|
| | | Price | Downpayment | Amount of each installment | |
| Counters | $ | $ | $ | $ | $ |
| Storage shelves, cabinets | | | | | |
| Display stands, shelves, tables | | | | | |
| Cash register | | | | | |
| Safe | | | | | |
| Window display fixtures | | | | | |
| Special lighting | | | | | |
| Outside sign | | | | | |
| Delivery equipment if needed | | | | | |
| TOTAL FURNITURE, FIXTURES, AND EQUIPMENT (Enter this figure also in worksheet 2 under "Starting Costs You Only Have To Pay Once".) | | | | | $ |

**Have you talked to a banker about your plans?** _____

## How about a partner

If you need a partner with money or know-how that you don't have, do you know someone who will fit—someone you can get along with? _____

Do you know the good and bad points about going it alone, having a partner, and incorporating your business? _____

Have you talked to a lawyer about it? _____

## How about your customers?

Do most businesses in your community seem to be doing well? _____

Have you tried to find out whether stores like the one you want to open are doing well in your community and in the rest of the country? _____

Do you know what kind of people will want to buy what you plan to sell? _____

Do people like that live in the area where you want to open your store? _____

Do they need a store like yours? _____

If not, have you thought about opening a different kind of store or going to another neighborhood? _____

# GETTING STARTED

## Your building

Have you found a good building for your store? ____

Will you have enough room when your business gets bigger? ____

Can you fix the building the way you want it without spending too much money? ____

Can people get to it easily from parking spaces, bus stops, or their homes? ____

Have you had a lawyer check the lease and zoning? ____

## Equipment and supplies

Do you know just what equipment and supplies you need and how much they will cost? (Worksheet 3 and the lists you made for it should show this.) ____

Can you save some money by buying secondhand equipment? ____

## Your merchandise

Have you decided what things you will sell? ____

Do you know how much or how many of each you will buy to open your store with? ____

Have you found suppliers who will sell you what you need at a good price? ____

Have you compared the prices and credit terms of different suppliers? ____

## Your records

Have you planned a system of records that will keep track of your income and expenses, what you owe other people, and what other people owe you? ____

Have you worked out a way to keep track of your inventory so that you will always have enough on hand for your customers but not more than you can sell? ____

Have you figured out how to keep your payroll records and take care of tax reports and payments? ____

Do you know what financial statements you should prepare? ____

Do you know how to use these financial statements? ____

Do you know an accountant who will help you with your records and financial statements? ____

## Your store and the law

Do you know what licenses and permits you need? ____

Do you know what business laws you have to obey?       _____

Do you know a lawyer you can go to for advice and for help
with legal papers?       _____

## Protecting your store

Have you made plans for protecting your store against thefts
of all kinds—shoplifting, robbery, burglary, employee steal-
ing?       _____

Have you talked with an insurance agent about what kinds
of insurance you need?       _____

## Buying a business someone else has started

Have you made a list of what you like and don't like about
buying a business someone else has started?       _____

Are you sure you know the real reason why the owner wants
to sell his business?       _____

Have you compared the cost of buying the business with the
cost of starting a new business?       _____

Is the stock up to date and in good condition?       _____

Is the building in good condition?       _____

Will the owner of the building transfer the lease to you?       _____

Have you talked with other businessmen in the area to see
what they think of the business?       _____

Have you talked with the company's suppliers?       _____

Have you talked with a lawyer about it?       _____

### MAKING IT GO

## Advertising

Have you decided how you will advertise? (Newspapers—
posters—handbills—radio—by mail?)       _____

Do you know where to get help with your ads?       _____

Have you watched what other stores do to get people to buy?       _____

## The prices you charge

Do you know how to figure what you should charge for each
item you sell?       _____

Do you know what other stores like yours charge?       _____

## Buying

Do you have a plan for finding out what your customers want?       _____

Will your plan for keeping track of your inventory tell you
when it is time to order more and how much to order?       _____

Do you plan to buy most of your stock from a few suppliers rather than a little from many, so that those you buy from will want to help you succeed? ____

## Selling

Have you decided whether you will have salesclerks or self-service? ____

Do you know how to get customers to buy? ____

Have you thought about why you like to buy from some salesmen while others turn you off? ____

## Your employees

If you need to hire someone to help you, do you know where to look? ____

Do you know what kind of person you need? ____

Do you know how much to pay? ____

Do you have a plan for training your employees? ____

## Credit for your customers

Have you decided whether to let your customers buy on credit? ____

Do you know the good and bad points about joining a credit-card plan? ____

Can you tell a deadbeat from a good credit customer? ____

### A FEW EXTRA QUESTIONS

Have you figured out whether you could make more money working for someone else? ____

Does your family go along with your plan to start a business of your own? ____

Do you know where to find out about new ideas and new products? ____

Do you have a work plan for yourself and your employees? ____

Have you gone to the nearest Small Business Administration office for help with your plans? ____

If you have answered all these questions carefully, you've done some hard work and serious thinking. That's good. But you have probably found some things you still need to know more about or do something about.

Do all you can for yourself, but don't hesitate to ask for help from people who can tell you what you need to know. Remember, running a business takes guts! You've got to be able to decide what you need and then go after it.

*Good luck!*

---

**Source:** "Checklist for Going into Business," *Small Marketers Aid No. 71* (Washington, D.C.: Small Business Administration, 1977)

---

**FIGURE A-2.  Checklist for increasing gross margin.**

I. Increasing your markon
   A. Buying for less
      1. Do you take advantage of all discount opportunities?
      2. Do you watch purchases under seasonal rebate agreements so that they will not fall below limits?
      3. Do you keep your transportation costs to a minimum by using the most economical common carrier, packing methods, and consolidations?
      4. Do you concentrate your purchases with key suppliers?
      5. Do you actually use the facilities of a resident buying office to obtain better values?
      6. Could you realize savings by placing orders further ahead?
      7. Could you realize savings by placing blanket orders?
      8. Have you an undeveloped opportunity to use private brands to compete with national brands?
      9. Do you resist special quantity price concessions, for merchandise that will not turn over for a long period of time?
   B. Selling for more
      1. Do you take every opportunity to buy exclusive merchandise?
      2. Do you price every item on its merits (rather than applying an average markup on most goods)?
      3. Are goods costing the same put into stock at different prices when there is a difference in value in the customers' eyes?
      4. Could you raise price line endings slightly without detracting from your sales volume?
   C. Promoting higher-markup goods.
      1. Do you know the markup of each price line and in each classification?
      2. Do you make an adequate effort to feature in your advertising those price lines and items that bear a long markup?
      3. Is your long-markup merchandise adequately displayed in the store?
      4. Are your salespeople trained to give special attention to the higher markup goods in stock?
      5. Do you give rewards for selling high markup goods?
      6. Do you avoid giving valuable space to slow sellers?
II. Curtailing your reductions
   A. Buying
      1. Will your markdowns be reduced by rising wholesale prices?

2. Do your buyers make careful buying plans before they go to market?
3. Do your buyers frequently overbuy promotional merchandise, later forcing you to take heavy markdowns on remainders?
4. Are your stocks peaked well in advance of the sales peak?
5. Do you curtail reorders at the peak of the selling season?
6. Are you developing classic lines with a long life?
7. Are merchandise shortcomings leading to customer returns and markdowns? (If so, demand higher quality standards.)
8. Do you place your orders on time so that you will have the proper merchandise in your store when the demand is great?
9. Do you concentrate your buying on what you know will sell instead of experimenting with fringe sizes, colors, fabrics and types of merchandise?
10. Do you "test" new merchandise in small quantities before the beginning of a season and then concentrate heavily on the items that were successful?
11. Do you buy "items", where possible, instead of full lines?
12. Do you follow up your orders carefully to check for better deliveries?
13. Do you refuse to accept past due merchandise when the demand falls off?
14. Do you receive merchandise at regular staggered intervals as opposed to receiving it "when ready"?

B. Selling
1. Are your salespeople adequately presenting the older goods in your stock?
2. Do you have a good followup system to ensure that goods don't become slow sellers?
3. Do you carefully instruct your salespeople in the selling points of merchandise that is slow moving?
4. Are your salespeople using forced selling methods that lead to returns and eventual markdowns?
5. Do you provide your salespeople with proper rewards for selling slow moving merchandise?

C. Control
1. Do you have any opportunities to increase your stock turn and reduce the length of time goods are on hand before being sold?
2. Do you take your markdowns early enough?
3. Do you take them too soon?
4. Do you set the first markdown low enough to move most of the goods marked down?
5. Have you established special markdown prices?
6. Do you have a system of good physical control of stock that avoids shortages?
7. Do you reorder well enough in advance to avoid being out of best sellers?
8. Do you avoid unnecessary markdowns on staple merchandise that can be carried over to next year?
9. Do you keep a record of markdowns by sizes ... to avoid errors in future ordering?

III. Increasing your cash discounts
A. Are you getting the largest possible cash discounts from your suppliers?
B. Do you pay all your bills on time so as to obtain the discounts offered?
C. Are you taking advantage of anticipation opportunities?

IV. Lowering your workroom and alteration costs
   A. Are charges to your customers desirable, and are they adequate?
   B. Is your workroom being run as economically as possible?
   C. Would it be feasible to eliminate your workroom operation?

**Source:** John W. Wingate and Seymour Helfant, "Small Store Planning for Growth," *Small Business Management Series No. 33,* 2nd ed. (Washington, D.C.: Small Business Management Administration, 1977), pp. 96–99.

**FIGURE A-3.   Checklist for interior arrangement and display.**

I. Layout
   1. Are your fixtures low enough and signs so placed that the customer can get a bird's-eye view of the store and tell in what direction to go for wanted goods?
   2. Do your aisle and counter arrangements tend to stimulate a circular traffic flow through the store?
   3. Do your fixtures (and their arrangement), signs, lettering, and colors all create a coordinated and unified effect?
   4. Before any supplier's fixtures are accepted, do you make sure they conform in color and design to what you already have?
   5. Do you limit the use of hanging signs to special sale events?
   6. Are your counters and aisle table *not* overcrowded with merchandise?
   7. Are your ledges and cashier/wrapping stations kept free of boxes, unneeded wrapping materials, personal effects, and odds and ends?
   8. Do you keep trash bins out of sight?
II. Merchandise emphasis
   1. Do your signs referring to specific goods tell the customer something significant about them, rather than simply naming the products and their prices?
   2. For your advertised goods, do you have prominent signs, including tear sheets at the entrances, to inform and guide customers to their exact location in the store?
   3. Do you prominently display both advertised and nonadvertised specials at the ends of counters as well as at the point of sale?
   4. Are both your national and private brands highlighted in your arrangement and window display?
   5. Wherever feasible, do you give the more colorful merchandise in your stock preference in display?
   6. In the case of apparel and home furnishings, do the items that reflect your store's fashion sense or fashion leadership get special display attention at all times?
   7. In locating merchandise in your store, do you always consider the productivity of space—vertical as well as horizontal?
   8. Is your self-service merchandise arranged so as to attract the customer and assist in selection by the means indicated below:
      a. Is each category grouped under a separate sign?
      b. Is the merchandise in each category arranged according to its most significant characteristic—whether color, style, size, or price?
      c. In apparel categories, is the merchandise arranged by price lines or zones to assist the customer to make a selection quickly?
      d. Is horizontal space usually devoted to different items and styles within a category (vertical space being used for different sizes—smallest at the top largest at the bottom)?

e. Are impulse items interspersed with demand items and *not* placed across the aisle from them, where many customers will not see them?

9. Do you plan your windows and displays in advance?
10. Do you meet with your salesforce after windows are trimmed to discuss the items displayed?
11. Do you use seasonal, monthly and weekly plans for interior and window displays, determining the fixtures to be used and merchandise to be displayed?
12. Do your displays reflect the image of your store?
13. Do you budget the dollars you will set aside for fixtures and props to be used in your displays, as well as the expense of setting them up and maintaining them?
14. Do you keep your fixtures and windows clean and dust free?
15. Do you replace burned out light bulbs immediately?
15. Do you take safety precautions in setting up your fixtures?
17. Do garments fit properly on mannequins and fixtures?

---

**Source:** John W. Wingate and Seymour Helfant, "Small Store Planning for Growth," *Small Business Management Series No. 33.* 2nd ed. (Washington, D.C.: Small Business Administration, 1977), pp. 100–102.

---

**FIGURE A-4. Checklist for increasing transactions.**

I. Stock assortment
  A. Unit control systems
    1. Do you have an adequate system for checking on staple items?
    2. For other than staple items, do you have an adequate unit control system in operation?
    3. Do you have an effective system for checking on slow-selling stock?
    4. Do you have an effective system for spotting potential fast-selling stock?
    5. Do you keep a close check on customer demand by a want slip system?
    6. Do you keep adequate records to help you plan for next year's purchases?
    7. Do you plan your inventory so that you will always be "in stock" at peak periods?
    8. Do you make use of electronic data processing (EDP) to ensure good inventory control, at the low rates available to small retailers?
  B. Balance of stock
    1. Is the stock in each of your merchandise classifications balanced to the rate of sale in each?
    2. Is your stock balanced by price line, color, size, and type?
    3. Do you have too many price lines?
    4. Are your prices and price lines the right choice to meet your competition?
    5. Do you carry deep stocks in each of the running styles?
    6. Do you carry deep stocks in heart sizes, colors, and materials?
    7. In fringe sizes, colors, etc., do you deliberately keep low stocks and depend on substitution to avoid lost sales at these points?
    8. Do you keep a proper balance among the following classes of stock: Staple, assortment, prestige, and clearance?

9. Do you maintain a basic stock assortment even in dull months?

C. Selection

1. Do you avoid stocking items from different suppliers and in different brands that virtually duplicate one another?
2. Do you select each item in stock with a distinct customer group or target in mind?
3. Do you choose items for promotion that have outstanding merit in price, fashion, or utility?
4. Do you place adequate emphasis on special value promotions, neither too much nor too little?
5. Do the characteristics of the stock give your store a clearly defined personality or image that attracts people in the trading area?
6. Do you keep in close touch with all new market developments by cooperating with a buying office or voluntary group and by seeing all salesmen who call?
7. Do you carefully select the lines you carry since you can't be all things to all people?
8. Do you know your competition, their strengths and weaknesses?

II. Promotion

A. Outside publicity

1. Do you promote best sellers?
2. Do you make adequate use of the appropriate media: Newspapers, direct mail, signs, radio—TV, press publicity, stunts, special sales inducements, sampling, house-to-house selling, home and club demonstrations, mail and telephone selling?
3. Do you use the most appropriate newspapers?
4. Do you have adequate promotion each month of the year?
5. Do you advertise on the right days of the week?
6. Are your ad layouts eye-catching?
7. Does the ad copy inspire interest, desire, and action; and, above all, is the copy believable?
9. Does your store have adequate window space?
10. Are your show windows well planned and compelling?
11. Do you use one large ad for better effectiveness rather than a number of small ads?
12. Do you keep a record of what your competitors advertise?
13. Do you tie in with local merchants' community sales efforts?
14. Do you promote your store as the type of store you want it to be to the kind of customers you want to attract?
15. Do you promote your strong points in the types of merchandise you carry and the services you offer?
16. Do you maintain an excellent relationship with your regular customers, while still going after new customers?
17. Does your advertising copy sell your store as well as the item?
18. Do you include related merchandise, when possible, in all your ads?
19. Do you present the main benefits of the merchandise you advertise?
20. Do you include your store's name and address in all your advertising?

B. In-store publicity

1. Do you maintain adequate ensemble displays that coordinate items?
2. Do your salespeople suggest to customers the coordinations featured in displays?

3. Do you make effective use of advertising blowups?
4. Are your signs effective?
5. Do you use handbills at store entrances to attract customers to specials in the store?
6. Do you take the best advantage of interdepartmental selling?

C. Layout
1. Are the merchandise lines properly located in your store and easily accessible?
2. Is each merchandise line adequately serviced?
3. Are your fixtures up to date?
4. Is the lighting good?
5. Is the majority of your fast-selling merchandise always on display, available for customer inspection without the intervention of a salesclerk?
6. Are informative labels, listing major selling points, attached to all items for which customers may need the information?
7. Are your impulse goods so placed as to be seen by customers shopping for demand items?
8. Do you limit your reserve stock area if you are paying a high rental?

D. Sales
1. Is your salesforce well chosen?
2. Is your salesforce adequately trained in merchandise information and in customer handling?
3. Do your salespeople get adequate merchandise information?
4. Do you provide your salespeople with sufficient premiums, rewards, and contests to maintain their interest?
5. Do you give considerate attention to their suggestions and grievances?
6. Is each of your buyers a good leader?
7. Do you train your salesforce to substitute items when styles and sizes are sold out?
8. Do you get on the floor often enough to stimulate your salesforce— and learn what your customers are demanding?
9. Do you motivate your salesforce to do an outstanding job?
10. Do you teach your salesforce to increase the size of their sales through the use of multiple unit pricing, when it is available?

E. Customer Services
1. Do you make it convenient for customers to exchange merchandise or obtain refunds?
2. Do you have a liberal refund policy?
3. Do you offer gift wrapping?
4. Do you sell gift certificates?
5. Do you encourage charge accounts?
6. Do you have lay-away services?
7. Do you accept telephone orders?

**Source:** John W. Wingate and Seymour Helfant, "Small Store Planning for Growth," *Small Business Management Series No. 33*, 2nd ed. (Washington, D.C.: Small Business Administration, 1977), pp. 90–95.

**POSTAGE AND MAILING DATA**

The United States Postal Service classifies all mailable material into four categories. Pertinent details for each of these classifications follow.

### First Class

This category gets the fastest transportation service of all. Included are handwritten and typed letters, postcards, greeting cards, statements, bills, checks, and money orders. Business reply mail is also considered first class. If the item weighs more than 13 ounces, it is then called "Priority Mail." The maximum allowable weight for priority mail is 70 pounds; the maximum size permitted, 100 inches in length and girth combined. Envelopes and packages must be clearly marked "Priority Mail" on all sides.

Heavy mailers may wish to "presort" their first class mail to save postage. To enjoy this benefit, an annual fee must be paid. In addition, each mailing must consist of at least 500 identical pieces, must be presorted according to postal regulations, and each individual letter or package must carry the words "Presorted First Class."

### Second Class

This is generally used by newspapers and periodicals that are issued at least four times a year. Application must be made for a second-class entry permit, and specific post office requirements must be met. Bulk mailings are usually made by the publication. However, there is a separate rate for mailing individual copies of newspapers and magazines.

### Third Class

Mail sent under this classification costs less—and moves more slowly—than first-class mail. The classification is often referred to as "advertising mail." It includes circulars, self-mailers, brochures, catalogs, and other printed materials—as well as parcels that weigh less than one pound. Two rate structures exist: a single piece and a bulk rate. There is no maximum limit on size.

To earn the lower bulk rate, the following conditions must be observed:

- A bulk mailing fee of $40 must be paid annually, in advance.
- Mail must be presented in quantities of not less than 200 pieces or weigh less than 50 pounds.
- Mail must be properly ZIP-coded and presorted.
- Postage is to be prepaid by meter stamp, permit imprint, or precanceled stamps.
- Mail must carry these identifying words: *Bulk Rate* (or *Blk Rt*).
- Shipments must be accompanied by either Form 3602 (Statement of Mailing Matter with Permit Imprints) or Form 3602-PC (Bulk Rate Mailing Statement—Third Class Mail).

### Fourth Class

This category is also called "parcel mail" or "parcel post." It is a service for parcels and packages of one pound or more in weight. Domestic fourth-class mail charges are based on both weight and distance factors. The country is divided into eight parcel post zones, each requiring a different rate scale. Fourth-class packages that are sent between the larger post offices in the continental United States are limited in weight to 40 pounds and in size to 84 inches (length and girth combined). Those traveling to and from the smaller post offices may be both heavier and larger—up to 70 pounds and up to 100 inches.

Books, catalogs, and sound recordings travel within the fourth-class category at a special rate. There is also a bulk rate available; this requires a minimum of 300 pieces mailed at the same time, provided that they are separated by zones. A lower, "presort" rate can also be obtained if at least 500 identical pieces are mailed. (Consult your post office for further details.)

**Other Pertinent Facts**

Some other common postal service terms are explained briefly below.

1. Business reply mail. Mailers use this to encourage responses. Such mail is turned over to the sender from any post office in the country. When received, both the regular first-class rate and a small business reply fee are charged. An annual permit is required as well as a postage trust account. (An "advance deposit" trust account will cost you less per piece returned.)

2. Certified mail. This is used for items of no intrinsic value and is handled in transit as ordinary mail. A return receipt is available for an additional fee; this provides proof of delivery.

3. C. O. D. (collect on delivery) service. May be used in connection with parcel post, or first- and third-class mail. When the recipient is to pay for the merchandise sent, the carrier collects the amount due plus a C. O. D. fee. This fee includes insurance protection. The service is limited to a maximum of $400.

4. Insurance. This is available on third- and fourth-class mail and on merchandise sent via first class. Limit to $400.

5. List correction. The post office provides a series of list correction services, as well as a list sequencing service (where the addresses on a mailing list are sorted into a carrier route sequence).

6. Plant load. When a very large mailing is prepared for one or several destination points, the postmaster may send a vehicle to your place of business to pick it up. The mail is then taken directly to its destination.

7. Precanceled stamps. These may be used only at the post office that issued your permit for using such stamps (Form 3620, "Application for Permit"). Their use reduces the time and costs of mail handling in connection with second-, third-, and fourth-class mail and with postcards.

8. Presorting. For each advance in the degree of presorting by a mailer, more time is saved in processing the mail. Faster handling is also accomplished by traying the mail—in trays furnished free by the post office. Such mail may be bundled and labeled, or trayed and sacked, depending on your preference and the post office's recommendation. Presorting saves postage, when properly prepared according to requirements.

9. Registered mail. Offers security for valuable and irreplaceable items, with insurance protection up to $10,000 and a return receipt (for an additional fee).

10. Special delivery. This applies to all classes of mail, at an extra fee. Such mail is also delivered on Sundays and holidays.

11. Special handling. Useful for items requiring special handling; available only for third- and fourth-class mail at a small additional fee.

The following information has been excerpted from "Postage Rates, Fees, and Information," Notice 59 (Washington, D.C.: United States Postal Service, March 1981).

1. *Size Standards for Domestic Mail*

   Minimum size: Pieces that do not meet the following requirements are prohibited from the mails:

   a. All pieces must be at least .007 of an inch thick and
   b. All pieces (except keys and identification devices), *which are ¼ inch or less thick,* must be:
      (1) Rectangular in shape,
      (2) At least 3½ inches high, and
      (3) At least 5 inches long.
      NOTE: Pieces *greater than ¼ inch thick* can be mailed even if they measure less than 3½ by 5 inches.

   Nonstandard mail: all first-class mail weighing 1 ounce or less and all single-piece rate third-class mail weighing 1 ounce or less is nonstandard (and subject to a 9¢ surcharge in addition to the applicable postage and fees) if:

   a. Any of the following dimensions are exceeded:
      Length—11½ inches,
      Height—6 inches,
      Thickness—¼ inch, or
   b. The piece has a height to length (aspect) ratio that does not fall between 1 to 1.3 and 1 to 2.5 inclusive. (The aspect ratio is found by dividing the length by the height. If the answer is between 1.3 and 2.5 inclusive, the piece has a standard aspect ratio.)

2. *Postage Rates*

   a. First class: Letters, 18¢ the first ounce, 17¢ each additional ounce; postcards, 12¢.*
   b. Third class (circulars, books, catalogs, and other printed matter; merchandise, seeds, cuttings, bulbs, roots, scions, and plants, weighing less than 16 ounces):

   | | | | |
   |---|---|---|---|
   | 0 to 1 oz. | $0.18 | Over 6 to 8 oz. | $0.92 |
   | Over 1 to 2 ozs. | 0.35 | Over 8 to 10 ozs. | 1.14 |
   | Over 2 to 3 ozs. | 0.52 | Over 10 to 12 ozs. | 1.36 |
   | Over 3 to 4 ozs. | 0.69 | Over 12 to 14 ozs. | 1.58 |
   | Over 4 to 6 ozs. | 0.70 | Over 14 but less than 16 ozs. | 1.81 |

   For bulk rate, consult postmaster.

*Effective November 1, 1981, first-class postage rates changed to 20¢ the first ounce for letter mail and 13¢ for postcards.

c. Fourth class: Parcel post, zone rates. (Consult postmaster for weight and size limits; see zone rate chart.)

3. *Special Services—Domestic Mail Only*

a. Insurance (additional fee for covering against loss or damage, besides postage):

| Liability | Fee |
|---|---|
| $   .01 to $20 | $0.45 |
| 20.01 to $50 | 0.85 |
| 50.01 to $100 | 1.25 |
| 100.01 to $150 | 1.70 |
| 150.01 to $200 | 2.05 |
| 200.01 to $300 | 3.45 |
| 300.01 to $400 | 4.70 |

b. Registry (for maximum protection and security):

| Value | For articles covered by postal insurance | For articles NOT covered |
|---|---|---|
| $   0.01 to $100 | $3.30 | $3.25 |
| $100.01 to $500 | 3.60 | 3.55 |
| $500.01 to $1,000 | 3.90 | 3.85 |

For higher values, consult postmaster.

c. Certified mail: $0.75 fee, in addition to postage.

d. C.O.D.: Consult postmaster for fee and conditions of mailing.

e. Special delivery (in addition to required postage): For first class, up to 2 lbs., $2.10; more than 2 but not more than 10 lbs., $2.35; more than 10 lbs., $3.00. All other classes, $2.35, $3.00, and $3.40, as per above weight categories.

f. Special handling (third and fourth class only, in addition to required postage): 10 lbs. and less, $0.75; more than 10 lbs., $1.30.

**MAIL ROOM DATA**

All mail room information in this section has been excerpted from:

Customer Services Department, United States Postal Service, "Modern Mailroom Practices," *Publication 62* (Washington, D.C.: U. S. Government Printing Office, August 1977).

## MAILROOM FURNISHING & STAFFING

### Locate your mailroom where the action is

For maximum efficiency, your mailroom needs to be easily accessible to your employees as well as to Postal Service employees delivering and picking up your mail. Don't hide the mailroom away from the flow of traffic. Whenever possible, locate your mailroom at the lowest practical level of your building so gravity fed chutes can be used to move mail quickly down to the processing area. It is also a good idea to locate Telex or facsimile machines and copying machines in or near the mailroom since this location usually stays open longer than other service areas.

### Staff your mailroom properly

Because today's mail system requires equal parts of brain and brawn, many companies have changed their qualifications for mailroom employees. Mailroom supervisors are now being treated as middle-level managers and are expected to perform as such. The mailroom is no longer a testing ground for untrained youths. Pick your mailroom employees for their intelligence, good vision, a degree of maturity and willingness to tend to details. By recognizing the mailroom as a vital link in a company's communication system, you'll enjoy a high level of efficiency and productivity.

### Furnish functionally

Take advantage of the several lines of furniture specially designed for mailroom use. Their rugged construction and specially set height make them ideal for use by standing mailroom employees. It's a sure bet you'll recoup your investment many times over in employee efficiency and improved productivity.

### Mechanize repetitive chores

Automated metering, opening, inserting and wrapping equipment can speed business mail through your mailroom and free employees for other tasks. A good postage scale, for example, can pay for itself time and time again by eliminating over-postage and speeding postage calculations (most let you read the postage directly from the scale). Check your present equipment to see if it's as modern as it should be for your mailing volume.

**249**

## POSTAL SERVICES AVAILABLE

### Match our services to your needs

Express Mail Service offers guaranteed overnight delivery to many cities throughout the country. For next business day delivery of messages to one or many addressees, use MAILGRAM which offers "the impact of a telegram at a fraction of the cost." Other services (first-class mail, parcel post, 2nd- and 3rd-class mail, etc.) provide delivery according to published service standards which your Postmaster or Customer Service Representative can provide.

## POSTAGE

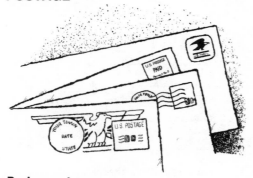

### Paying postage

Postage for first-class mail and parcel post can be paid with stamps, postage meter imprints or strips, or be a preprinted permit imprint. In addition, you can purchase embossed stamped envelopes for first-class letters from the Postal Service. Postage for third-class mail is generally paid by a preprinted permit imprint (except for small volumes of third-class mail). Your Postmaster or Customer Service Representative can assist you in determining the most efficient way to pay postage.

### Save postage costs by presorting

You can save postage on first-class mail by presorting mailings of 500 or more pieces according to five- and three-digit ZIP Codes.

Each address must be ZIP Coded and the mailing presorted and bundled by 10 or more pieces to the same five-digit ZIP Codes, 50 or more pieces to the same three-digit ZIP Codes, and the residue made up to states or mixed states. Bundles should be banded and placed in USPS trays. Postage can be paid by either postage meter or permit imprint. Your Customer Service Representative or postmaster can assist you in taking advantage of this opportunity for savings and better service.

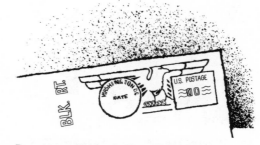

### Do you qualify for bulk mail savings?

You're eligible for special bulk mail rates if you mail 200 identical pieces or more at a time. This includes printed letters, folders, booklets, catalogs, and other similar materials which are not first- or second-class mail. Check with your Postmaster or Customer Service Representative for details—and tips for keeping your bulk mail costs to a minimum.

## Monitor your postage meter

If you use a postage meter, run a frequent check on it to be sure that meter impressions are legible and do not overlap. Metered mail must be presented for mailing only on the date shown on the metered postmark, so get in the habit of advancing your meter's date the first thing each day.

Remember to face all metered mail in the same direction and bundle five or more pieces. Pressure-sensitive bands for wrapping bundles are available from your Customer Service Representative or Postmaster. Large volumes of metered mail should be faced and trayed.

## Double check your scales

Inaccurate mailing scales can cause a company plenty of trouble. A scale that reads "high" means you're over-paying postage. A scale that reads "low" means embarrassing "postage due" for your customers. Here's how to check your weight: place nine pennies on your postal scale. They should weigh exactly 1 ounce. If they don't, remedy the situation pronto!

## Save unused envelopes for refunds

Envelopes or meter tapes printed but for some reason not used (e.g., wrong denomination) are worth saving. Your local post office will give you a 90% rebate for them. Or, if their total value exceeds $250, you'll get a *full* refund—minus $10 per hour for processing the refund (minimum $25 fee). Check with your local Postmaster or Customer Service Representative for details.

## LETTER MAIL PREPARATION

## Be choosey about envelopes

One easy way to help insure delivery of your mail is by using the proper envelopes. Too small envelopes may break during processing. Too large first-class envelopes may be mistaken for third-class. Keep an ample supply of various size envelopes on hand so you can match the envelope size to its contents. And when you have to use large, flat first-class envelopes, be sure they have a distinctive green diamond border design for easy first-class identification.

Envelopes should be light colored so as to contrast with the address impression for easy machine reading. They should be rectangular, no smaller than 3½″ x 5″ and no larger than 6⅛″ x 11½″.

### Be a separator and presorter

Your mail gets on its way faster if it's separated and marked before it reaches the post office. By separating your first-class mail from other mail, and your local mail from out-of-town mail, you save the Postal Service steps in handling it. Further presorting by ZIP Codes saves many additional steps. Wide rubber bands are available for banding bundles of separated and presorted mail. When volume merits, trays, sacks and labels are also available. A presort rate applies to some first-class mail—see page 3.

Metered mail users can save two steps by marking bundled or trayed mail "Local Metered Mail" or "Out-Of-Town Metered Mail" or by using pressure-sensitive bands available from the Postal Service. And remember, you must bundle five-or-more letter-size, meter-imprinted envelopes.

### Make a mailing schedule—and stick to it

Make a point of knowing when your post office dispatches mail. Then arrange your mailing schedule accordingly. If you use a street or building lobby mail box, check the collection times listed. Often you can save a full day on delivery time by posting your mail just a little earlier. If you miss the last collection, take your mail directly to the post office—this extra effort will be rewarded by quicker delivery.

### Mail early—and often

Since post offices generally receive most of the day's mail around 5 p.m., get your employees in the habit of picking up any signed correspondence at noon and mailing it before they go to lunch. This will get your mail to its destination significantly faster (with less chance of error) than "rush hour" mailings. You can avoid afternoon tie-ups, too, by posting your mail just a little earlier than usual.

### Equipment and materials available on loan

The Postal Service will loan sacks and trays to large volume customers and will provide sack and tray labels and tags. In addition, the Postal Service has dozens of helpful free booklets available upon request to help business customers use the mails more profitably. A list of several of these is provided at the back of this booklet.

## ADDRESSING

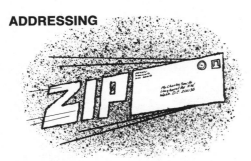

### ZIP Codes save processing time

ZIP Coding (mandatory for bulk mail) can mean a day or two faster delivery of your mail. In some locations, our sorting machines are able to "read" ZIP Codes and automatically sort several thousand pieces of mail per hour at each operator station. So make the most of this innovation, since non-ZIP Coded mail must be held for conventional sorting at slower speeds. (Make sure your ZIP Code appears in your return address, too.) You can ZIP Code your mailing lists by using the *National ZIP Code Directory* or the ZIP-A-List computer tape file. Or, the post office will help you ZIP Code your mailing lists.

### Automate your mail

With a typewriter or properly-prepared addressing plates and a few simple rules, you can prepare your mail for automatic machine sorting—and in turn enjoy faster processing of your letters. The address area on all mailed materials should be blocked, with all of the lines having a uniform left margin. City, State and ZIP Code should appear in that sequence on the bottom line.

*Example*
GENERAL XYZ CORP
1000 MAIN ST RM 4325
DETROIT MI 48217

The delivery point for the mail, whether it be a street address or a box number, must be shown on the second line from the bottom, directly above the city, state and ZIP Code. When a station name is also shown it should be on the same line as the box number, except it may be entered on the preceding line when the station name and box number are too long for one line. When apartment numbers, suite numbers, room numbers, etc., are used, they should appear immediately after the street address on the same line. Accounting numbers, subscription and presort codes, etc., can be located within the Address Read Zone, but should be entered on the line immediately above the addressee's name. Be sure to keep the lower right half of the envelope free of printing or symbols.

Addresses should be placed at least one inch in from the left edge of an envelope. The bottom of the last line (city, state, ZIP Code) should be at least ⅝ of an inch up from the bottom edge of an envelope. Use blockstyle type fonts (no italic, script, artistic, or proportionally-spaced fonts) and type addresses in upper-case letters without punctuation. Addresses should also have a uniform left margin.

Window envelope inserts should be prepared so that nothing but the address appears in the window. There should be at least ¼ inch between the address and the left, right and bottom edges of the window when the insert moves to its full limits in the envelope.

### Dual addressing

You can now use both a box number for your business reply mail *and* include your street address to let prospects know where you are. With this new "dual address" system, your mail will be delivered to the address located directly above the City-State-ZIP Code line. Be sure the ZIP Code used is the correct one for the *delivery* address.

*Example*
GENERAL XYZ CORP
1000 MAIN ST
JEFFERSON STATION  PO BOX 3302
DETROIT MI 48214

### Keep your lists current

Mailing lists need to be up-dated from time to time for maximum efficiency. Your local Postmaster can help you do this. If you send your mailing list to any local Postmaster, he'll check the names against his local address lists for correctness. Names submitted for verification must be on 3 by 5 inch cards or data processing cards, and only one name and address shown per card. Another way to "clean" your mailing lists is by simply printing "Address Correction Requested" on your outgoing envelopes. Undeliverable items under two ounces will be returned to you with a corrected address or the reason for non-delivery. A fee is charged for these services.

Many companies make one or two "double post-card" mailings to their mailing list each year, asking recipients if they would like to continue receiving mailings. Those who do simply return the reply half of the card, and this is used to up-date address plates and make any corrections. Companies with computers can borrow and copy magnetic tape with ZIP Code information from the Postal Service at no charge.

Internally, make it a company policy to route change of address notices to the mailroom so mailing lists and addressing plates can be corrected.

When arranging cards into carrier delivery sequence, a new service enables mailers who meet certain specific requirements, to obtain missing addresses and delete undeliverable addresses. Requirements of this new service are outlined in the Postal Service Manual, section 122.53.

## TRANSPORTING MAIL

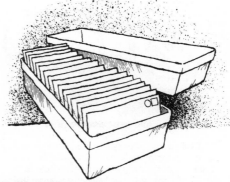

### Switch to trays for modern mail convenience

First-class mail gets faster processing through the postal system when it's trayed. The Postal Service provides trays to mailers free of charge, where available and when volume dictates. Just place your first-class mail in them with address and postage facing in the same direction instead of throwing the mail helter-skelter into a mail sack. Traying saves culling and facing mail at the post office . . . so your mail gets on its way faster. It's a simple step that really makes a difference.

### Package & sack third-class bulk mail

The Postal Service requires that all third-class bulk mail be sorted by ZIP Code and, where volume warrants, sacked before it goes to the post office. This saves the post office time-consuming sorting and allows faster delivery. Also remember all bulk mail must be ZIP Coded except in special situations. Check with your Postmaster or Customer Service Representative.

## PARCELS/PACKAGING

### Packing pointers

All packages containing easily breakable articles should be marked "Fragile." The package's contents should be surrounded with sufficient cushioning material to keep it from moving inside and to protect it against impact from the outside. Excelsior, flexible corrugated fiberboard or felt are commonly used cushions for heavy materials. Cellulose materials, shredded paper or expanded foam are often used for lighter materials. Check your *National ZIP Code Directory* or ask your local post office for the free pamphlet "Packaging For Mailing."

Since your parcels will be processed through the highly-automated National Bulk Mail System, be sure they have ZIP Codes on them. Otherwise, they'll be delayed.

### Metering parcels

If you're using a postage meter, position the meter strip to overlap the corner of the address label.

### Piggyback a letter with your package

You can enclose a first-class letter in parcels without paying first-class postage for the entire package, if you simply mark the package "First-Class Mail Enclosed" and add the first-class letter postage to the parcel's postage. Or, as an alternative, tape your first-class letter—with its own postage on it—to the front of the parcel.

## ASSISTANCE

### Discuss your mail with peers and pros

As a business customer, you're eligible to participate in Postal Customers Councils, an organization of mailers and postal officials who meet to discuss matters of mutual concern. Through films, lectures, question and answer periods, and through various training and orientation sessions, you and your employees can gain a better understanding of mailing practices and procedures.

### Postmasters and Customer Service Representatives—Your personal mailroom consultants

Whenever specific mailing questions arise, your Postmaster or Customer Service Representative is available for assistance. They can help in working out programs for the most efficient, and least expensive, mail delivery system. They can also give you the details and rates on all of our products and services and provide descriptive literature.